GW00771343

PEOPLE AND PROPERTY

People and Property

*

EDWARD L. ERDMAN

B.T. BATSFORD LTD · *LONDON*

To my wife, Pamela, for withstanding
my prolonged rapport with a dictaphone

First published 1982

ISBN 0 7134 3790 1

Photoset by Servis Filmsetting Ltd, Manchester
and printed in Great Britain by
The Pitman Press Ltd
Bath
for the publishers
B.T. Batsford Ltd
4 Fitzhardinge Street
London W1H 0AH

CONTENTS

*

LIST OF ILLUSTRATIONS

INTRODUCTION

⁂

During my so-called retirement, I decided it would be fun to write a book. As a professional man and not a risk-taking entrepreneur, my personal biography alone would not, I thought, prove celebrated or lurid enough to produce a bestseller. But I have been blessed with a good memory; the book is, therefore, a collection of authentic anecdotes about the colourful personalities I have met in the course of a 50-year career as an estate agent and valuer dealing with all types of property and people.

The stories are not confined to business or real estate. They are about people and are written to give the reader a brief pen picture of the character of the entrepreneurs I have known a long time. Humour is an essential ingredient of the book – and the incidents related are all true. Many characters within the pages were born in humble circumstances and became national and international figures of high standing. I hope some of the stories behind their success will prove interesting and entertaining to young and old.

Some of my reminiscences spotlight episodes in the personal lives of individuals who have worked hard and taken risks to create wealth for themselves and others by establishing commercial empires to manufacture, distribute and export merchandise, to rebuild bombed sites and to erect buildings to serve some of the needs of the community at home and overseas.

I have included some of the enterprising men I have met who tried but failed. Here, too, are stories about other professional men for, although not entrepreneurs as such, several of them sought out and promoted a large number of projects, deals and company takeovers for their entrepreneurial clients. Others could not resist the temptation to become entrepreneurs themselves.

The first chapters contain a brief history of my family background and the reasons why I entered the profession. Later I describe my experiences as an office boy over 50 years ago followed by my early days in the profession and my first meetings with important clients.

Grateful thanks are due to colleagues and clients, too numerous to mention, who have supplied information and photographs. And my apologies are due to many other friends whom I have been unable to include due to lack of space.

Last, but not least, my thanks are due to my loyal and long-suffering secretary, Claire Bonner, who has coped with the pressures of other work and my incoherent dictation in order to record my intermittent memories of the past.

EDWARD ERDMAN *London 1982*

I

AN OFFICE BOY IN THE TWENTIES

*

I was born in Highbury, London, nearly within the sound of Bow Bells. My only sister, Vera, and I had a happy childhood thanks to affectionate parents who were devoted to each other. They did everything possible for us within the limits of their often fluctuating financial resources. My father had an exceptional ability for painting and drawing and, as a boy, he displayed such outstanding promise that a well-known artist offered to adopt him in order to help him to develop his talent. My grandparents feared that the life of an artist was too hazardous and they insisted that he should serve in their drapery store instead. My father was artistic – more of an intellectual than a commercial man – and liked reading classical books and history rather than concentrating on business. He would enthusiastically embark upon a number of business projects and then, after a short time, would lose interest. Easy-going by nature, he found that more than one of his undertakings failed and folded up. During his life, he opened drapery shops in north London, a car hire company off Theobalds Road in Holborn, a cloth merchants' business with an office in Bow Lane, Cheapside, and then tobacconists' and gift shops in Edgware Road and Praed Street, Paddington. His pleasant personality ensured that he was well-liked by everyone. My mother was equally popular but she did the worrying for my father. When I came home from school, their constant discussions concerning money problems may perhaps have helped me to become objective and cautious on financial matters at a young age. I thoroughly enjoyed my life at school but made no serious effort with my studies and my best subject was football. At the age of 16, I had a childish whim to become a lawyer and I had romantic dreams that one day, I would be a famous judge. The first step was to catch up on my school subjects and I managed to agree a special fee at a cramming school in Chancery Lane which coached backward pupils for professional examinations. My parents readily agreed and for six months I worked intensively, often until late at night. Although over-anxious, I managed to pass the examinations and arranged an appointment to see an eminent firm of city solicitors. They were prepared to accept me as an articled pupil on payment of £200 but without salary for five years which was the custom at the time.

My mother had a multi-millionaire uncle, Reuben Gliksten. In the 1920's, millionaires were scarce and treated with some deference. Gliksten was a tough, self-made man with a large timber yard in Stratford adjoining the canal linking with the London Docks. He was a strong man in every way and was twice commended by the Metropolitan Police for helping them with arrests. He and his wife, Sophie, lived with their three sons in a large house at Highbury New Park in north London. They had a carriage and pair with a coachman named Charlie. Gliksten was a shrewd, hard working man who boasted of the fact that he toured his timber yard at 8.00 a.m. each day and greeted each member of his staff by christian name. He often visited us in the evenings, usually removed his shoes and went off into a sound, noisy sleep whilst his wife – who was very entertaining – did the talking. Although he did not give my family any money, he was always ready to offer advice. When he spoke, no one would ever argue. Indeed, when he heard the result of my application to become an articled clerk, he turned to my parents in my presence and said 'You cannot afford to make your son a solicitor'. The following morning, without further comment, I applied for a job as an office boy. So in 1923, I was engaged by a firm who – by fate or good fortune – were estate agents and auctioneers known as Gordon Thomas & Co of 63 Margaret Street, Oxford Circus. I had begun what was to be my chosen career. Fifty years later, my son, Timothy, decided to take a Bachelor of Law degree and qualified as a solicitor but may seek other fields to conquer.

At Gordon Thomas & Co, my starting salary was 5/– a week which, in those deflationary days, was probably my maximum worth. Gordon Thomas, my principal, was a dedicated professional who maintained a large, hand-written diary recording every call and conversation. He received his early training at Davis & Co, surveyors, whose professional practice was founded in 1901 by the former David Isaacs – a blunt, honest member of the profession – at 64 Berners Street where it remained for almost 80 years. Only recently in 1979, the present senior partner of Davis & Co, Richard Wilks, arranged to move the practice to 9 Margaret Street. Incidentally, Richard Wilks joined David Isaacs as an office boy in 1926 at a salary of 15/– a week and became a partner in 1937. A comparison of my salary as an office boy in 1923 of 5/– with Richard Wilks' salary of 15/– in 1926, shows that the spiral of inflation had already started.

Margaret Street was in the sector of the West End of London which was fast becoming the centre of the textile trade. Many tailors and cutters migrated there from the East End to establish workrooms and showrooms for the wholesale ladies' fashion trade serving the leading retail stores. The Rag Trade area extended roughly from Upper Regent Street behind the stores of Peter Robinson, the former Waring & Gillow and Bourne & Hollingsworth in Oxford Street and included such thoroughfares as Great Castle Street, East Castle Street, Market Place, Wells Street, Great Titchfield Street, Margaret Street, Mortimer Street and Berners Street. My first employer's offices in Margaret Street were partitioned into two rooms, the general office in the front for the staff and the office occupied by

Gordon Thomas himself at the rear. There were several negotiators but no female typists. Therefore, among my duties as an office boy – and as a self-taught, two-fingered typist – I received dictation direct from Gordon Thomas and from his senior assistants, John English, who subsequently set up on his own account as Pritchard & English in Great Portland Street, and Arthur Muddiman who left the profession to become a detective. My role as a typist and my seat next to the partition separating the principal's office, enabled me to learn speedily about every activity taking place in the office. I often hoped that the sounds and the excitement which appeared to generate from the principal's office on the visits of a particularly good-looking lady client might melt the frosted glass partition which obscured my view.

After a short time, I found myself typing rent demand notices, entering payments in a simple doubly-entry rent book and also typing agreements and counterpart agreements on engrossment paper for lettings. Two guineas were charged by the firm for the preparation of agreements in addition to collecting the appropriate duty for stamping. I typed so many of these agreements that I am still able to remember the clauses and repeat them, parrot fashion. Carbon copies of letters were not accepted as legal evidence in those days. Another of my duties was, therefore, to place a damp cloth on all outgoing letters in the letter book and put them through a copy press to obtain facsimiles with the signature of the writer. If the cloth sheets became too damp, the typing would smudge badly, which sometimes delayed my return home. I gained experience answering the telephone, despatching the post and obtaining keys to conduct applicants over vacant workrooms and showrooms. In addition to this, as office boy I was given the usual menial tasks including making the tea, washing up, running errands, dealing with the mail and taking the principal's suits and trousers for renovation to Harry Hall, the well-known tailors and riding-habit makers who were in Oxford Street at that time. When I called to collect at Harry Hall's and tendered the cash I had been given, I was always informed that the bill would be debited to the account and Gordon Thomas looked puzzled when I returned his money. It was later discovered that the account was held by a Mr George Thomas, registered in the books as 'G. Thomas', who had been paying the account for Gordon Thomas for several years. These general duties may perhaps have helped me in later years to carry out with complete serenity most exacting instructions from particularly demanding clients.

Gordon Thomas was an engaging character and inspired confidence as a reliable agent of integrity. Most transactions were concluded by personal contact with principals and a verbal acceptance and handshake by the parties was seldom broken; their word was considered to be their bond. While strict economy was observed with no boardroom lunches or, in fact, no boardroom, many agents liked to conclude a deal over a drink, usually a pint in the local. On more than one occasion, I spotted the principal walking out of the saloon bar of the Cock Tavern on the corner of Margaret Street and Great Portland Street in company with a well-satisfied client. Personal contacts were all important and some agents developed a type of 'Hail-fellow-well-met' style with a buttonhole and a jaunty manner; others attracted clients because of a reputation for sound advice and service. My early experiences in conducting tough East End tailors and other rag trade clients over premises probably gave me my first insight into the art of negotiating and bargaining. In fact, gown firms, from modest beginnings in the East End of London, became leaders of the fashion industry and some are large public companies today. Luncheon vouchers were, of course, unknown, but even on my limited salary at that time I could afford a light lunch, occasionally at a Lyons café on the corner of Margaret Street and Upper Regent Street. The coffee, tea and crispy rolls were excellent value and served to a high standard by first-class trained waitresses called 'nippies'. Talking with a junior member of another firm over lunch one day, I heard that the largest and most important estate agents dealing with commercial property were located on the south side of Oxford Street in Maddox Street and around Hanover Square. Trades and professions tended to congregate in particular areas in those days – and agents were no exception. Property dealers often made personal calls on foot, without appointment, and could conveniently visit more than one firm of agents in this small area.

The trend towards Maddox Street was started by Mr William Hillier and Mr Thomas Parker of Regent Street, who subsequently acquired the practice of May & Rowden of 27 Maddox Street. In 1921 the merged firm was established at this address. It was the most prominent shop agency firm at that time – much of its early success due to the drive and ability of the late Stanley Edgson and Douglas Overall. They were far-sighted leaders of their profession and eventually, in 1939, laid the foundation stone of their new office building, 77 Grosvenor Street, where it stands today. History repeated itself and other agents left Maddox Street and followed them into Grosvenor Street. Stanley Edgson was a dynamic personality and was mainly responsible for expanding the practice. He was also a first class auctioneer. He became Mayor of Westminster and managing director of a public property company, Central Commercial Properties – the controlling shares of which were subsequently acquired from his family by the famous Jack Cotton. Stanley Edgson's life-long partner was Douglas Overall, who became managing director of Sterling Estates, another quoted company. Douglas was a charming man, well liked by everyone. Until his death at more than 80 years old, his tall figure could be seen visiting his former practice to give a kind, encouraging word to some of the younger men. Many years ago, Douglas – a keen golfer – became president of the Auctioneers' & Estate Agents' Institute and was asked to open their Golfing Society. He duly appeared on the course (overlooked by a crowd of spectators) and, in commanding manner, gave an enormous whack at the ball. He missed it completely but retaining his poise and dignity, drew himself up to his full impressive height and took another mighty swing – only to miss again amid silence from the crowd. Douglas, with stiff upper lip, calmly turned to the caddy and exclaimed 'That is a damn long course isn't it?' Other partners continued the practice of Hillier Parker May & Rowden over the years. Peter Edgson, Stanley Edgson's son, ultimately became senior partner and, upon his retirement, joint senior partners were appointed, Herbert Burnige and Leonard Jarrad. Herbert Burnige retired in 1979 and became a consultant.

By 1924, I was anxious to progress and to make more money. I wanted to deal with properties in all parts of the West End and the suburbs rather than those limited to the West End textile area. Therefore, in 1924, I applied for a post with Douglas Kershaw & Co. I was impressed at the time with their offices in Princes Street, Hanover Square, a few yards from Regent Street. In the traditional style of a large West End estate office of that era, the ground floor was narrow but long, containing a formidable line of desks. Every desk was occupied by a senior negotiator representing different departments of the firm, with one or more chairs at the side for the use of clients. It was impressive to listen to the buzz of activity created by the negotiators' voices, cross talking on their telephones. But I remember thinking that it would be easy to overhear confidential business between one desk and another. However, behind these desks were the private partitioned offices of the partners who could only be seen by special appointment. The senior partners of Douglas Kershaw & Co at that time were Douglas Kershaw, the founder, Charles Gooch and Frederick Sainsbury. I waited nervously before being interviewed by Fred Sainsbury. Due to my limited experience, I did not feel justified in applying for a permanent post and I asked Mr Sainsbury to accept my application on the basis of one month's trial as a junior negotiator. Fred Sainsbury said that they had no vacancies for negotiators but that he would grant me one month's trial as a canvasser in the West End Department.

My job was to hunt for business. I was not allocated a desk inside the office because I was expected to be out all day seeking instructions and making calls on shops in the West End. Another of my duties was to solicit instructions in every street in the West End where another agent's board appeared on shops or offices. Then I would return to the office to fill in printed instruction forms with details of the properties I had been able to get on the books. My completed forms were passed to the West End manager. Nowadays, of course, soliciting business by direct personal call and touting for instructions on premises where other agents' boards are on exhibition would be regarded as improper and unprofessional conduct. Before 1931, however, it was recognised as normal practice. For my new job I wore a bowler hat and stiff white collar and armed myself with a smart walking stick. But, as a young man of just over 18, I was shy and self-conscious and I had to summon all my courage to make these calls, some of which are still imprinted upon my memory. The experience gave me exceptional knowledge of every thoroughfare in the West End and, no doubt, cured my shyness the hard way. After bungling my approach to several large stores, I gradually adopted a fairly stereo-typed method; I walked in boldly and asked in a confident voice to see the chairman, managing director or owner. When asked if I had an appointment, my answer was no, but my mission was special and personal. Having wormed my way into an owner's private office, my usual opening statement was: 'I have a point blank question to put to you – are you prepared to sell this building if you secure a satisfactory price?' I either received a complete rebuff – sometimes impolite – or a tentative expression of interest. In the first case, I would walk out smartly, but in the second case I would continue the dialogue by ear and prepare an instruction form recording my conversation to enable one of my firm's partners or senior negotiators to follow up. I managed to secure an average of at least six properties to place on the books every day, passed the probationary trial period and became a regular member of the West End Department of Douglas Kershaw & Co.

Douglas Kershaw also had a Suburban Department, managed by Charles Morse – a bright, experienced and active negotiator. At that time the multiple shop business was thriving and private retail traders were being bought out rapidly by multiple companies. As a junior canvasser in the West End Department, I was rather overawed by Charles Morse and had little contact with him. Then I heard that he was leaving the firm to start in practice on his own account at 13 Maddox Street, taking his principal assistant with him. I therefore asked Fred Sainsbury if I could transfer to become a negotiator in the Suburban Shops Department. Thus, with little or no knowledge of the suburbs, I found myself at a senior negotiator's desk in the Suburban Department, answering telephone calls all day from applicants who were enquiring about shops where we had boards or who had received particulars of premises. Details of available shops were registered on a card index system under each district. By fumbling through these cards, I quickly grasped the range and nature of the Suburban Shops Department. This experience was augmented by travelling to the suburbs, preparing location plans and letting a number of shops. But I became involved in a dispute over personal commission with the manager of the office and gave in my notice.

Abruptly leaving the practice of Douglas Kershaw & Co (which many years later, in the time when Albert Berger was in control, merged with Walker Son & Packman), I decided to call on Charles Morse, Kershaw's former manager, who had set up on his own account. He immediately engaged me as a negotiator at a much improved salary and, in 1927, I became manager of his office. Life was not to be plain sailing, however. I learned that Charles Morse had a financial partner who had backed his business with comparatively limited capital and, as commissions came in slowly, the firm found itself in financial difficulty. The practice closed down and Charles Morse told me that he had made arrangements to be taken over by Dudley Samuel & Harrison of 29 Maddox Street. Part of his arrangement was that I accompanied him as his assistant and that we were to carry on the same type of practice dealing with suburban shops. He had sent a letter to all our clients stating that the practice of Charles A. Morse was to be merged with the firm of Dudley Samuel & Harrison. The former practice of Charles A. Morse, including me as one of the fixtures, was allocated a ground floor room at the rear of 29 Maddox Street and we soon set up our department to deal with multiple shops. Dudley Samuel & Harrison were not entrepreneurs but, as a highly commercialised practice of estate agents, they introduced many deals to entrepreneurs. The partners, Dudley Samuel and Amyas Harrison, were on the first floor with their respective secretaries. Amyas Harrison, a former army officer, was a professional valuer and estate agent. One of Mr Harrison's personal friends was a Mr Richard Smee and it always amused me when I answered the telephone to hear his rather high voice remark: 'Smee speaking'.

Dudley Samuel was a likeable, rather eccentric character who came from a wealthy background and no doubt provided the finance to set up the firm. Shrewd and down-to-earth, he hated red tape, pomp, devious negotiation or hypocrisy and he was sometimes so blunt and direct as to be embarrassing. He was ready to admit honestly that his office was engaged in commercial rather than in professional work. He did not attempt to concentrate on valuation, surveys or management, but only on sales and lettings. The firm had no time for lame-duck negotiators. Wages were low but we received a percentage of the firm's commissions on transactions we initiated and completed. Dudley Samuel's business philosphy insisted the practice made the maximum profit with minimum investment of capital and risk. It was made clear to everyone that we were to go out on the prowl and get business and, every Friday night, the secretary came round with her notebook to record the transactions we had carried out during the week. Those with too many blank weeks were not retained on the staff. I can remember what happened when a recession was anticipated in the property market. The firm took steps immediately to reduce everyone's salary. I went to see Dudley Samuel and refused to take a cut in anticipation of a bad year; but I undertook to make a reduction at the end of the year only if my figures proved to be bad – and I turned out to be one of the fortunate ones. The atmosphere of the firm, paying only for success, bred an independent type of negotiator, many of whom – including me – left to start their own practices or to become successful entrepreneurs.

Among them were John Snell, Jeffrey Pilcher, Norman Hirshfield, Victor Behrens, Ray Davis, Harry Hyams who founded Oldham Estates, Walter Flack who founded Murrayfield, Maxwell Joseph who founded Grand Metropolitan Hotels and Joseph Gold who set up Centrovincial Estates. Whilst I did not always agree with the firm's policy, I had very happy times with Dudley Samuel & Harrison. Eventually I was given the position occupied by my senior and close friend, Charles Morse, and became the manager. Morse then left to start up a property investment company.

We all liked Dudley Samuel our senior partner. At that time, he lived in Hampstead with his attractive wife, Rhoda, who was a talented artist. He owned a luxurious coach-built Delage car and his antics with his chauffeur, William Ruff, always caused amusement in the office. I recollect travelling down to Brighton with him when he was supervising the building of Embassy Court, a block of flats on the seafront. Temperamental and a little impatient, on the journey down, he turned to his chauffeur and exclaimed: 'William, hurry up – we shall never get there.' To which William replied in a dull voice: 'Yes Sir.' A few miles further on, he said: 'William, slow down, you are going too fast past the crossroads.' With the same expressionless tone, William replied: 'Yes Sir.' After Dudley Samuel had left the car and I was about to follow, William said in a conspiratorial whisper: 'I always say Yes Sir to the governor – he is off his rocker.' On another occasion, I was told by William that 'the governor' was a impetuous driver and that William was terrified sitting next to him when he decided to take the wheel. A further vivid memory concerns the day I was summoned to Dudley Samuel's room to work out some figures in the presence of Mr Lewis, chairman of Lockwood & Bradley, the tailors. My employer suddenly stood up, pulled out his key chain with a bunch of keys from his trouser pocket and unlocked the cupboard in his desk. Mr Lewis seemed surprised when he produced from it a paper bag bearing the name of Mash & Austin, the Covent Garden fruiterers and took a bite from an apple. He then offered one to Mr Lewis who, as a rather formal gentleman, curtly refused and seemed to be slightly put out.

At that time the office opened until 1.00 p.m. on Saturday but, unlike local suburban house agents, little work was done. Many of the staff turned up in plus fours or sports jackets, with their football togs or cricket bags. Dudley Samuel himself usually appeared with his binoculars slung over his shoulder to go to a race meeting. I have never been keen on horse racing due to an unfortunate experience while at Dudley Samuel & Harrison. Charles Morse, then manager of the Suburban Shops Department, asked me to take a chance one Wednesday morning and go with him to the Derby. It was assumed that we would not be seen and could be visiting a suburban shopping centre on business. I recollect paying 22/6d for entrance to the Silver Ring (which I could ill afford) and then had the misfortune to bump straight into my boss, Dudley Samuel, who pretended not to see me. I backed a loser in every race, suffered a torrential rain storm with no overcoat and had to queue up in the open for a long time to get the train back. Soaked to the skin and completely broke, I thought I would get the sack when I returned. I believe the combination of circumstances probably dampened my ardour for racing for evermore. Fortunately, Dudley Samuel took a liberal view and graciously refrained from mentioning the incident.

2

COLOURFUL CHARACTERS OF THE PAST

*

The famous J.A. and R.M. Phillips were cousins of my principal, Dudley Samuel. Their father was David Phillips who had a small estate office known as Phillips, Phillips & Co in Oxford Street above Tottenham Court Road Tube Station. Here both boys received their early training, but their personalities and careers were entirely different. J.A. Phillips was affectionately known as Jackie, and his brother Reggie was sometimes known as 'Dipy' Phillips, from the initials of his company, Development on Investment Principle. I am told that Jackie was initially in his father's management department collecting a large number of weekly rents and that, even in these early days, he liked to place a few shillings on the horses. Reggie was reputed to have an eye for attractive ladies, but hated horse racing or gambling. They both became prominent property developers – Reggie Phillips ultimately setting up impressive offices at 22 Conduit Street, Mayfair, as a development organisation. J.A. Phillips opened offices as an estate agent in 1924 at 123–5 Oxford Street on the corner of Wardour Street. He employed the late David Levy and his brother, Joseph Levy (who became D.E. & J. Levy) and Henry Joel, now in practice on his own account.

While at Dudley Samuel & Harrison, I met Jackie Phillips on several occasions. Extrovert, and something of an actor, he was renowned for his big betting on racing – he was also a racehorse owner and one of his horses, 'Real Estate', ran in the Derby – and he was a heavy poker player at the Eccentric Club in St James's. He seemed to enjoy creating a sensation when he entered the office with his sprightly bearing, confident commanding manner, sporting a curly brimmed bowler and a buttonhole. Although he wore a deaf aid, Jackie Phillips always appreciated a joke, sometimes at the expense of others. At that time, Hillier Parker May & Rowden had offices at number 27 Maddox Street and Dudley Samuel & Harrison were at 29 Maddox Street. One day he swept into No. 29, went straight upstairs without being announced in the general office and, in a deep, dominant voice, said to Miss Cohen, Dudley Samuel's secretary: 'I wish to see Mr Stanley Edgson,' – knowing full well that the latter was the senior partner of Hillier Parker May & Rowden. Miss Cohen, somewhat overawed by his presence, said in an apologetic voice: 'I am sorry, Sir, but you are in the wrong building.' Jackie Phillips replied: 'Who are you then?' and, when Miss Cohen told him Dudley Samuel & Harrison, he said in a casual manner: Well, Dudley Samuel will do. When asked for his name, he said: 'Tell him Lord Roxburgh is here to see him.' Poor Miss Cohen was terrified and rushed into Dudley Samuel's office to make the announcement. Dudley Samuel roared with laughter and thoroughly enjoyed the joke. It was disconcerting to attempt to negotiate with Jack Phillips as he always complained that he was unable to hear you. He seemed, however, to have an uncanny knack of hearing any aside not intended for him. I recollect waiting at 24 Pall Mall when, due to a fracture of his leg, he was carried into his office by two members of his staff. One of the two senior staff performing this wearisome task remarked to the other, jocularly in an undertone – thinking Jack would not hear – 'Shall we drop the blighter?' To their embarrassment, like a flash, Jack said in a stern voice: 'What did you say?' This injury occurred when Jack invited his staff to his home at Virginia Water. Among the festivities, he organised some races with prizes, but gave himself a good start on age qualification. 'Nippie', the office boy collided with him and one member suggested this was deliberate! Although J.A. Phillips ran an estate office using spectacular red agency boards with white lettering, he was more of an entrepreneur and speculator than a professional agent. In his early days he spent hours at the London Auction Mart, bidding for properties and re-selling at a profit. He lived in style, bought his cigars from the famous tobacconists, Fribourg & Treyer, who are still at 34 Haymarket, London W1 and was undoubtedly one of the leading entrepreneurs and developers of his time.

In 1925, the original Old Curiosity Shop of Charles Dickens fame in Portsmouth Street, at the rear of the Law Courts, was put up for auction. There were rumours that it was to be bought by American millionaires and transported brick by brick to the United States. J.A. Phillips vowed in public that this would happen only over his dead body. He attended the sale at the London Auction Mart and acquired the freehold for some £2,000. Joe Levy congratulated him on his return to the office and Jack Phillips's retort was: 'I shall now test you as a negotiator; go and let it at £350 a year.' Joe Levy tells me he let it as the Curiosity Shop at £250 rising to £320 a year. For his pains, Joe received a personal commission of £2. 18s. 0d – ten per cent of the fee payable to the office – as recorded in the commission book which he treasures as one of his sentimental possessions today. History has repeated itself and a further reference to the Old Curiosity Shop appears in another chapter. It is significant that Joe Levy and the late David Levy – the two brothers who worked for Jack Phillips – set up in practice in somewhat similar style. They have also promoted their own developments and have been extremely successful, building up a large public company, Stock Conversion Investment Trust.

Whenever I go down Portland Place past Broadcasting House, I think of Jackie Phillips. He purchased this site – formerly the house of Lord Waring – erected a new building and let it to the BBC. He made a profit of more than £500,000 on the deal which was a large sum in those days. His many other developments included Golden Cross House, Trafalgar Square and Aldford House, Park Lane. After making a fortune, it is sad to relate that, when the slump came in 1939, he died penniless and bankrupt. Jack Phillips, although an inveterate gambler, was a character and an individualist who played for high stakes and relied entirely on his own judgement.

*

In the thirties, it was customary for most people to wear a hat. In fact, a professional or important business executive would have looked undignified without one. It was also the invariable custom for ladies to wear hats, to and from work, in church and on formal occasions. I recollect the late Sir Hugh Fraser remarking that if a man applied to him for a job and appeared without a hat, he would reject him instinctively. Because of my involvement with multiple shops in high street positions, I met many shopkeepers including the Specterman family who seemed to have a near monopoly in popular-priced ladies' millinery at that time. They traded as Franks and had shops in sought-after positions in Kilburn, Wood Green, Harlesden and other centres. Their relatives had similar millinery shops in key positions in Hammersmith, Ilford and elsewhere. One of the younger but precocious members of the family who looked older than his age and who shall remain nameless, instructed Dudley Samuel & Harrison to sell a short lease of a small shop in Stratford Broadway. I was successful in arranging the sale to Jeromes Limited, a multiple firm of photographers who had a large number of branches at that time – before everyone had their own camera. A deposit of £40 was lodged by Jeromes with the firm but the scale commission was £70. When the transaction was completed, I arranged for the sum of £40 to be transferred from the client's account to the credit of the firm and simultaneously rendered an account for the balance of our commission of £30 to the client in question. Despite submitting many accounts rendered, no payment was made and one day, the client walked into the office and said: 'Erdman, your bosses are rich, forget the extra £30.' I was indignant and arranged for the firm to take legal proceedings. I was even more surprised and frustrated when the gentleman in question pleaded that he was an infant under 21, so we lost the case and had to pay costs.

A few years later the same man bought job stocks of ladies' gowns and sold them off in high streets by taking on temporary tenancy empty shops due to be rebuilt. I arranged such a letting to him on behalf of Montague Burton Limited, the multiple tailors. Burtons had taken a site at Deptford Broadway which they were prepared to let for one month pending rebuilding, the rent to be paid in advance in accordance with their standard form of printed agreement for such tenancies. When Mr X called at the office to complete with the cash and with his stock of gowns outside in a van, I accepted the money for the rent, allowed him to sign the agreement, but then decided to take the law into my own hands. I refused to hand him the keys of the shop until he paid the £30 in cash he owed the firm. He was furious, called me many impolite names, threatened me physically and said he would report me to Montague Burton. I stood firm although I realised I was strictly out of order. For I knew that Mr X was anxious to get the keys as each day of trading on a short tenancy like this was vital to him. This kind of unprofessional conduct is not taught at the College of Estate Management at Reading University. He stalked out of the office several times to speak to his friend in the van and eventually returned and almost threw £30 at me, note by note, interspersed with imtemperate language. I thanked him with a smile and handed him the keys. He had a good sense of humour and his parting words were: 'I caught you, now you have caught me and it is my turn next.' He has since prospered and matured and when he passed me by chance one day, he gave me a knowing grin and said: 'Hello, governor of Maddox Street.' He is now older, wiser and successful.

*

I recollect Jack Bateman being engaged by Dudley Samuel & Harrison as a junior negotiator. He was a born entrepreneur and totally unsuited to being a professional surveyor. He was a tall, good-looking young man, a rugger player with a public school background. I was asked to take him under my wing in the Suburban Shops Department and to show him how to canvass by personal call. I have a clear recollection of driving with him down to High Street, Walthamstow, on a cold day. I told him how to approach the shop traders, excluding the multiples, and arranged that I would make calls along one side of the busiest part of the High Street and he on the other. When I returned to the car after completing my calls, to my surprise he was sitting stretched out and, with a broad grin, said he had had little success. I suspected that he had made very few calls, if any.

Some time after this, I walked out of the office at 29 Maddox Street, crossed the road and passed the offices of another firm of surveyors at 16 Maddox Street, P.W. Talbot & Co. When I greeted their senior partner, Godfrey Palmer, I saw him wave to Jack Bateman on the other side of the road. I said to him: 'Do you know Jack?' and he said: 'Yes, he works for us.' Thus in his very young days Jack Bateman had conceived the idea of working for more than one firm at the same time and drawing salaries from each. I subsequently heard that he was also working for Trevor & Morris, later to form part of J. Trevor & Sons at 33 Maddox Street. Jack was using three different visiting cards and being paid by all three firms unknown to each of them. This was his version of the three card trick. He had such a pleasant style that it was difficult to take offence with him, but shortly after this he left our employment as he found professional life too slow and he had the urge to make his fortune. Our next encounter was some years later when he was chairman and managing director of a company called Bateman's Office Cleaning Service which entered into contracts with a great many offices in the West End and the City of London. In addition, he supplied towels for office staff, and I believe he concluded a deal with the Initial Towel Company and sold his office cleaning company for a handsome profit. Having seen the office cleaner absent through sickness on many occasions, he had cashed in on the idea of contract cleaning with a large staff of Mrs Mops and supervisors. Subsequently he formed Bateman's Catering Company to supply canteens and directors' dining rooms. He ultimately sold this to Maxwell Joseph of Grand Metropolitan Hotels for a large sum. Also, in the early 1950's, he started the first two/three-year car hire purchase plan, with rebate at a time when there was a big Government credit squeeze. Standard Motor Car Company took up this system and apparently placed all their car business through his company, Industrial Motors. Within five months, I understand it had a turnover of approximately £15 million but the Government brought in legislation to prevent such arrangements and Jack sold the company to United Dominions Trust.

In September 1979 I asked Jack Bateman, now known as Major Bateman, whether he would have any objection to my mentioning his escapades in his early days as a junior in Maddox Street, nearly 50 years ago. He roared with laughter and said he would have no objections whatsoever. He is now engaged in catering and wholesale fruit and vegetable distribution in the New Covent Garden Market at Nine Elms.

*

In my comparatively young days in the business, Claude Leigh was a prominent figure who had made a fortune by his own good judgement and ability. His father had a small estate office in east London which he joined, but he soon left the professional side of the business to become a property owner in his own right. He had original ideas and, as early as 1929, he floated a public company, The Metropolitan Housing Corporation Limited, which acquired large estates of houses and flats in Lambeth, Stepney, Camberwell, Battersea and other London suburbs. Some of these properties lacked bathrooms and modern conveniences. He also formed a company called Claude Leigh (Management) Limited to administer and manage these estates. He was a far-sighted man and these companies – 50 years later – became the foundation of the present MEPC (Metropolitan Estates and Property Corporation) which, by 1979, was the second largest public property company in the United Kingdom. It is interesting to compare the gross profit on the copy of the 1952 Accounts (see fig. 8) of nearly £½ million with the 1980 gross profit amounting to over £10 million. Claude Leigh devised a novel plan for the improvement and modernisation of houses to avoid their becoming slums. He set up a maintenance and improvement company which supplied baths, hand-basins and kitchen equipment to his tenants on a hire purchase basis without increasing rents, which were controlled by the Rent Acts. He was socially minded and, even in those early days, he appreciated the benefits of knowing his tenants and looking after their welfare and amenities and he arranged many social meetings and children's camps for them. However, in spite of his efforts to improve the dwellings owned by his company and at the same time pay reasonable dividends to his shareholders, the Rent Act over the years made his task almost impossible. Later in life Claude Leigh arranged the takeover of the London County Freehold and Leasehold Property Company Limited, with its large portfolio of flats in Kensington and elsewhere together with commercial properties. Victor Cullen and Gordon Dashwood of that latter company became members of his board. He had a flair for making spot valuations, despite the formal valuations and advice given by his well-qualified directors, Charles Lush, Dick Shepherd and Walter Philp. Cyril Sweett, the quantity surveyor, was also on his board for a time. In more recent years, Dick Shepherd followed Charles Lush as managing director, strongly assisted by Maxwell Creasey. From the company's headquarters, then at 16 Hanover Square, Claude Leigh and his board changed their policy, decided to sell off their residential properties and to concentrate on first-class commercial buildings.

The company also expanded overseas and Claude Leigh selected one of his favourite bright young men, Peter Anker, to set up in Canada. Peter Anker was vigorous and expansive, thriving on carrying out large-scale developments. He formed a highly successful subsidiary company for MEPC in Canada and also carried out developments in other parts of the world on behalf of the company. Claude Leigh died in 1964 and, after Dick Shepherd retired, Peter Anker was recalled from Canada to become managing director. Peter Anker, with the support of Maxwell Creasey, initiated a large number of extensive and ambitious developments at home and abroad. During the subsequent property crisis in 1973, the company suffered severe setbacks due to extensive outstanding loans overseas and in the United Kingdom and its development programme was curtailed for a time. This did not perhaps suit the expansive policy of Peter Anker, who returned to Canada. Chris Benson has since become managing director with the strong and able assistance of Maxwell Creasey and the company – under the chairmanship of Sir Gerald Thorley and with a formidable board of directors – is now based in Brook House, Park Lane. It has regained its place as one of the leading public property investment companies, perhaps the second largest in the country, developing many office blocks and shopping centres.

As a young negotiator, I was somewhat overawed when I met Claud Goddard for the first time. He was a leading member of the profession and senior partner of Goddard & Smith of St James's. He was a typically autocratic Victorian boss who wore a bowler hat and dressed in a style befitting a professional gentleman of that era – although the loop on his bowler hat and rubicund complexion caused him to be nicknamed in some quarters as the 'cabby'. He usually arrived at the office in his immaculate landaulet with chauffeur in leggings and tailored livery. The front of the car where the driver sat was open, with two impressive silver headlamps on either side, while Claud Goddard was snugly covered in the back seat with a fur rug. I am told that, when he was approaching the office, it was customary for the commissionaire on duty, a Mr Hatcher, to open the door of the front office and to shout 'Heads Down' which was the signal for everyone to be diligently at work. After the rug was unfurled and Goddard alighted with the help of his chauffeur, in order to create the appropriate impression with his staff it was his custom to dash quickly through the office and dive up the first flight of stairs without stopping. But the staff noticed that when he reached the top stair, he was obliged to stop and recover his breath to open the door of his private office. Nowadays, in complete contrast, most junior members of professional firms are no longer terrified in the presence of the senior partner and it is not unusual for a junior typist passing the senior partner of a firm on the staircase to greet him with a casual 'Hello'.

Claud Goddard was a great property man and built up a large professional practice with many personal clients of high standing including the late Sir Edward Mountain, chairman of the Eagle Star Insurance Company who, in latter years, was followed by Sir Brian Mountain and more recently, Sir Denis Mountain. Sir Edward Mountain had close links with Philip Hill who set up an issuing house in St James's known as Philip Hill & Partners. This grew into a merchant bank – formerly Philip Hill, Higginson Erlangers Limited and now the well known Hill Samuel – with Lord Keith of Castleacre and Sir Harry Moore, at that time plain Kenneth Keith and Harry Moore, as principal directors. In turn, they had close links with Second Covent Garden Property Co Ltd, a public company which carried out a large number of shop property developments in its early days with Woolworths and other chain stores as tenants. The name was changed to Hill Samuel, now one of the leading international merchant banks, on the merger with M. Samuel & Co headed by Lord Bearsted and the Hon Peter Samuel and assisted by William de Gelsey. In more recent years, William de Gelsey joined the Orion Bank and I always used to enjoy his cocktail parties which were thronged with city financiers as well as elegant young ladies.

Claud Goddard had strong support from his partners, Alec Brownfield-Pope and George Bourner, who in turn became senior partners and are mentioned in another chapter. One incident underlines Claud Goddard's style. His firm was instructed to carry out a survey and valuation for one of the largest brewers with pubs throughout the country. Claud Goddard received an urgent message from the brewers' chairman stating that he and his board wished to see him personally. They were duly shown into his office by appointment and the chairman said: 'Mr Goddard, before you proceed with this valuation, will you tell us whether your office has ever carried out a brewery valuation?' Goddard sat up in his chair and replied in commanding and measured tones, pointing downwards: 'Sir, if you knew what was in the bottom drawer of this desk, you would be amazed'. No-one knew what was in this bottom drawer, but the brewers left the office fully assured and the valuation was carried out. I am told that Goddard did not blink an eye-lid, although one or two of the staff were hot around the collar when they escorted the chairman and managing director of the brewers out of the office, knowing that the firm had never valued a brewery previously.

A former senior partner of the firm, Alan Ongley, remembers when, as a junior and a somewhat inexperienced surveyor, he was terrified when instructed to jump into a car with Claud Goddard to journey to Slough. He sat nervously beside the principal, hardly daring to say a word, crouched on the far corner of the back seat. The car stopped abruptly at a factory owned by J. Lyons & Co at Slough and Claud Goddard alighted, followed by Alan Ongley. Without any preliminaries, Goddard walked round the factory at a fast pace calling out, without taking a breath: 'Eaves heights, loading facilities, roof, heating, draining, lighting, area, car parking.' He then came back to the car and said to the startled Alan Ongley: 'I shall want your full written report by 9.00 tomorrow morning.' Alan Ongley was completely bewildered, but was too frightened to question his nerve-wracking boss. However, by a stoke of good fortune, he remembered that one of the surveyors at the head office of J. Lyons was a friend of his. He was able to call upon his friend at 7.00 the following morning to borrow a copy of a full survey report describing the property in detail and to hand his own report to Claud Goddard at 9.00 a.m. as instructed.

Harold J. Colebrook, a well-known property owner, was a neighbour of Claud Goddard at Fulmer, Bucks, and was reputed to be responsible for building the whole of this picturesque village in order to preserve the amenities. In later years, Harold Colebrook moved into a house called Penn Wood and it is a coincidence that this later became the home of Sir Robert Bellinger – a boyhood friend of mine who became Lord Mayor of London. Claud Goddard had extensive stabling and grounds adjacent to his mansion at Fulmer. His hobby was horses and he was famous for the many trophies he won at Olympia and elsewhere in four-in-hand competitions. I am told that he gave up this hobby and fell out with Harold

Colebrook following the large number of trophies won by Colebrook's daughter. Harold Colebrook was a discriminating property man of good taste as well as good judgement. He owned, among other buildings in the West End, the Burlington Arcade in Piccadilly and Stanbrook House in Old Bond Street. The Burlington Arcade is now owned as an investment by the Prudential Assurance Company whose Estates Department are renowned for selecting sound investments. Among other deals undertaken by Harold Colebrook was the purchase of the exclusive Connaught Hotel in Mayfair. This was introduced to him verbally by Yates & Yates, the auctioneers of Hanover Square, the purchase price being £250,000 – a substantial sum in those days. Harold Colebrook acquired the shares of the company and notified Cecil Levy, the senior partner of Yates & Yates, that he had completed the purchase. He then sent him a cheque for his professional fees – the whole matter being dealt with on trust by two gentlemen who considered it unnecessary to confirm the undertaking by letter. It follows that Harold Colebrook was a charming man of his word and Cecil Levy was a traditional professional man who retained old-world courtesies. Subsequently, in order to raise capital, Harold Colebrook wished to sell off the freehold of the Connaught with a created ground rent, instructing Yates & Yates. In spite of the hotel's location in Mayfair, all the investment institutions rejected the purchase of the freehold ground rent because they regarded a building with a licence for intoxicating liquors unsuitable for inclusion in their portfolios. How the world has changed! Cecil Levy, however, was able to sell the building to the Trustees of the Duke of Westminster's Estate who owned all the adjacent property and he had little difficulty in coming to terms with Geoffrey Singer who was then Chief Estates Surveyor to the Grosvenor Estate.

3

THE MAN WHO FINANCED MY START

*

I first met Walter Sawyer at the offices of Dudley Samuel & Harrison after he had sold out a chain of hardware shops known as Hopes Limited to Timothy Whites & Taylors. He had many financial interests and wished to invest some of his capital in real estate. He was a mature, diminutive, dapper man with an air of confidence and considerable wealth. He lived in Totteridge and had landed estates in Ferring-on-Sea with beach rights. His offices were at 3 St James's Square under the name of Whitehall Properties Limited and, after I had taken over from Charles Morse as manager of the Suburban Shops Department at Dudley Samuel & Harrison, I handled a number of properties for Walter Sawyer and we established a bond of mutual trust. He was a gentleman of good manners and good taste, thought and spoke quickly, appeared casual and was not aggressive like some of the other tycoon clients I have met.

Walter Sawyer would not deal with any other member of the firm but me, and one day he asked why I had not thought of starting my own practice. I had to admit that my professional ideas were somewhat different from my employers', but I had no capital to open my own office. He asked me how much was required, to which I replied £1,500. Walter Sawyer said in a flash: 'Find an office, tell Dudley Samuel and I will open an account for you at my bank, the National Provincial Bank in Piccadilly and £1,500 will be credited to your account.' He also introduced me to his accountants, Vincent & Goodrich – an old-established professional city firm and a partnership of undoubted integrity – with somewhat austere and well used offices in Queen Street, Cheapside. At that time the senior partner was 'Grandfather' Alan Clarke Vincent and my affairs were dealt with by 'Father' Peter Clarke Vincent. On his retirement his eldest son, John Clarke Vincent, took over and, on his retirement, his younger brother, Robert Vincent, replaced him. He still acts for my firm, but the independent firm of Vincent & Goodrich has become a large modern partnership by merging with other accountants. It is now known as Buzzacott & Co with elaborate, more expensive offices in Salisbury Square House and specialist partners dealing with taxation, trusts and corporate matters. Though the organisation has completely changed during the years, their integrity remains intact.

I asked Walter Sawyer about a partnership agreement and he said: 'I shall trust you to give me a share of your profits.' The trust between us was a great thrill and incentive to me and I took immediate action. First, I saw Dudley Samuel, who offered me a partnership to stay with the firm but, seeing that I had made up my mind to leave, and in fact, had already agreed to take offices at 35 Maddox Street, he decided to take a generous view and I left on a friendly footing. He asked if I had invited any of the firm's staff to go with me. My answer was 'no' but I made a request to invite Miss Gertrude A'Brook, a young, rather self-effacing, shy and serious-looking teenage girl, who was plainly dressed but whose underwear always protruded below her skirt. She was regarded by many in the office as inefficient and stupid. Incidentally, it was customary in those days to address your secretary with the prefix 'Miss', unless, of course, she had worked for you for many years. I thought that with experience and training Miss A'Brook would prove to be a good secretary. Dudley Samuel seemed almost relieved to lose her, so I invited her to meet me at Fullers Tea Shop in Regent Street. Miss A'Brook appeared, amazed to be asked to become my secretary at a salary three times as much as she was then paid – £1 10s 0d a week – but I wanted her to look smart and to buy a complete new outfit. I would pay for this, on the understanding that she would act and feel her importance as my secretary. She was elated and became a first-class, efficient and trustworthy secretary who looked after my affairs with loyalty and complete trust up to the outbreak of war in 1939.

The ground floor and basement offices at 35 Maddox Street were well situated alongside Hillier Parker May & Rowden, Dudley Samuel & Harrison and J. Trevor & Sons. I rented them from the Washington Singer Estate (the owners of the Singer Sewing Machine Company) at a modest rent and, on 18 June 1934, I set up practice as Edward Erdman & Co. The enormous enthusiasm generated by starting a new, young, agent's practice in the right location, ready to give whole-hearted service to clients and with the energy and the will to work all hours, operating within a rigid policy to rely only on professional fees and not to participate in property dealing, resulted in immediate success. In 1934, I found myself sitting in my newly acquired office at 35 Maddox Street with some inexpensive, mass-produced office furniture, two Royal manual typewriters and my former secretary, Gertrude A'Brook – looking quite attractive in her new, more fashionable outfit and completely transformed from a junior typist to a fully-fledged secretary. I had previously visited the sales department of the London Telephone Service to secure a good telephone number and I obtained Mayfair 4444. I did not realise at the time that this would produce callers for the London Clinic and Debenhams. Our telegraphic address became All Fours London – but we always managed to keep both feet on the ground. I had also recruited a totally inexperienced but bright young office boy named Gooden, who joined me straight from school and whose future progress exemplified his name. Len Gooden is now one of the senior members of a well-known firm of auctioneers in Bromley, Kent. My next step was to engage some staff and I dictated an advertisement for keen young negotiators with previous experience. Salaries were low and I was fortunate to attract the services of some first-class men whose loyalty and help enabled me to lay the foundations of the practice. I specialised in shop property and was lucky that an enormous expansion of multiple retailers was taking place at that time. The multiples were able and willing to pay good prices to buy out private shopkeepers who owned and occupied shops in sought-after locations. There was also the opportunity to promote the development of new shopping parades in growing districts. In addition, many shop property speculators felt free to utilise our services, knowing that there would be no breach of confidence and that they could rely upon our professional integrity.

The first negotiator was Stanley Behrens who, at the age of 19, was already a seasoned campaigner from estate offices in Hampstead and Baker Street – in both of which he felt the opportunities for progress were far too limited. The Behrens family is well known in the property industry. Stanley's cousin, Clive, is a director of Land Securities Management and joint managing director of Ravenseft Properties, part of the giant Land Securities Investment Trust. He is a keen golfer and has been appointed president of the Surrey County Golf Union. Clive's brother, Victor Behrens, who has been closely connected with the Chichester Festival Theatre since its inception, has had his own successful practice for many years in partnership with Bertie Sandhurst who recently retired. At that time, Victor – like me – as a young man was employed by Dudley Samuel & Harrison to whom I had just given notice. He therefore gave Stanley Behrens the tip that I was starting my own office and Stanley took the initiative to approach me before my advertisement appeared. From his first day at Edward Erdman & Co, Stanley was keen and enthusiastic with a determination to succeed – and his energy has not diminished. He is an individualist, preferring to initiate transactions rather than be involved in the red tape of office routine and staff management. He helped build up the rapidly expanding shops side of the practice, based on the goodwill generated with well-known retail companies wishing to expand. Edward Mowle joined me only a few weeks after Stanley Behrens. He had previous experience with two other firms, including the eminent City surveyors, Matthews & Goodman, whose senior partner at that time was the celebrated Sir Roy Matthews who, after a distinguished career, has retired to the Isle of Man. Eddy Mowle, a man of strong principle and high standards, was a perfectionist, most meticulous and reliable, and his organising ability was a great asset to the development of the practice. The practice went from strength to strength. I engaged a number of young men as junior negotiators – Henry Rosswick, Hector Perkins, Ted Stringer, Bertram Sandhurst, Laurence Knight, Leonard Jackson, Eric Buswell, Richard Stephenson, Gordon Hand, Boris Prevezer, Joseph Fooks, Len

Gooden and others. I gave training lectures after hours almost every evening in the early days from 6.30 – 9.00 p.m. and departments were set up. I doubt if young men would be keen to work such late hours nowadays.

In the first two years, I was lucky enough to pay my backer, Walter Sawyer, a good return on his investment and to repay the whole of the capital he invested. After this, to my amazement, he said: 'You can now keep the practice, it's yours.' I shall never forget his generosity as he had the moral right to share the profits of the practice for evermore. I shall always be grateful for this gesture which, in itself, was an inspiration for further effort as I became the sole owner of the practice. I employed additional staff and secured adjacent premises at 37 Maddox Street. I was proud to carry out the conversion linking both buildings. A solid mahogany door in the centre was bought at a discount from my clients, J. Glikstem & Sons, now the International Timber Corporation. This central door and the railings I installed in 1937 are still to be seen at 35–7 Maddox Street today.

After I had established my practice, my cousin, Edward Footring, set up in practice as Footring & Co at 12a Maddox Street, quite close to my office. Edward Footring became an extremely able solicitor and the fact that we shared a Maddox Street address was convenient. I could call at his office for instant legal advice and, sometimes I introduced some of my clients to him. But Maddox Street developed a bad name for prostitutes. There were a number of flats above many of the ground floor offices and the street's reputation centred on estate agents' activities during the day and prostitution at night. Above Edward Footring's second-floor offices were four flats, each occupied by a lady of easy virtue. Much to his annoyance, visiting cards were plastered on the door bells at ground-floor level leading to the flats above – with names like 'Yvonne' and 'Paula'. To be fair, there was no evidence of the ladies' activities during the day, but at night, after most of the offices had closed, many of them would promenade along Maddox Street with their small dogs on a lead. One night, when Edward Footring was walking home briskly, wearing his bowler hat and carrying his brief case and umbrella, he was wrapped in thought and wore a stern expression on his face. One of the Maddox Street ladies accosted him with: 'Good evening dear – would you like a cup of tea?' Recognising her as Paula, who lived on the third floor above his offices, he pointed a remonstrating finger and said: 'I'm not thirsty, your name is Paula and you live on the third floor at 12a Maddox Street.' The lady in question thought she had fallen foul of the law and, not only did she hurry down Maddox Street, but also swiftly vacated her apartment in the morning – and was never seen again.

Edward gave up his practice on the outbreak of war and joined the army. After the war, with the rank of major, he returned to London and joined, as a partner, Harris Chetham & Co of Stratford Place, a solicitors' practice which had been established for well over 100 years, now known as Chethams. Many of his pre-war clients consulted him again and he was soon busily engaged. Arthur Chetham, a fine Victorian gentleman lawyer who was nearing retirement age, called Edward into his office after the first fortnight and asked how he was progressing. He replied that all was under control but that, after 6.30 at night, when the office boy had gone, he had to fold and post his own letters. This had not happened in the past. Arthur Chetham replied: 'I have never been satisfied with the office boy', called his secretary and asked: 'How long has the boy been with us ?'. '45 years' was the answer. Chetham grunted to himself: 'I told him not to get married and that it would be too much for him.' The 'office boy' was then about 60. The senior partner of Chethams is now John Franks, an able and quick fire solicitor of the old school who likes personally to handle the affairs of his clients – whatever the problem – without despatching them to other specialist departments. His senior conveyancing partner is Leslie Mitchell, a charming man who is in semi-retirement.

Edward Footring built up a great reputation at Harris Chetham & Co – so much so that one of his influential clients, A.L. Oppenheim, enticed him to leave the practice to become managing director of a public company. Due to various mergers, Edward then had an interlude in the financial world as a director of several public companies but, at heart, he was always a professional lawyer and eventually returned to his old profession. He joined Titmuss, Sainer & Webb, the well-known City solicitors whose senior partner is Leonard Sainer. Leonard became chairman of Sears Holdings Limited, the empire of the late Sir Charles Clore, and is mentioned elsewhere in the book.

4

MASTER BUILDERS

*

During the 1930's, London was expanding and a large number of housing estates sprang up in the suburbs. The men who built literally thousands of houses between the wars were pioneers in their own right. One of them is that remarkable figure, Sir Frank Taylor, whose career reads almost like a fairy tale. I find it hard to imagine that Frank Taylor, with his charm, courtesy, soft speaking voice and sophistication, started from modest beginnings by building two houses in Central Drive, Blackpool, in 1921. One house was for his parents and the other was sold after arranging a bank loan. He then built another 85 with a further loan. After this, he turned his attention to the London suburbs, building houses on 120 acres of land at Grange Park, at Hayes End, Southall, Perivale, Kenton, Stanmore, Edgware, Ruislip, Eastcote, Sudbury and elsewhere.

In 1935, he transformed this vast growing enterprise into a public company known as Taylor Woodrow Building & Civil Engineering Contractors. The Taylor Woodrow Group now includes many subsidiary companies constructing buildings in the United Kingdom and abroad. There are associate companies in France, Italy, America, Canada, Australia, Africa, India and Malaysia. In 1956, Frank Taylor married his former secretary, Christine, who, apart from her charm, has great ability. A member of the main Taylor Woodrow Board (having been with the firm for 35 years), it is said that whenever Lady Taylor travels the world with Sir Frank, she packs slacks and wellingtons in her luggage, ready to inspect any muddy site. To possess the leadership and drive necessary to create such a huge empire, Sir Frank – like other men of his stature – has an inner compulsion of service, high principles and unbounding energy which is an inspiration to others. Still at the helm as its president in 1980, he must sometimes reflect on the phenomenal success of the Taylor Woodrow Group which happened as a result of his efforts to build two houses in Blackpool 60 years earlier. It is worth mentioning that he is the sole founder of the Group – there has never been a Mr Woodrow within the organisation. Woodrow is a family name. The team spirit Sir Frank fosters among his employees is portrayed by the four-man trade mark of his organisation. He is seen in the photograph outside Taylor Woodrow's international headquarters in Ealing, next to the sculpture by David Wynne known as 'Team Work.'

Another outstanding character was a young builder named George Wimpey, who moved into premises under railway arches in Hammersmith in 1880 and set up a small stonemasons' yard. His early success was in road construction and the maintenance of the former London Tramway system. After a productive partnership with Walter Tomes – a skilled mason – George Wimpey's health failed and he died in 1913 aged 58. His three sons and Tomes managed the company until the First World War, when they joined up. The business slipped into decline and in 1919 they sold the company to Godfrey Mitchell, a young captain recently returned from France. The company's first involvement with private-house building arose through its contracts with speculative housebuilders to construct roads and sewers on numerous housing estates.

Godfrey Mitchell (now Sir Godrey Mitchell and president of the Wimpey Group) soon realised that, as far as building operations were concerned, Wimpey could do the job more efficiently than 'spec' builders. Just as important as technical efficiency was practical knowledge of the market. Mitchell decided, therefore, that the secret of success was to build the right houses in the right places and at the right prices. Wimpey's first practical experience of speculative house building came when he acquired land for a dozen houses at Greenford in Middlesex. The first scheme was a success; a second of 26 houses was also successful. After a third scheme of 200 houses, Mitchell arranged for Wimpey to set up a development organisation to include legal services, land survey, architectural, civil engineering and publicity departments – all under one roof. He had, therefore, placed the firm in a favourable position to take advantage of the house-building boom of the 1930's. During the ten years up to the outbreak of the Second World War, Wimpey was building 1,000 homes annually and when war broke out in 1939, the company had completed 10,000 houses. The tradition of performance continues. In 1978, I understand that Wimpey Homes Holdings Ltd built 6,000 houses for local authorities and sold more than 10,000 to private occupiers. Now a large, international organisation, George Wimpey & Co has formed signficant links with many leading property development companies. At present the Wimpey Construction Company is one of the largest in the UK, with a turnover of about £1,000 million. Like Taylor Woodrow, this vast company has branches throughout the world, including France, Spain, Canada, America, the Caribbean and other countries. It is a pity that the hard-working builder, George Wimpey, is not here to see the effect of his early labours.

*

Another distinguished building contractor who turned a small family firm into a civil engineering and building organisation of international proportions was Sir John Laing, who, like others, started from a modest background. Sir John had no difficulty in blending a successful business career with high-standing, Christian, religious principles. In later years, during a period of outstanding success, he avoided luxury and led a modest life with an emphasis on service to others. His strong beliefs and social conscience inspired the growth of his organisation and Laings are now one of the largest contractors in the country. After completing small building jobs for farmers around Carlisle, he built a large housing estate locally and decided to set up in Mill Hill, north-west London. He then built a large number of houses in the London suburbs, including Golders Green, Colindale, Sudbury, Woodford, Canons Park, Boreham Wood, Elstree, Cranford, Shooters Hill, Blackheath and Enfield. Laings, on occasions, produced slightly more expensive houses, with special attention to finishes and landscaping. These homes were sometimes known as 'Laings' Little Palaces.' A founder member of the National House Builders Council formed to improve housing standards, Sir John died in January 1978 aged 99. He was fortunate in being followed into the business by two able sons – Sir (John) Maurice Laing, who joined the firm in 1935, and Sir (William) Kirby Laing in 1937. Sir Maurice is, among other appointments, a director of the Bank of England.

Laings' present management has expanded the organisation and a large amount of commercial development is undertaken in the UK and overseas. The company has separate contracting, property development, housing and international divisions. At present, it also continues to build modern shopping centres – one of the first of which was the Bull Ring at Birmingham. Unique in its time, the Bull Ring involved a capital outlay of many millions. Due to transport and town planning requirements, Laings – who won the scheme by tender – were obliged to construct the centre on a complicated layout with shops on five different levels and with several access points from adjoining buildings including the bus station, market, car park, main thoroughfare and station. The shops were offered for letting too early during the construction period when the site was full of scaffolding. It was, therefore, difficult for retailers to visualise the final layout and prospective tenants proved hard to find. Maurice Robson, property director of Laings at that time, then instructed my office as letting agents. Adverse early publicity could have been disastrous, but we found Laings the ideal clients who gave us maximum backing. They created a local letting office and spent a lot of money on publicity when the building was finished – and thus every shop was let, many to leading multiple firms. I have always felt that clients of a lesser calibre might have felt a sense of panic at the lack of tenant-response before building work had been completed.

*

Leo Meyer, who founded the Ideal Building and Land Developmen

Company, was perhaps one of the largest housebuilders of the 1930's. He built as many as 5,000 houses a year, ranging in price from £370 upwards, in more than 100 estates around London and the Home Counties. He concentrated on low-cost popular housing and operated as Ideal Homesteads, one of his chief subsidiaries. The late Leo Meyer was a rugged invidualist. His career began with a company called Blackwell & Meyer which went into voluntary liquidation. A man of his word, he swore that, if he ever came into money again, he would pay off all his creditors in full. Within two or three days – following the flotation of Ideal Building & Land Development Company – he invited all his creditors to see him and paid them in full. They responded by presenting him with a gold cigarette case inscribed: 'To the whitest man we ever met.' Leo Meyer's son, James, upholds the family tradition and is chairman and joint managing director of Federated Land & Building Company of Dorking – a public property development company which produces housing estates and commercial buildings.

*

Richard Costain is another famous name in the building industry who, assisted by other members of his family, built up an international construction and civil engineering group known as Richard Costain Limited. He also made a substantial contribution to housing between the wars and one of his outstanding developments of 2,500 houses in Romford, Essex, was known as Elm Park Garden City. Richard Costain conceived the idea of designing and building an entire 'Garden City' at the time when a new underground station was built to offer commuters fast electric trains to the City, connecting to all parts of London. The cost of a quarterly season ticket to and from the Mansion House was then only £3 19s 9d. Socially-minded, he created a self-contained town with local shops, a recreation hall and sports fields and, in order to promote residents' social amenities, he sponsored a Gardens Guild, tennis, football and Men's Clubs, dancing, amateur entertainment and other social events. New residents were welcomed to membership of the Residents' Association to have a voice in the affairs of Elm Park. In the 1920's and 1930's social changes produced the concept of communual living and developers responded by building blocks of flats. Costain was responsible for building – between the wars – Dolphin Square, one of the largest flat developments in London, overlooking the Thames between Chelsea and Vauxhall Bridge. It contains 1,250 self-contained flats with communual facilities such as swimming pool, gym, squash courts, restaurant, open space for recreation, shops – including a hairdresser's – library with a large car park, garage and even a children's nursery. In recent years, Costains has developed a mining division and has expanded its operations to the USA, Australia, Germany, Jordan and Zimbabwe. The company still builds, on average, 2,000 houses annually.

A large number of blocks of flats were built by Reginald Toms and Anthony Somers of the Bell Property Trust – probably the most prominent and successful developers of medium priced purpose built flats in the 1930's. Reggie left the Air Force after the First World War. Originally from farming stock, he was a skilful engineer and seized upon the idea of buying obsolete War Department motor parts and vehicles for conversion into roadworthy lorries and coaches. Success enabled him to run private bus services before passenger transport services were nationalised. He created Blue Bell coaches and Red and White coaches, building London's first coach station at Clapham in which he subsequently sold his interest. Through the introduction of the late Sir Brian Mountain, then chairman of the Eagle Star Insurance Company, Reggie met Anthony Somers, an economist and financial man engaged in hire purchase, and together they formed the Bell Property Trust for the purpose of carrying out flat development. With this in mind, Reggie formed his own architectural practice around 1930 known as Toms & Partners. William Biggs, the architect, subsequently joined the firm. He was a good designer and also a practical man of outstanding ability. While acting for the Bell Group, he designed the huge block of over 500 flats known as Park West, near Marble Arch. A spectacular block – almost as large as Dolphin Square – it has been in the news a great deal for one reason or another.

Apart from the large portfolio of modern flats, through a number of small companies Reggie Toms and Tony Somers bought out thousands of small suburban houses at low prices from building societies and other mortgagees. Reggie Toms left Toms & Partners in 1939 but William Biggs continued the practice throughout the war, building aircraft factories and other wartime emergency installations. Reggie had amassed a large fortune and I am told that he came to the rescue of the Hawker Siddely Aircraft Company – builders of Hurricane fighter planes – when it was in difficulty. Due to post-war Government legislation, building flats on any scale was no longer a commercial proposition so Toms and Somers settled abroad. Toms was a great collector of oriental carpets and tapestries and is said to have had the finest collection in the world. He died in 1968 at the age of 85 leaving a huge fortune. Tony Somers is still active and, since the end of the war, has built houses and flats in Nassau, on the French and Italian Rivieras and in Paris.

At that time, Edward Stone, the surveyor and architect, was practising as Norfolk & Prior. He had a flair for spotting sites with redevelopment potential and was prominent in designing many cinemas and theatres in the late 1920's including the Whitehall, Piccadilly and London Casino. A friend of Lord Austin of Austin Cars, he designed the British Leyland Longbridge Works at Birmingham. He used to joke that he built Ansells Brewery in Birmingham at the same time because the factory staff worked so hard on the Austin Sevens that they needed proper lubrication! After

Stone's sudden death in 1948, William Biggs arranged the amalgamation of both architectural practices – which became known as Stone Toms & Partners – and is still active today. The firm designed a large number of office blocks including the Empress State Building at Earls Court and the Associated Television complex at Elstree.

*

Christopher Hutley, known as Tony Hutley, was good looking, charming, witty and ex-public school. He was dubbed 'the handsome Mr Hutley' by the Press. George Farrow was a Cockney boy from a modest background who had an outstanding flair for finance and organisation and together, he and Tony made an excellent team. In the early 1930's, Tony had been secretary, accountant and technical adviser to a group of small companies specialising in land development and speculative house building in Petts Wood, Kent. George Farrow became his assistant. In 1938, they formed a company – Farley Properties Limited – and began property development on a small scale, gaining valuable experience before the outbreak of war. Tony served in the Army and George in the RAF, the latter completing his service as a sergeant under the education and vocational scheme. He learned accountancy, company and mercantile law and passed the final exams of the Institute of Chartered Secretaries. Whenever they met during the war, they analysed and discussed the future of the property market in peacetime. They decided that, once the war was over, there was money to be made in selling houses to sitting tenants. Suitable houses could be purchased as investments at a price equivalent to about one third of the cost of the land plus the total cost of building. They agreed to confine themselves to houses built between 1928 and 1939. They even managed to acquire a few houses during the war without capital, having persuaded the mortgagees to debit the interest and credit the rents received between 1939 and 1945. After demobilisation, they began operating on these lines from Petts Wood. Their capital consisted of their demobilisation gratuities, but with unbounded enthusiasm and the will to work, they promptly started selling off their wartime acquisitions piecemeal to sitting tenants with considerable success. With complete trust in one another, they entered into a written unconditional partnership agreement for life. They were willing to work hard up to any hours of night to sell to sitting tenants. This usually meant calling well after office hours when husbands had returned from work. They eventually became one of the biggest, specialised house-selling agents to sitting tenants in the business.

In 1947 they purchased a company known as A. Peachey & Company Limited – a quoted public company – whose balance sheet consisted of 130 houses, seven shops, some land of dubious value and losses of nearly £70,000. They acquired the controlling interest by borrowing from the bank the whole of the capital required. Tony became chairman of the group and George managing director. In the early days, they started with a profit of £500, but increased this consistently until profits rose to a record £1¼ million. In the hey-day of their sitting-tenant sales, when low interest rates prevailed, everybody received a good deal. For instance, tenants could often buy houses on such a basis that the weekly outgoings – less than the rent – were based on a 30-year mortgage at three and a quarter per cent. Although the Peachey Property Group was criticised by both Labour and Tory MPs of the time for selling to tenants, today there may be thousands of people or their heirs who can look back on what was probably the best financial transaction of their lives. It is ironic that a similar process is currently being undertaken by the Greater London Council and the present Government is much in favour of sitting-tenant sales. Tony and George used to purchase properties in single lots, such as one transaction of 4,600 houses and another of 3,000. They built up a first-class door-to-door specialist salesmen team which started work at 6.00 p.m., and it was not unknown for them to sell and complete 100 houses a week. They were able to arrange simultaneous mortgage facilities for tenants by having standing arrangements with building societies. Their greatest achievement was the personal negotiation they conducted to acquire the Bell Property Group and its consolidation with the Peachey Group to form the Peachey Property Corporation. The acquisition of the Bell Property Trust and associate companies gave the company control of a large portfolio of first class modern blocks of flats in Hampstead, Streatham and elsewhere and, of course, Park West – the huge block of flats including shops at Marble Arch. In later years, this became a major asset. In time, because of the scarcity of suitable houses and flats, the two men turned their attention to more traditional forms of commercial property development and investment. Again, they were successful. Tony died in January 1961 and George succeeded him as chairman. He continued to build up the company, undertaking several commercial developments. But after a heart attack in 1964 he was forced to slow down and three years later he resigned as chairman and managing director to live abroad for health reasons; Eric Miller succeeded him.

*

Another outstanding personality was Charles Peczenik. A man of great taste who lived to a ripe old age, he designed and built expensive luxury blocks of apartments and, in particular, some of the magnificent residential buildings in Grosvenor Square. He developed 1–3 Grosvenor Square on the corner of Grosvenor Street as a luxurious block of flats. It was acquired by the American Embassy and, when the Americans moved into their new Embassy on the west side of Grosvenor Square, the building was taken over by the Canadian Embassy, who occupy it today. A feature of the building, apart from its attractive elevation, is the spacious hall and impressive staircases leading to the flats. Peczenik was also responsible for the construction of 48 Grosvenor Square. The building bears a plaque inscribed with his name – although the official seal of the London County Council is missing from the inscription. He built several other palatial luxury blocks of flats in the West End including an impressive block in Mansfield Street, close to Portland Place. He moved in fashionable circles and paid seasonal visits to the French Riviera and Deauville. I last saw him there when he was over 90 – keen and alert as ever but, sadly, in a wheelchair.

Sidney Kaye, the architect responsible for, among other buildings, the Hilton Hotel at Hyde Park Corner, tells me that when he began preparing working drawings for a new block of flats at 17 Grosvenor Square, he decided to consult Peczenik for the benefit of his experience and advice. Peczenik was then 94 and Sidney remembers the advice he was given: 'Remember, my boy – le premier impression.' Peczenik was, of course, referring to the lavish entrance halls and massive staircases of his developments, although the flats within them may not have come up to such a high standard. In some, for instance, the baths were particularly high, saving, perhaps, the expense of a hole in the floor slab to take the waste trap from the bath.

Another developer and building contractor with whom I had dealings was Harry Neal. Between the wars, he built two luxury blocks of flats at 45 and 47 Grosvenor Square, two blocks of flats known as Albion Gate in Bayswater Road facing Hyde Park, 7–11 Princes Gate and the block known as Melton Court opposite South Kensington Station. In addition, his company built Hobart House at 40 Grosvenor Place – now occupied by the Coal Board.

*

Walking down Regent Street today, it may be hard to believe that in 1937–38, many well built Crown properties on the west side were empty and to let. Some occupiers during the slump even complained they could not pay the rates. One of the vacant properties was 211 Regent Street, formerly a 'Maison Lyons' of the caterers, J. Lyons & Co. The leasehold interest was owned by George West Limited forming part of the Aquascutum Group – the chairman of which was the late Isidor Abrahams. At that time, Aquascutum concentrated on waterproof clothing and raincoats.

Henry Rosswick, the senior negotiator dealing with offices in my Maddox Street office managed to obtain a definite offer to rent 211 Regent Street at £3,500 a year from Hoover Ltd who had some offices at Upper Regent Street, close to Oxford Circus. This was quite an achievement but one small point had to be settled before the solicitors were instructed. It concerned the allowance of about £300 to be given to Hoovers against the first payment of rent to cover certain dilapidations. In order to conclude the transaction, Henry Rosswick thought that it would be a good idea if he fixed an appointment for Isidor Abrahams to visit Hoover's offices in Upper Regent Street to agree the sum and shake hands on the deal. Abrahams and Rosswick duly arrived for this meeting and the receptionist informed them that there was likely to be a delay as Hoover's directors were engaged in an emergency meeting. Abrahams – an important man in his own right and rather sensitive – was irritated by the delay. He also seemed to think that American executives were less polite than their English counterparts. After waiting more than ten minutes, he became incensed, passed some derogatory remarks about American business courtesies, stated that the transaction was at an end and stamped out of the office – followed in hot pursuit by a most perturbed Rosswick, who walked all the way down Regent Street imploring Abrahams to change his mind, pointing out that a letting like this was impossible to repeat. But to no avail. A pallid and drawn Rosswick returned to the office and asked me to intervene. As it was about noon, I decided it might be better to talk to Isidor Abrahams after lunch when I hoped he might have calmed down a little. I first telephoned the chief executive of Hoover's and, after a chat, asked him whether, as a favour, he and his colleagues would be willing to visit Abrahams at the latter's office as a compromise. In order to reinstate the negotiations which were in Abraham's best interests and at the same time, to appease his ego, I felt justified in adopting a rather exaggerated method of negotiation. I telephoned Abrahams and started the conversation by saying: 'I am ringing you up to congratulate you.' There was complete silence at the other end of the phone. I then said that his firm attitude had caused Hoovers to go on with the deal without asking for further concessions and they were now prepared to 'eat humble pie' and to call to see him at his offices. I fixed the appointment, met Hoovers with Abrahams at his offices and the deal was concluded.

The sons of Isidor Abrahams, Sir Charles Abrahams and Gerald Abrahams – after returning from active service in the Air Force and the Army respectively in 1945 – expanded and developed the business into an international clothing manufacturing firm of national importance. They have both been honoured for public service.

*

Victor Kempner, a property consultant who runs a property investment company, is married to Bunny – formerly a ballerina with Sadlers Wells – whose sister is Dame Alicia Markova. Before the war, as a bachelor fond of the odd diversion from work, he took inexpensive trips to Paris at weekends by cross-channel steamer and train. Victor's parents were a little conservative, and because they believed Paris to be a bad place for a young man, Victor concealed from them his occasional weekend visits. I recollect reading a story in the *Daily Express* about a young Englishman who had been arrested by mistake in Montmartre. It was Victor. After leaving a club with friends, he was arrested by two French detectives and taken to a police station. A few hours later, still with no explanation whatsoever, Victor and his friends were unceremoniously shown the door and released. I believe that to this day he is puzzled as to why he and his party had been arrested. Victor was always a refined gentleman and, having recovered from this indignity, the next day he boarded the cross-channel steamer to return to Dover. In the bar during the crossing, he met a pleasant fellow with whom he passed the time of day – including an account of his arrest in Montmartre. To his horror, his name and the entire story appeared on the front page of the *Daily Express* the following morning. The friendly gentleman in the bar was Geoffrey Cox, the paper's Paris correspondent. He later became Sir Geoffrey Cox, editor and chief executive of ITV who was responsible for the introduction of News at Ten. Victor's parents were shaken and not amused.

5

SUCCESS AS SOLICITOR AND SOLDIER

*

I have pleasant memories of first meeting the late Lionel Wigram in connection with shop property development in Ruislip. He was a tall, handsome young solicitor with a forthright and fearless character and an obvious flair for property. His legal practice, Wigram & Co, was established first in Langham Street and then in a Georgian house in Queen Street, Mayfair. The office was furnished in fine taste with some excellent pine panelling. Lionel Wigram was first in the news in 1938 as a result of a large deal he carried out with the Bute Estate in Cardiff. As a Territorial Officer, he was called up in 1939 and had a most distinguished career in the Royal Fusiliers during the Second World War. I am told he masterminded the adopted method of battle drill for the individual infantry soldier and I am sure that its disciplines saved many lives. I also understand he organised a group in Italy made up of Italian irregulars and which he called the 'Wig Force'. He was killed in action in Italy in 1944 after he had reached the rank of Lieutenant Colonel.

Lionel Wigram worked closely with a friend of his, Francis Winham, who set up a surveyor's practice known as Royds & Co in a similar house in Queen Street a few doors away. Francis Winham – a quiet and careful man – was extremely able, but disliked publicity of any kind. If he was asked how he felt, he used to reply that he was feeling all right but that was not to say he was well. He wore the same soft, trilby hat for years and because of its age, a hole appeared in the top. When it was suggested that he bought a new one, his reply was: 'That hat is the most expensive one I have ever had because, when I go to lunch or out in the evenings, I leave it in the cloakroom and each time I tip the attendant. It has already cost me hundred of pounds and I see no point in going to the expense of buying a new one.' Francis Winham purchased, developed and let many shops to multiple firms. He became wealthy and a leading shareholder on the board of Shop Investments Ltd, a publicly quoted company.

Henry Denton, a shrewd and well-known figure in the property world, was a colleague of Lionel Wigram and was closely associated with both Lionel and Francis Winham until the latter died in 1968. Henry Denton was partly responsible for building up Shop Investments Limited and was engaged in the acquisition of the Bute Estate and the building up of the company which purchased the estate called Western Ground Rents Limited. He ultimately arranged a merger of Shop Investments Limited and other companies with Amalgamated Investments and Property Company Limited and became a member of the board of this latter company under the chairmanship of the late Gabriel Harrison. The untimely death of Gabriel Harrison – a charming and dynamic character – after the property crash in 1973 caused the collapse of Amalgamated. Henry Denton shares my view that if Gabriel Harrison had been living today, he would have been able to place the company on the road to full recovery. Henry Denton was also engaged in the development of two buildings in Bond Street known as the Time and Life Building and the Westbury Hotel. He was a member of the hotel board for more than 20 years, at the end of which the Westbury was taken over by the present owners, Trust House Forte Limited. Respected as a man of considerable judgement and experience, Henry was also chairman of the United Kingdom Property Company Limited and on the boards of many other companies. A keen horse-racing man, Henry Denton was at Ascot one year in a box with some friends. In walked Sir Jack Cohen of Tesco Stores with his wife, Cissie, to have a drink and a chat. Jack Cohen had a horse running called 'Tesco Boy' and an indiscreet guest present asked him if he thought his horse had any chance. The owner of the box, somewhat embarrassed, waited agog for a racing tip straight from the owner's mouth. Jack Cohen, hesitating before answering, replied dryly: 'I only wish I knew'. Henry Denton is still to be found at Wigram & Co, but has sold their offices in Queen Street and moved to Queen Anne Street.

*

In the thirties, I had occasion to meet Oscar Deutsch – a remarkable man of small, unassuming stature but possessing enormous drive and energy. The son of emigrants from central Europe, he was born in Birmingham and educated locally at the King Edward Grammar School. Fascinated by the cinema from an early age, he was the creator of the Odeon Cinema chain, devising a unique method of financing the building of each cinema by forming a separate company in the town, raising local finance with leading citizens and shopkeepers. He started as a metal merchant, had six cinemas of his own which grew to 26 cinemas in 1933, and it was his aim to build 300 by 1937. I am told it probably only cost between £50,000 and £100,000 to build a cinema in those days and the decor was economically done by Mrs Deutsch. The idea was to build an Odeon of fairly uniform appearance in most of the provincial cities and suburbs as well as in the West End and all parts of London. Because larger cinema groups could monopolise the best film rights, Oscar Deutsch sold 50 per cent of his shares to United Artists – the film distributors of the USA. He died prematurely in 1941 at the age of 48, but by this time he had opened 142 Odeons throughout the country, had another 25 under construction and more in the pipeline. Lord Rank, formerly J. Arthur Rank, was on his board and ultimately took over the company which now forms part of the Rank Cinema Group.

A particular Odeon story springs to mind. Deutsch gave instructions to negotiate possession of an island site he had acquired in the East End of London for another Odeon. There was a number of dilapidated terraced houses on the site occupied by many tenants – among them retired seamen and dockers paying low weekly rents. A few years before, agents had failed to come to terms with the tenants who sub-let rooms to their friends in the hope that each would receive a capital sum to vacate. The local church hall was hired and all the tenants invited to a meeting. They were informed frankly that the site was required for an Odeon cinema and that a generous but uniform sum would be paid for possession of each house. If this was rejected, Odeon Cinemas would abandon the project. Pandemonium broke out in the hall as the tenants and occupiers started to argue heatedly among themselves. It was impossible for those on the platform to restore order, but suddenly a huge, fierce man with a stump on one leg and a crutch, yelled above all the voices of everyone and restored them to order. An old seaman, he was asked on to the platform and invited to form a Tenants' Committee and to become its chairman. As a result, he quickly arranged for everyone to vacate the properties and move to better accommodation in Essex. The Odeon cinema was duly built.

*

In the late 1930's, if a property investment company owned prime income-producing properties, let to banks and first-class concerns, it was next to impossible to float it on the Stock Exchange – the yield to potential shareholders being too low. Morris Bloom, who at one time owned a chain of opticians, conceived the idea of overcoming this problem by forming United Investors Co-operative Society – known as UNICOS – registered under the Friendly Society Act, which permitted national advertising to invite subscriptions by the general public. Around 1936 the Canadian Pacific Railway had acquired freehold houses forming nearly the whole of the east side of Berkeley Square for the purpose of building a hotel. The late Sir Howard Frank, senior partner at that time of Knight Frank & Rutley, was acting for the Canadian Pacific Railway. He approached architect Gordon Jeeves who, assisted by Cecil Eve, designed a hotel on the site. Canadian Pacific decided not to proceed and sold the site to UNICOS. They had accumulated considerable funds from the public and Morris Bloom approached Hector Hamilton to co-operate with Gordon Jeeves's practice in designing Berkeley Square House – a modern office building with showrooms on the ground floor. In order to carry out this ambitious and comprehensive development, Morris Bloom negotiated the purchase of additional houses in Bruton Street – one of which was the birthplace of the present Queen. Then, with the co-operation of Sir Robert

McAlpine & Sons, the contractors, he produced his building. Construction work was completed in record time – starting in 1937 and completed a year later at a cost of £1 million. Our present-day building industry, please note.

Berkeley Square House contains about 300,000 square feet of offices on eight floors, plus showrooms and banking halls on the ground floor and extensive car parking. Bloom was courageous to undertake building what was probably the largest office block in Mayfair before the war. Architect Cecil Eve tells me that after the building was let to the Ministry of Works – just before the outbreak of the war in 1939 – Westminster City Council required that the garages be converted into a First Aid centre. Elaborate air-raid safeguards had also to be installed. Ironically, in 1938 the Council sent two German experts to liaise with the architects and advise on how to gas-proof the building! Through failing health, UNICOS developer Morris Bloom eventually emigrated to Rhodesia, where he undertook some further developments prior to his death. His Berkeley Square House is undoubtedly a London landmark, containing Jack Barclay's Rolls Royce showroom, many banks and other showrooms on the ground floor and well-known international firms occupying the offices. The building was subsequently acquired by Central & District Properties Limited controlled by John Rubens and Barney Shine. This company later merged with Town & City Properties. After the property crisis of 1974, Barry East, then chairman of Town & City, resigned in favour of Jeffrey Sterling. Four years later, in order to reduce outstanding loans, he sold Berkeley Square House for more than £37 million to a consortium of the British Rail Pension Fund and Airways Pension Fund. It is interesting that Berkeley Square was at one time a high-class residential area. Indeed, some of the original properties on the west side built round 1750, are still in existence. Lord Clive of India, George Canning and Horace Walpole are listed as among the Square's former residents.

In recent years I negotiated the sale of the Samuel Estate to the BP Pension Fund, which contained the freehold ground rents of almost all the houses on the west side of Berkeley Square including those occupied by the Claremont Club and Annabel's, together with the majority of the houses in Charles Street, Hill Street and adjoining thoroughfares. The income from these ground rents was low and when I arranged the sale for £6m, I was crowing like 'the Nightingale who sang in Berkeley Square.' Since this time, the value of the estate has inflated to such an extent that when I now cross the Square, I feel somewhat deflated.

*

At the time when the shop property market was strong and booming, some speculators with good judgement and a nose for the right property were able to make profits without investing their own capital. Their method was to 'line up' the purchase of a freehold property at a keen price and then to induce a friendly purchaser to take over the contract – he paying the whole of the purchase price upon completion but allowing the introducer either 50 per cent of the profit upon re-sale for the introduction, or 50 per cent of the shares of a joint company formed for the acquisition. Some entrepreneurs, without any capital outlay, found themselves wealthy through their 50 per cent stakes in companies which made a large profit. Such arrangements ceased to be acceptable when the market started to fluctuate.

One of the early entrepreneurs was the late Arthur Fawke, a shrewd judge of shop property values who did many such deals in the 1930's. An unusual character, he looked like a typical retired gentleman to be seen round clubland in Pall Mall wearing a well-tailored Savile Row tweed suit and bowler hat. Of slim athletic build, he carried a walking stick, never wore an overcoat and had great charm. He claimed to be a descendant of Henry Fulk, great grandson of William of Normandy, Count of Anjou and later Henry II of England and France, the first Plantagenet. Racing, speculating and the countryside took most of his time during weekends. His club life-style enabled him to cultivate a large number of friends and he would visit estate offices in the West End in order to seek out freehold shops at keen prices. Then he would meet the owners direct and come to terms with them on a shake of hands. A man of his word, he befriended many wealthy people and shared deals with them. They relied upon him and never bothered to inspect the property.

In this way – which might be termed precarious – Fawke was able to earn his livelihood to support a large family. After he had carried through a few remunerative deals, he tended to disappear to the country for a spell and would not be seen in the West End for several weeks. He befriended, among others, Louis Denempont, one of the directors of Woolworths at that time. And, although I was not all that keen on horse racing, he persuaded me to join him at Northolt Races at which Mr and Mrs Denempont were running one of their horses called 'Careless Rapture'. Both men handed me large sums of cash to place with the bookies on their behalf on 'Careless Rapture'. They wished to disguise their identity so that the odds would not shorten drastically. I had little money at that time and was told by my hosts that, as a headstrong young man with little knowledge of racing, I should follow them as experienced racehorse owners. I walked away to buy a newspaper to get some tips and the newspaper man said gruffly: 'King Fish for the second race.' I accordingly backed King Fish which won the race, 'Careless Rapture' lost and Mrs Denempont fainted.

Among Arthur Fawke's friends was Bert Hillman, a jovial, well-proportioned butcher from Smithfield who had a number of shops. Although in private life he lived in luxurious style, he still enjoyed wielding the axe in his butcher's shops. I carried out several pleasant transactions with him in association with Fawke.

As a member of the Territorial Army attached to the Kings Royal Rifles, I was called up one week before 3 September 1939. Rather hurriedly, I left the staff at 35–37 Maddox Street. Later, nearly everyone else was called up with the exception of Henry Rosswick, manager of the West End Department, and he ultimately took over our empty offices and practised there as Henry Rosswick & Co. My first company commander was a young captain known as Toby Low. An inspiring leader, he became one of the youngest Brigade Commanders in the Army. As Sir Toby Low, he became MP for Blackpool South after the war and ultimately Lord Aldington, a director of GEC and many other important concerns. In the early days of the war – when I had reached the exalted rank of corporal – I was sent on a leadership course for officers and NCO's. On the same course was Lord Hailsham, the present Lord Chancellor, who was then a lieutenant in the Tower Hamlet Rifles, part of the London Rifle Brigade, a sister unit of ours. It is good to forget the war years. But I remember receiving a letter from Charles Morse who looked after the office equipment for me asking what to do with 20 Royal typewriters which he had difficulty in storing during the bombing of London. I was in North Africa at the time and told him to sell the lot. If I had thought of subsidising my army pay, I should have requested him to hire them out.

*

I was released from the Army at the end of 1945 with a gratuity of £250 and a civilian suit which was not tailored in Savile Row. I set about looking for an office to re-start the practice and I recollect an amusing incident in Maddox Street outside my old offices at Nos 35–37. I was confronted by the lady who ran the café opposite (now part of Healey & Baker's premises) who exclaimed: 'I told Mr Rosswick not to take your offices as I knew you would be back.' While searching the West End, by chance I bumped into Jack Taylor, a former junior member of my staff who had put on a great deal of weight. I shook hands and said: 'You are looking very prosperous,' and he replied: 'I am about to retire,' I thought this a strange coincidence as I was about to start. Jack Taylor was well spoken, had an engaging personality and, apart from being a good pianist and successful composer, he was an able negotiator. Tempted by high living, however, he owned a racehorse called 'Garter Club' and lived lavishly. He eventually ruined what might have been a successful career in estate agency by becoming involved in criminal prosecution.

After walking round the West End, I managed to secure one room as an office at the rear of the first floor at 125 New Bond Street, a few doors from Grosvenor Street. In December 1945 it was extremely difficult to obtain the services of a window cleaner or painter. Fortunately, I spotted a window cleaner finishing a job in Bruton Street. A hat inscribed with his window cleaning company's name provided cover for the decorations he was carrying out illicitly at a time when, because of rationing, it was impossible to get anything without a licence. Uninvited, he volunteered the information that he was an old sailor – after which I said: 'Follow me, mate, I am an old soldier.' Not only did he clean my windows but he also redecorated the room. I paid him well.

On the off chance, I called on a former client, Harry Stanley, who had offices in Princes Street, Hanover Square and who was also in business with Eric Lightfoot – former secretary of Associated British Cinemas. Stanley wished me good luck in my new office and offered to loan me some nice mahogany furniture. 'You can use it and pay me for it in due course' he said. I was grateful for this kind gesture and I soon moved in, duly paid for the furniture which was good antique mahogany and is still used by the firm. I wrote to some of my former partners in the Army. The first man to turn up was Ted Stringer, looking very smart in captain's uniform of the Royal Ulster Rifles with a double Sam Browne belt. Rather shyly, he announced he had married a nurse – Alice – whom he met in India. I managed to get the London telephone service to reinstate my previous number of Mayfair 4444 and, almost within weeks, several former members of the firm had returned from the Services and no less than nine people were working in the same single room. It was an enormous thrill to reopen the practice. I felt young again and the six years that had elapsed seemed like just a few months.

During the first few weeks, with no register of properties and no staff, I walked down Grosvenor Street – a few doors from 125 New Bond Street – thinking of my old canvassing days to see if I could initiate some business. I secured the services of a temporary secretary and my first move was to write to John E. Snell, a former colleague and previously employed at Dudley Samuel & Harrison who had set up on his own account in Bond Street. He had a board on display at 51 Grosvenor Street – a fine old residential house which had been converted for office use by the Government during the war. Snell informed me that the price was £27,500 for a 42 year lease. I asked whether his client would consider an offer of £26,500 and whether he could claim a sum for dilapidations from the Ministry for repairs during its temporary wartime occupation. John Snell said yes, I then telephoned Bert Hillman, the butcher client and friend I had met pre-war through Arthur Fawke. I told Bert that I could secure this property for a bargain £26,500 and recommended he bought it and allowed me to resell on his behalf. He said: 'As a soldier, what the hell do you know about property values? But I have always trusted and relied upon you and, if you think it is a good deal, go ahead.' I did so and this was my first deal after the war. Arthur Fawke's son, Leslie, had qualified as a solicitor, acted on Hillman's behalf and followed in his father's foot-steps.

Within a short time, I was able to resell the building to another pre-war client – A.L. Oppenheim – for £42,500 and Hillman was happy with his quick profit of £16,000. The two commissions for the purchase and resale were my first fees on restarting the practice. In 1946, about six months from the end of the war, business was on the upturn and I let the property for Oppenheim to C.C. Wakefield, the oil firm, at a rental of £7,500 a year. As a result, I was able to secure for Oppenheim a fixed term mortgage of £60,000 at 5½ per cent interest. Having paid £42,500, Oppenheim finished up with £17,500 cash in hand and a net income of more than £4,000 a year after mortgage interest. Not a bad deal!

The additional fees were more than welcome and stabilised the re-establishment of the practice. This was an unusual transaction to take place only about six months after the end of the war. Following my approach to John Snell regarding 51 Grosvenor Street, I called upon Edgar Lane of Lane Saville & Co, well-known Mayfair agents who acted for the owners of No 61 up the road. Edgar Lane shook hands warmly and asked what my intentions were following my release from the Army. I told him I was re-establishing my practice to which he replied: 'I wish you luck – things are highly competitive and I think you will have a tough job.' Number 61 Grosvenor Street was a comparatively small leasehold property let in several floors to produce an income after paying ground rent to the Grosvenor Estate. Lane asked what my clients would pay for it and laughingly handed me his valuation tables, asking which I would use to capitalise the value. I chose the six per cent table as there were reversions and this threw up a price of £12,000 which he agreed he would recommend his clients to accept. I promptly telephoned my old friend, Charles Morse, who had joined Whitehall Properties and recommended the purchase. He agreed and I later resold the property for him at a profit.

My third deal was a property at 43 Conduit Street. After this, I began writing to several pre-war clients, and happy reunions of my former members of staff took place as, one by one, they were released from the Services. The single room at 125 New Bond Street housed, at one time, 11 of us, including Ted Stringer, Eddy Mowle, Stanley Behrens and Hector Perkins. The practice became brisk as a large number of our pre-war clients, although not in touch with us for six years, were loyal and ready to place their business in our hands again. It became vital to secure other premises and I was able to agree a deal with Charles Morse to purchase the leasehold interest of the upper part of 10 Hanover Street with possession of the first floor. Three flats above us were occupied by ladies of easy virtue, although the sub-lease was in the name of a man who resided in the country. I needed possession of these upper floors, and furthermore it was not conducive to our professional practice to share a door-plate with cards inscribed with ladies' christian names above the door bells. I had toughened up after six years in the Army and I decided to take practical steps to ensure we would no longer share the premises. Every time I saw a man standing at the entrance ringing the bell to one of the upper flats, I appeared on the first landing and demanded sternly: 'What do you want?' This had an electrifying effect on these gentlemen; they immediately disappeared at a sharp pace and, for obvious reasons, within a short time the ladies moved out.

About nine months after the war had ended, I received a Mr Green in my office – quite unannounced and without appointment. This was 'Slasher Green', a sergeant in my former unit who was an amusing, somewhat rough, Cockney lad. He told me he was running a car hire service, was prospering, but had called on me for some advice. Having offered to take some premises for his car hire service, he had paid a deposit of £250 to a Mr X (whose name was quite well-known) and the gentleman in question had refused to return it to him. He therefore intended to call on the party in question to 'push his face through the window.' I told him to play it cool, to make sure he got his deposit back and later, if he wished to push the gentleman's face through the window, this was a matter for him. I bumped into Slasher about three months afterwards and heard that he had carried out both parts of my advice in order of priority and that it was most effective.

6

A PERSONAL INDISCRETION

*

In 1946, I received a call from a solicitor friend, Herbert Bishop, to assist in his election campaign. I first met him soon after leaving school. A good athlete and sportsman, he was full of fun and lacked commercial ambition. Herbert's father was a highly successful solicitor in a north London partnership, was politically active and became chairman of the local Conservative Association. Herbert finally qualified as a solicitor but, as an outdoor man, he preferred to deal with litigation and to appear personally in Court, Groomed by his father for a political career, he attended various courses and, after his father died, became a prominent member of the Southgate Council. An extrovert, he was honest, loyal and good natured, liked to have fun and was far from being studious or intellectual. He enoyed a pint of beer and developed a strong voice as a street corner speaker on politics. But, although he was adopted three times as Conservative candidate, his prospective seats were all Labour strongholds. His straightforward style appealed to many constituents, but he had little chance of success in North Hackney, Edmonton and Greenwich where I endeavoured to help him. Herbert's 1946 election campaign sparked off one of my more foolish indiscretions.

He was contesting Hackney North against the well-established Labour candidate, David Weitzman QC. Disappointed that the local paper, the *Hackney Gazette* appeared to be pro-Weitzman, he invited me to a Hackney Tradesmen Association dinner presided over by a local vicar and held in the first-floor restaurant of a pub called 'The Crown & Castle' on the corner of Kingsland Road and Dalston Lane. My function was to sit next to the editor of the *Hackney Gazette* so that I could praise the virtues and life of Herbert Bishop in the cause of good publicity. To this day, I remember opening the conversation by asking whether the editor thought he could increase his circulation if I handed him a photograph of the prospective Conservative candidate dressed in a tight bathing costume bending down to pick up a sixpence. This opening remark, combined with a plentiful supply of drink, enabled us both to have a hilarious evening. It was unusual for me to be affected by drink but, when the dinner was over, a concerned Herbert asked whether I felt all right to drive. I told him – emphatically – I had never felt better.

I drove my Jaguar slowly along Essex Road, Islington, towards my bachelor flat in Park Street, Mayfair. But, before reaching Islington Green,

I remember looking hard at the tram lines. I suspect my subconscious was telling me not to drive and I thought I showed great presence of mind by driving down a narrow, deserted cul-de-sac, turning off the engine and slumping over the steering wheel in a deep sleep. I awoke with a start to find myself in a small compartment with tiled walls – a cell in Islington Police Station. Thinking the matter was a huge joke, I was led somewhat unsteadily out of the cell to see the contents of my pockets displayed and recorded by two police officers – one having warned me that anything I said would be taken down in evidence. I was a bit truculent and, when asked if I wished to call my doctor, I answered: 'What the hell for?' When asked if I would object to being examined by the police doctor, I replied: 'I don't care a hoot if William the Conqueror examines me.' One of the officers then asked: 'Why did you park your car?' and I answered: 'Because I was tight.' The next question was: 'What had you been drinking?' My reply came swiftly: 'After the meal, I finished with ten brandies.' The police doctor did his examination and asked me to walk along a white line – I am not sure whether I was off balance. I spent the rest of the night in a sound sleep on a wooden bench covered with a blanket, reminiscent of my Army days. Jangling keys and a police sergeant shouting 'Breakfast Up' awoke me and after having a mug of tea, I was discharged on my own recognisance of £25 to appear at Old Street Police Station at 10.00 a.m.

I drove straight to the office to leave a tactful note on my secretary's desk. Freda Stones – the soul of discretion – was my secretary for 20 years and the message read: 'I shall not be in the office first thing as I have an appointment in the City.' After a bath and change at my flat, I presented myself at Old Street Police Station. There, for the first time, I realised the gravity of the situation. I was shown to the section reserved for prisoners, where a kindly policeman advised me to ask the magistrate for the case to be remanded to allow me time to instruct a solicitor – advice for which I was eternally grateful. When the statements I had made when giving evidence the night before were related word for word in Court, there was uproarious laughter and the magistrate threatened to clear the Court unless silence was maintained. I immediately instructed Sidney Rutter, a solicitor who had developed a reputation for dealing with criminal cases and police court work, who briefed, on my behalf, Sir John Maud QC subsequently Judge Maud, and his junior, Victor Durand QC. I was advised to have the case heard before a jury and, at the London Sessions, Sir John Maud made such an impassioned speech emphasising my war service that I felt more like a hero than a criminal. The result was a fine of £25 and a licence endorsement. The Judge looked at me squarely over his glasses and asked what the topic of conversation had been with the prospective Conservative candidate over dinner. I replied: 'The Town and Country Planning Act, my Lord' at which he commented: 'How dull.' Fortunately, in later years, I have developed a preference for Perrier water.

I spent many happy times yachting with Herbert Bishop at Mersey Island where he owned a quaint cottage called 'Periwinkle' named after the blue plants in Essex growing out of the slate roof. He eventually became more settled, married Lorna and, as a family man, concentrated on his legal practice. He also became involved in property development with two former clients, with whom he formed a property company. However, his love of sailing together with despondency concerning the UK's Labour administration prompted him to sail with his family to Barbados, where he has remained ever since.

*

I always used to arrange a Christmas party for my colleagues and I shall never forget the reaction of some of them when I invited my young fiancée, Pamela, to the party held at a club in South Molton Street to introduce her. The disparity in our ages and the fact that Pamela was an attractive fashion model and professional dancer provoked whispers: 'It will never last.' They were wrong!

With the practice operating at high speed, business was good and I sought permanent offices. I wrote to Sir Bruce Bruce-Porter, physician to the former King. He owned the leasehold interest in 6 Grosvenor Street, previously his private house. An amusing Irishman of 80, he bounded up the stairs of 10 Hanover Street to see me, demanded to know who my client was and why I had written to him. I told him that we needed the premises for ourselves. He said: 'You are the first agent who has spoken the truth to me. I am willing to let you the whole building at a rent of £1,000 a year.' Legal proceedings were pending with sub-tenants who had carried out illegal sub-lettings without consent and, apart from the first floor, each floor was let on terms which Sir Bruce Bruce-Porter was unable to confirm. I decided to take a chance and enter into the lease. Despite a higher bid made by other agents, Sir Bruce kept his word. So, in 1946, we moved to some of the upper floors of 6 Grosvenor Street, a few doors from New Bond Street.

Rationing was still in existence only a year after the war and it was difficult to get a good steak. An exception to the rule was a private-members club known as the Garter Club at 52 Grosvenor Street. As I had a healthy appetite and was working hard, I decided to join and, for this purpose, met the proprietor, a charming Frenchman known as Captain Leo Ponté. He was a Basque, partial to the opposite sex and sported the ribbon of the Legion of Honour. He and his good looking wife, Rosemary, ran the club on efficient and high class lines as a luncheon club during the day and offered dinner and cabaret at night. The food was excellent and as the practice was doing well and the club was only a few yards away, I endeavoured to lunch there daily. So too did several other well known estate agents but I tended to keep rather to myself as at that time my main objective was to re-build the practice and I seldom sat at the bar where one could meet other members. Incidentally, Rosemary's sister, Kitty, was then married to John Mills, a famous character who owned Les Ambassadeurs Club. I have vivid recollections of visiting this magnificent house in Hamilton Place at the request of Tom Bond of Barclays Bank. It was then the private residence of Captain Leonard Plugge, an inventor, former MP and at one time director of Radio Normandy who died at the age of 92. The meeting included Captain Plugge, John Mills, Jean Simmons and Stewart Grainger, the film stars, to add some glamour.

One day, Leo Ponte approached my table while I was lunching at the Garter Club and asked if he could join me for a brief chat. He said his members included many well known estate agents but he decided to talk to me as he felt I was a quiet man who would not betray his confidence. At the bar, he said, stood his landlord who wanted £70,000 for the leasehold interest of his building. Leo thought that he would probably settle for £60,000 so he asked me if I could get him a mortgage of £50,000. I replied: 'Don't take a mortgage – why don't you sell, take back a lease and I will resell the leasehold for £65,000 giving you back the whole of your capital outlay – if you will take back a lease at a rent of about £5,500 a year.' A shrewd businessman, he looked at me very hard and I could almost see him thinking: 'I wonder if it is too good to be true?' However, he was a tough negotiator and told me he would not take a penny less than £75,000 with a leaseback of about £5,000 'but keep the door open'. There and then he acquired the leasehold interest and I re-sold it for him at the full price to Second Covent Garden Properties with the leaseback to Ponte. I continued to lunch at the club at my own expense and a year later, Leo approached me again and said – with a twinkle in his eye – he was worried that if anything happened to him, his family would be obliged to honour the commitment of a long lease at a high rent for 56 years. I explained that the only solution was to sub-let the entire building to a firm of high standing. I succeeded in doing this at £7,500 a year to C.C. Wakefield, the castrol oil firm which occupied the adjacent building, 51 Grosvenor Street. The managing director and some of the board members lunched regularly at the Garter Club and, after C.C. Wakefield had signed the lease of the entire building, Leo Ponte, over a bottle of champagne, was able to negotiate an underlease of the ground floor and basement so that he could continue to run the Garter Club. His legendary continental charm was enhanced by a slight French accent and I shall always remember him describing the development charge introduced in the Town & Country Planning Act 1947 as 'Devilment Levy'.

Leo's fertile mind dreamed up yet another idea; he asked me if I could sell off the 56 year profit rent of £2,000 per annum he received from C.C. Wakefield. Investor trustees then bought this for around £20,000 so Leo had ingeniously bought and sold his house making money every time but still remaining in possession of his club. He made yet another profit when he eventually sold the club to Rico Dajau. Rico Dajau was a famous West End nightclub and restaurant maestro who, at one time, ran the Bagatelle in Mayfair and the Society Restaurant in Jermyn Street. A great showman, his antics and cabaret attracted a clientele of celebrities including the former Duke of Marlborough, Sir Charles Clore, Felix Fenston, Prince Radziwill and Lord May. It was here that I met Sir Freddie Laker, then quite a young man and well before his Knighthood. A jovial individual with a smiling face and friendly manner, he had even then an inner impulse for success and as a former flyer, an uninhibited burning desire to improve aerial communications. His early life had been modest and comparatively uneventful. But when I met him the characteristic which stood out was that of a practical man – not a back room financier – who knew about flying and machines having learned the hard way. He was too young to be in the RAF in 1939 but being extremely patriotic, almost single handedly won a 'Battle of Britain' in peacetime by fighting the international airlines business monopoly and winning the right to fly his planes to America bringing down the price of fares to help everyone see the world. He was an outstanding example of what an individual with grit and determination can achieve, but it was unfortunate that his financial resources were inadequate and he was ultimately brought down by the big guns of the banks.

Gradually, I obtained possession from all the other tenants at 6 Grosvenor Street with the exception of Colonel Vandeleur who occupied the top floor as a flat with a protected tenancy. The only grounds on which I would obtain possession of this was by providing the Colonel with similar alternative accommodation at the same rent. I found a first floor flat in Gloucester Place at a rental of £400 a year. This I was prepared to under-let to the Colonel for £100 a year – as it suited me to secure complete possession of 6 Grosvenor Street. My solicitors carefully prepared a case to comply with the conditions of the Rent Act and I had photographs taken of the Colonel's flat and entrance and of the flat in Gloucester Place with measurements of each room. Grosvenor Street had by now become a semi-office area. To enter the top floor flat, it was necessary to walk through our office whereas Gloucester Place was a residential thoroughfare. I retained Lionel Blundell, QC, an expert on the Rent Act, to act on my behalf. The Hearing was in the County Court in St Martin's Lane and at one point in the proceedings, Counsel for the Colonel invited the Judge to visit both properties so that he could make appropriate comparisons. The judge agreed to visit our office building in Grosvenor Street first and then – with me and my legal representatives – Gloucester Place. We stood outside the Court, ordered two taxis and the Judge appeared without wig and glasses – he looked quite a sporting type wearing a soft trilby hat and a club tie. He had a keen sense of humour and on looking out of the first floor window of the flat in Gloucester Place, seeing the stark back wall and a dustbin, remarked: 'you could hardly call this the finest view in Europe'. On the return journey from Gloucester Place, the Judge became quite talkative and told us the story of a case which he had heard the previous week. He explained: 'It was a similar case to yours but the Plaintiff conducted the case himself and was a very well built and outspoken gentleman. When cross-examining the Defendant, he used bad language and suddenly accused him of being a bastard. I could not tolerate such language and said that if I heard any more of it, I would clear the Court. To my amazement, the Plaintiff accused me of being a bastard too. I therefore called the tipstaff and had the Court cleared. In a way, I was pleased as I love showjumping and my wife and I wished to go to White City that night. The suspension of the case enabled us to go as planned.' When we arrived back in Court, Counsel for the Colonel could see that he had lost his case and that the Judge would agree to the flat being transferred to Gloucester Place as there were really no grounds for refusal. Counsel therefore said he would concede the case, provided I agreed to pay a reasonable sum for the fixtures and fittings which the Colonel proposed to leave. We agreed terms and the Judge said he was pleased as there was another showjumping event at White City that night and he hoped that the early conclusion of the case would enable him to attend.

7

SHOPKEEPERS WHO BECAME DEVELOPERS

*

Edward Lotery was one of the pioneers of shop development at the time of the expansion of the London suburbs and extensions to the Underground railway system which brought a need for further shopping in these areas and a growth of multiple retailers. I first met him in the 1930's when I called at the headquarters of the family business, H. Lotery & Co in the East End. Loterys were a highly successful wholesale tailoring business specialising in uniforms and liveries. At that time, Edward was concentrating on a retail chain of shops trading as John Bright (Outfitters) Ltd. The name was appropriate as Edward was bright and energetic – athletic, broad-shouldered and handsome. When he turned his attention to shop development, he acquired many sites in the growing London suburbs. Unlike Cecil Fox (see page 50) – whose developments were situated in well-established suburbs – Edward concentrated on outlying districts securing sites in expanding green-field areas. His suburban parades were well built, simple, uniform blocks of shops, usually with two floors of residential accommodation above. Woolworths were the drawing power in these parades and Edward's policy was to entice Woolworths to lease a shop in the centre of each new development. He offered them a considerable rent-free period and a favoured rent over the first few years. Other multiple tenants would follow Woolworths. Therefore, in order to achieve a successful shopping parade with drawing power, Edward Lotery took a broad view and made cash allowances to multiple tenants to help them with shop fitting. He repeated this exercise in many areas in north-west London and many of the developments were designed by the same specialist architects, Fewster & Partners. Building costs were low at that time and Edward's shopping parades eventually became well-established positions which appreciated in value due to the rapid expansion of multiple companies.

A flamboyant and expansive character, Edward Lotery was highly successful and named his company Greater London Properties Limited. He ran it from an attractive and elaborate pine panelled office at 22 Conduit Street in London's West End. He became friendly with many expanding multiple shop tenants including Tesco Stores and others. By personally escorting potential tenants to see his properties, he often persuaded them to enter into a package deal to take several shops in each of his new parades. Jack Cohen, subsequently the late Sir John Cohen of

Tesco Stores, claimed that it was Edward Lotery who turned his firm into a multiple company. Edward enjoyed his success, had large parties in his house at Hampstead, played tennis and was a keen sportsman. One of his favourite places for lunch – where I joined him on more than one occasion – was the former Frascati's Restaurant in Oxford Street. The head waiter there found it good business to give Edward one more oyster than he had ordered as a gesture of goodwill. in 1938, Edward Lotery left England for California where I understand he has carried out some very successful developments. When I met him in more recent years, he appeared to have adopted a typical American style and it seemed that the way of life in the States suited him.

*

My first meeting with the late Cecil Fox was in the offices of Dudley Samuel & Harrison, although I carried out many transactions for him in later years. He had a retail tailor's shop in Rye Lane, Peckham, was methodical, dapper, well dressed, articulate and, by his own tenacity and personal effort, developed from owning one or two shops in Peckham into quite a large investor and shop developer. Cecil formed a private company known as the The Evelyn Property Investment Company Limited, the other main shareholder being his wife. He was married to one of the daughters of the Raphael Tuck family – manufacturers of greeting cards – and he led a simple and happy family life in Hampstead. One of his surprising pastimes was to gamble at roulette in France during his holidays and he claimed to have an unbeatable system. I do not think the croupiers in Cannes liked his safe method of betting. He had a flair for property which was self-taught and attended a large number of sales at the London Auction Mart. A hard worker, he inspected all the sites himself, called upon agents, dealt with tenants personally and conducted a large number of successful negotiations by direct contact. In the latter part of his career he built a number of shopping parades adjacent to existing shops in established London suburbs. He was a man of integrity, careful, keen and thrifty. Despite being well backed by his bank, he occasionally arranged for his company to re-sell a few of its properties to provide capital for further developments. Resale activities over the years caused the Inland Revenue to label the Evelyn Property Investment Company as a dealing company.

After a lifetime spent building up the company portfolio by his personal efforts, Cecil found himself in a difficult position as the shares in his private company were not a liquid asset which could be transferred to his family to realise in future years. Furthermore, nearly all the properties within the company were purchased cheaply years before and their book value was such that a huge tax bill would be payable should he try to sell them. In later years, for family reasons Cecil decided to sell his company shares, but most of the public investment companies rejected the proposition when they found that his was a dealing company with a large potential tax liability. In 1975, however, I was able to arrange an exchange of shares on his behalf to a publicly-quoted company, Town & Commercial Properties, whose chairman, John Hines, had the novel idea that Town & Commercial would retain the company intact, secure a mortgage on the properties and collect a good income from the equity – without selling off the properties and incurring tax. Cecil devoted all his time to dealing with nearly every negotiation himself and, after the bitter experience of putting his assets into a private company, he formed a new public company, Stem Properties Limited. He sold his shares before his retirement.

*

Maurice Mauray built up two vast empires in the course of his working life. Although small and slim, he was a forceful character, bouncing with energy. He was also a tremendous task-master. It was with Maurice that I first met Philip Gould, one of the most experienced 'battle inoculated' property managers. He perhaps has had more practical experience of dealing with multiple-shop property than most of his counterparts. The first empire Maurice Mauray built was a chain of ladies' gown shops with branches throughout the UK known as Wilsons (London & Provinces) Ltd. I recollect letting Maurice one of his first shops in King Street, Hammersmith, one of the busiest shopping thoroughfares in west London. Multiples were expanding at the time and paying what were then considered high prices to buy out private retailers whose shops were in busy locations. Maurice converted the premises into an attractive ladies' gown shop. J. Lyons, the leading caterers of the day, were next door and, on the other side of J. Lyons, Maurice opened yet another branch. He then acquired many more shops until he built up 130 branches in London and the provinces, all run from his head office in Edgware Road. In the 1930's the leading multiple ladies' costumiers with many branches in the suburbs were Style & Mantle, known as 'S & M'. The owner was Sigmund Cohen. Maurice Mauray was his son and followed his father into the Style & Mantle business. But, wishing to launch out on his own, he changed his name to ensure independence from the S & M name. Maurice was aggressive and tenacious in his desire to build an empire. Philip Gould certainly received some hard training – learning the art of conducting a tough negotiation under Maurice's direction. Wilsons (London & Provinces) Limited was eventually taken over by Great Universal Stores and Sir Isaac Wolfson became Philip Gould's commander-in-chief – perhaps no easier a boss to work for.

Sir Isaac Wolfson, one of the most enterprising and successful businessmen of our time, then proceeded to expand Great Universal Stores by taking over about 150 companies with branches in varying trades and carrying out expansions on behalf of these various companies. Philip Gould, therefore, had to negotiate and deal with shops all over the country and, in some cases, abroad. He thrived on hard training and has never flinched when the whip was cracked. With an exceptional knowledge of shopping centres and values, he is a living exponent of the subject, able to quote every detail in the Great Universal Stores portfolio from memory. The fact that Philip has held the position of head of the Central Estates Department of Great Universal Stores for about 20 years speaks for itself. GUS is a vast concern and Philip heads a substantial staff of surveyors with offices in Nottingham under John Guy, previously with Boots the Chemists, and in Leeds under Frank Leeson.

Having been bought by GUS, Maurice Mauray became restless and, using the large amount of capital from the sale, he built another empire. With his knowledge and experience of shop values as a retailer, he decided to become a shop property developer and, from a head office in Bournemouth, he set up City & Town Buildings Ltd. He then carried out a large number of successful shop developments in various parts of the country. Then, after building up a large portfolio with a substantial rental income, he sold the company to Second Covent Garden Properties. Maurice built a beautiful block of flats in Bournemouth with the intention of occupying the first floor himself. Constructed in continental style, it had a huge balcony with shutters for the winter months. He also had a flat at Fountain House, Park Lane, for use during the week. Although he developed the reputation of being an extremely hard man in business, Maurice's widow, Violet – a charming and well-preserved lady – told me recently in Cannes that her late husband was a wonderfully kind man. Her only complaint was that he refused to buy a new suit. Even their chauffeur complained that the governor's suits were getting threadbare – and it became impossible to have them cleaned. Maurice was either too busy or too thrifty to spend money on his own clothes and Violet was desperate when they received an invitation to attend an important formal party. Because of his diminutive figure, it was impossible for her to buy anything for him ready made, without complete alteration. Her daughter eventually came up with the bright idea of Harrods Boys' Department. There she apparently bought two suits which fitted Maurice perfectly.

*

A.L. Oppenheim, affectionately known as Abe, was another mercurial, dapper man. A shrewd Scot, he established furniture shops in High Road, Ilford, known as Goodways Limited. Like others, his retail experience caused him to turn to property development and he built several shopping parades in Barkingside, Borehamwood, Kingston and other parts of London. Hard working and energetic, he closed his furniture business and set up a private property company in the West End known as Suburban

Real Estates. He lived in a flat in Grosvenor Square not far from his offices in Upper Grosvenor Street. When I re-opened my practice after the war I met him once again and carried out many acquisitions on his behalf. After he had accumulated a large number of properties including shops in Oxford Street and a large, modern block of flats in Regents Park, he wished to distribute his private assets to his wife, two sons and twin daughters. I suggested he sold his shares to Second Covent Garden Properties, a public property company. Abe would not part with the schedules of his properties, insisting that these must be treated in confidence and could not even be seen by my secretary. I therefore had to spend several late evenings in his flat in Grosvenor Square copying out long schedules. After a trying negotiation, I eventually sold his shares to Second Covent Garden Properties. Although he was tough and by no means easy, I enjoyed dealing with a self-made man of character as he was straightforward and made firm and quick decisions. When I concluded the tortuous negotiations, I recollect him turning to me with a smile and saying: 'Tell me truthfully, am I difficult?' I replied: 'You are one of the most difficult clients I have ever met but any bloody fool can deal with an easy client and I have thoroughly enjoyed dealing with you.'

He had introduced me to one of his sons, the late Henry Oppenheim who had spent a great deal of his time in the States and had been at Columbia University. After being in London for a short time, he was re-united with an attractive young lady whom he had known in his youth, Sally Viner of the Sheffield cutlery family, and they were later married. Abe distributed the proceeds of his empire to his family and they acquired the silversmiths, Mappin & Webb. The main shareholders were Henry Oppenheim and Abe's two sons-in-law – Charles Burkeman, formerly in the textile trade, and Jarvis Astaire, who has since become a prominent figure in the television and sporting world. Boardroom disputes broke out from time to time as Henry and his brothers-in-law did not always see eye to eye, and the company was subsequently taken over by Sir Charles Clore. Henry followed in his father's footsteps, formed a public company called City Wall Properties, carried out a large number of developments and ultimately sold to the Rank Organisation. He acquired a country estate in Gloucestershire of more than 1,000 acres, known as the Sandhurst and Norton Estate where his wife, Mrs Sally Oppenheim, sat as Conservative Candidate in 1968. Sally Oppenheim is attractive, an able speaker and has become a prominent politician after defeating Joel Barnett, the former Labour Minister, at Gloucester. She was Consumer Affairs Minister in Mrs Thatcher's Government. Henry Oppenheim died in March 1980 after a severe illness, leaving a son and two daughters.

8

THE MAN WITH THE SIXTH SENSE

*

Joseph Littman, popularly known as Joe, was of Russian descent and, after his family had settled in New York, he came to London. His early life was hard and he had little time or money for education. He was married at a comparatively young age and brought up a family of seven children. We first met during the 1930's when I called upon him at Poppies – a ladies fashion shop in Edgware Road – which was owned by his wife's family. Quite large in stature, he struck me as Russian in appearance with a sallow and impassive face. His looks belied his keen and alert mind. He greeted me casually and bluntly summed up the proposition I had put to him while keeping an eye on a customer who was about to leave the shop without buying anything. She changed her mind – thanks to Joe's rushing to 'assist' his assistant in the middle of talking to me! He then made a substantial offer for the freehold property we had discussed, curtly shook hands and, with a knowing grin, said: 'My offer will be accepted.' Without the advantage of education – he could hardly sign his name – Joe instinctively knew how to deal with people. His judgement was excellent. He never said much but his manner inspired complete confidence. Shortly after we met, he expanded his business by acquiring a large shop in High Road, Kilburn, which was supervised by Mrs Littman at the same time as she cared for the children. This was just the beginning; Joe soon secured the confidence of his bank manager and proceeded to acquire a large amount of shop property and other commercial buildings. Mrs Littman, however, was apprehensive of her husband's large purchases and thought his advancement and initial success might end in disaster. He was a difficult man to pin down and see and I remember calling at Kilburn to find Mrs Littman holding one of the babies and looking very distressed. In strong terms, she asked me not to visit her husband – 'Don't sell him any more properties, you will ruin him', she said. When she learned I had called to present him with a rent cheque, I was invited to come in to have a cup of tea and await Joe's return. Kilburn High Road was a sought-after suburban shopping location in the 1930's and Joe bought many properties on each side of the road which he let to create investment income. Backed initially by his bank, he was later financed by the Royal Liver Friendly Society on a mortgage for a fixed term at 3¼ per cent interest. This provided a large profit income. I liked acting for Joe Littman and I liked his style. His

EARLY DAYS

1. My Mother and Father with Taffy on Brighton beach

2. A proud photo taken in 1913 of my Mother's wealthy Uncle and Aunt, Reuben and Sophie Gliksten, with their three sons, coachman and maid

GOODS ARE NOT TESTED AND IN THE EVENT OF ANY CLAIM SELLERS LIABILITY SHALL IN NO CIRCUMSTANCES EXCEED THE INVOICE PRICE OF THE DEFECTIVE PIECE(S)
ALL GOODS OFFERED SUBJECT TO BEING UNSOLD   PRICES SUBJECT TO MARKET FLUCTUATIONS

EXTENSIVE STORAGE WHARVES

TRAINS FROM BROAD STREET STATION
TO VICTORIA PARK STATION (L.M.&S.RLY)
BUS ROUTE Nº 6 FROM CITY

CONTRACTORS TO THE ADMIRALTY,
WAR OFFICE, LONDON COUNTY COUNCIL
& NUMEROUS MUNICIPAL AUTHORITIES
PRINCIPAL RAILWAY, TRAMWAY & BUS COMPANIES

SBAC

THE SOCIETY OF MOTOR MANUFACTURERS & TRADERS

J. GLIKSTEN & SON LTD

INCORPORATED

ESTABLISHED 1869

SEASONED TIMBER FOR ALL TRADES A SPECIALITY.

MAHOGANY, TEAK, WAINSCOT & GENERAL TIMBER MERCHANTS.

LARGE STOCKS OF ENGLISH TIMBER.

NATIONAL SCHEME FOR DISABLED MEN

CODES
6TH EDITION A.B.C. 5 LETTER
UNIVERSAL LUMBER.

TELEGRAMS
"GLIKSTEN, PHONE, LONDON"

TELEPHONE.
AMHERST 4444 (10 LINES)

REGD OFFICE. CARPENTERS ROAD, STRATFORD, E.15.
FEW MINUTES FROM VICTORIA PARK STATION, L.M.&S.RLY

3. J. Gliksten & Son: subsequently International Timber Corporation

4. Laying the stone of 77 Grosvenor Street in 1939: the late Stanley Edgson and Douglas Overall

AN EARLY ENTREPRENEUR

6. The Old Curiosity Shop

5. Jack Phillips at the Races

7. Claude Leigh, Founder of MEPC

METROPOLITAN ESTATE AND PROPERTY CORPORATION LIMITED

Directors:
CLAUDE LEIGH (*Chairman and Managing Director*).
H. N. HUME, C.B.E., M.C. (*Deputy Chairman*).
CHARLES S. LUSH. CYRIL SWEETT, F.R.I.C.S.
J. SCRIMGEOUR, O.B.E. S. H. SHEPPARD, F.A.I.
R. J. DICKINSON. W. E. PHILP, F.R.I.C.S.

Secretary and Registered Office:
BERNARD DUFTON, A.C.A., 16, Hanover Square, London, W.1.

Auditors:
THOMSON McLINTOCK & CO., Chartered Accountants, 33, King William Street, London, E.C.4.

Registrars and Transfer Office:
MARTINS BANK LIMITED, 68, Lombard Street, London, E.C.3.

REPORT OF THE DIRECTORS

for the year ended 30th September, 1952.

To be presented at the Ordinary General Meeting of the Company to be held at 16, Hanover Square, London, W.1, on 16th December, 1952.

The Directors submit herewith their Report and Accounts for the year ended 30th September, 1952.

	£	£
The excess of Income over Expenditure of the Company and its Subsidiary Companies for the year after charging all expenses, but before providing Leasehold Amortisation and Taxation, amounts to		524,459
Out of which has been paid:— Interest on Debenture Stock and Loans—Gross		123,794
		400,665
Deduct Taxation for the year:—		
Profits Tax	61,753	
Income Tax	190,928	
		252,681
		147,984
Deduct Provision for Leasehold Amortisation		24,368
Leaving a Balance of		123,616
Against which has been charged:—		
Dividends on Preference Stock for the year to 30th September, 1952, less Income Tax	36,028	
Interim Dividend of 2½% on the Ordinary Stock paid on the 16th June, 1952, less Income Tax	20,409	
		56,437
Resulting in an available balance of		67,179
To which should be added the balance brought forward from last year		86,830
Making a total available balance of		154,009
Out of this your Directors recommend the payment on the 16th December 1952, of a final Dividend on the Ordinary Stock of 4½%, less Income Tax making 7% for the year		36,737
Leaving to be carried forward to next year an amount of		£117,272

8. Copy Accounts, 1952

THE VICTORIAN BOSS & PARTNERS

9. (*right*) Claud Goddard

10. Alec Brownfield-Pope with his favourite horse, Birdbrook

11. A.W. (George) Bourner

GREAT MEN WHO BUILT HOUSES

12. Sir Frank Taylor by the sculpture 'Team Work'

13. Sir John Laing, founder of Laings

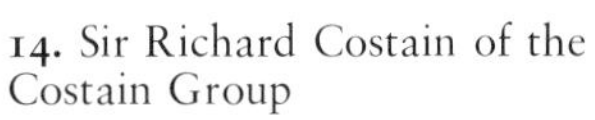

14. Sir Richard Costain of the Costain Group

15. Sir Godfrey Mitchell, Chairman of Wimpeys

16. Leo Meyer of Ideal Homesteads

17, 18. Tony Hutley (*right*) and George Farrow (*below*), founders of the Peachey Property Corporation who were followed by Sir Eric Miller (*foot of page*)

19. Sir Eric Miller

21. (*above*) William Biggs of Stone Toms and Partners

20. (*left*) Anthony Somers

22. Park West: *Evening News* advertisement. To Let in 1937 for £95 up to £330 p.a. rent

23. Park West: *Estates Gazette* advertisement. For Sale in 1979 up to £125,000

24. (*below*) Highlands Heath, Putney

25. 48 Grosvenor Square

26. Plaque without LCC inscription

27. 1–3 Grosvenor Square: Canadian Embassy (formerly American Embassy)

A BOLD DEVELOPMENT COMPLETED IN 1939

28. Morris Bloom, who formed UNICOS

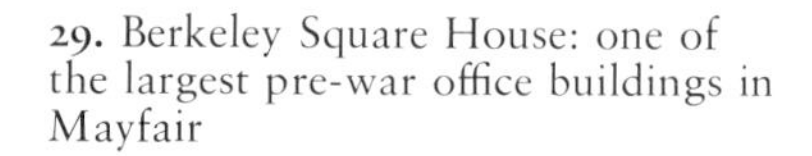

29. Berkeley Square House: one of the largest pre-war office buildings in Mayfair

30. The Connaught Hotel, Mayfair

31. An early staff Christmas party

COMPLETION OF MY MOST IMPORTANT NEGOTIATION

32. George Trott (*right*) of South Lambeth and Charlie Squires of Holborn, had a grandstand view from their scaffolding at Caxton Hall, Westminster, yesterday when Mr Edward Erdman and Miss Pamela Mason left after their wedding. (*Evening News*, 22 December 1949)

33. Edward Lotery

34. Cecil Fox (*centre*)

35. A.L. Oppenheim

36. Maurice Mauray

THE UNTUTORED MAN WITH THE SIXTH SENSE

37. Joseph Littman

38, 39. 54 and 55 Piccadilly – before and after

A FLAMBOYANT FATHER & SON

41. (*right*) Felix Fenston

40. Joseph Fenston

CREATION OF A NEW CENTRE – VICTORIA CENTRE, NOTTINGHAM

42. The late Leslie Marler

43. Hole in the ground

44. Dennis Marler

45. Ian Northen

46. Emmett clock and fountain – focal point of Centre

BUILT FOR THE MINISTRY

47. (*right*) 65 Davies Street, Mayfair in course of erection for the British Council

ANOTHER ROWLAND EMMETT DESIGN

48. Merrion Centre, Leeds

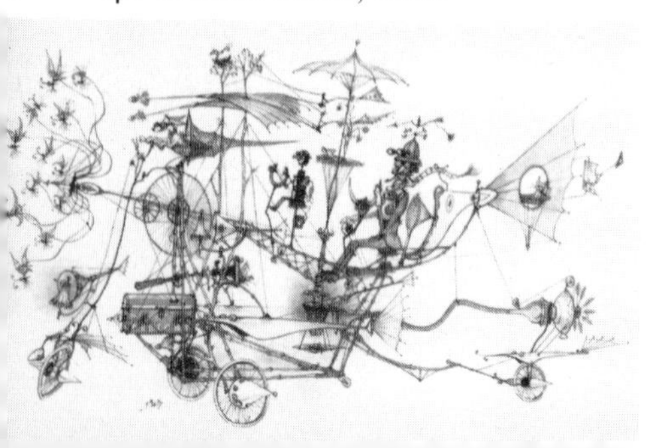

MARKS & SPENCER

49. Michael Marks (*on left*) and Thomas Spencer

50. Lord Marks

51. Lord Sieff

THE THEATRE KING

52. Prince Littler

53. Chestham Park Estate

54. Sir Montague Burton — Raymond Burton — Archie Wansborough — Arnold Burton — Bernard Burton

W.H. SMITH & SON

55. Sir Charles Troughton

56. Peter Bennett

57. Hugh McNearnie

58. Sir Isaac Wolfson

80 Birthday Greetings
to celebrate the eightieth birthday of
Sir Isaac Wolfson
Industrialist and Philanthropist
who integrated these concerns to form part of
THE GREAT UNIVERSAL STORES LIMITED

Acre Lane Estates
Adams Furniture (Canada)
Alexandra Hill Co.
A.N.D. Ltd.
E. Aston & Son
Barry Attwood Ltd
[illegible]
Ashley Russell
Associated Furnishers
Bainbridge (Lincoln)
Charles Baker & Co
Burrells of Staffordshire
F. Beavan Ltd.
Beck Jones
Victor Bell Estates Ltd.
Benzie & Co
Berrys
Black & Sons
[illegible]
Bones
Bowling Duke Estate Co
[illegible]
British & Colonial Furniture
James Broderick & Co
Brookside Electrical Co
Burberrys
Butterfields & Massies
Cavendish Furniture Co
Charles Ltd
J.T. Cheshire & Sons
J. Cook & Sons
Coorsh Bros & Co
Craig & Co (Hamilton)
Cross Bros Ltd
Cussons Ltd
[illegible]
Davies & Johnson Furnishers
Charles Dennes
Drages Furnishing
[illegible] Driver
Evans & Allen
The Garden Vale Mfg
Gardiner & Co (The Scotch House)
Garrett & Co
A. Gerstin & Co
General Guarantee Corp
Gill & Reigate Ltd
Glasgow & London Clothing Co
Global Tours
Godfrey & Co Ltd
Guilford Furnishing Co
Hall, Higham & Co
Hamilton & Crawford
Harpers (Downs)
Hector Powe
Heywoods
A.A. Holmes & Co
Hope Brothers
George Hopkinson
Houndsditch Warehouse Co
Jacksons Stores Ltd
Jax Stores Ltd
Jays Ltd (Oxford Circus)
[illegible] (Gloves) Ltd
John Temple
Joseph Johnstone Ltd
Jones & Higgins Ltd
R.H. Jones & Son
Katz & Co
Lawrie & Smith
The Leading London Tailors
[illegible] & Co
Lennards Ltd
Leslies Stores Ltd
Lindridge & Sons Ltd
Lindsay Hermitage Ltd
A.J. Lister (Leeds) Ltd
A.S. Little & Sons
T.L. McAdam
James McInnes & Co.
Hector McKenzie
A. McLeod & Co.
Masters & Co (Clothiers)
Midland Household Stores
[illegible] Ltd
J. & R. Millar Ltd
Fred W. Millington Ltd
Morrisons
Morses Ltd
Munn & Felton Ltd
Sharman & Neill Ltd
Newton Edwards & Co
New Universal Stores Ltd
Northern Bedding Co
[illegible]
Edward O'Brien Ltd
100,000 Chemises
Orchard Trust
Paige Gowns
F. Paton (Knitwear)
Penberthys
Phillips & Probert
Pickering Shopfitters
Pim Brothers
Playfair Shoes
Potter & Davies
Pollikoff Ltd
Premier [illegible]
Price Jones
Quality Furnishers
The Rego Clothiers
Rex & Co
Richard & Partners
The Royal Welsh Warehouse Co
Russell & Russell Ltd
Rylands & Sons Ltd
Alexander Sloan & Co
Smart Bros
Smith & McAndrew Ltd
Tom Snowden & Son Ltd
Sunray Printers Ltd
[illegible] & Co
F. Taylor & Son
Times Furnishing Co
Todd, Cunningham & Petrie
Town Tailors
The Trafford Mfg Co
[illegible] (Holdings)
Universal Furniture Products
Vertis Ltd
Vise Sons & Co
Wallace & Weir Ltd
Weaver to Wearer
Webbers Ltd
Weir & Sons
Whiteaway Laidlaw
Whitehead & Sons
Whitneys Ltd
Wickhams (C. Barker)
Willerby & Co
John Williams & Co
Willsons Ltd
John Woodrow & Son
Wool Products Ltd
Woolfs Furnishing Stores
Workwear Ltd
Hugh Wyllie Ltd
Woodhouse

and ultimately established
THE WOLFSON FOUNDATION
Good Wishes and warm thoughts from
[illegible]

59. Birthday greetings

60. Sir Leonard Wolfson

61. Rylands Buildings, Manchester

62. Lord McAlpine

63. The Hon. William McAlpine

64. The Hon. Alistair McAlpine

65. The Hon. David McAlpine

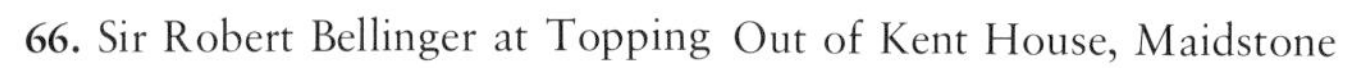

66. Sir Robert Bellinger at Topping Out of Kent House, Maidstone

incredible memory for figures and details more than compensated for his never writing notes.

After success with his Kilburn properties, he acquired a number of buildings in Oxford Street including a valuable block, formerly known as Commerce House and the Academy Cinema. He also bought the Café Marguerite – the site of which is now occupied by Marks & Spencer on the south side of Oxford Street. Other prospective purchasers of the Café were, apparently, wary of buying a restaurant as a going concern with a large wine cellar. Joe's comment was: 'So, I will own a restaurant and, if no one else wants the wine, I'll drink it.' After agreeing the deal, Joe said we should visit his Kilburn bank manager to borrow the money to complete. On the way, we stopped for a coffee in a restaurant called the Lombardy in Edgware Road. An extremely sophisticated French head waiter looked after us with great style and bonhomie. I thought his manner was polished and diplomatic and told Joe he was the head waiter for the Café Marguerite. Littman's immediate reply was an impassive: 'Get him.' I did, and the next time I saw this waiter he was manager of the Café Marguerite. He then occupied the same niche at other well-known restaurants in the West End, including L'Ecu de France.

Joe built an income producing portfolio worth hundreds of thousands a year. He was perhaps the originator of the leaseback method of finance which allowed him unlimited expansion without borrowing. Lord Cohen of the Alliance Building Society and George Bridge of the Legal & General Assurance Society, found him a reliable client and they were ready to back his judgement. One of his typical deals was buying at auction 54–55 Piccadilly near the Burlington Arcade. He outbid everyone by paying £63,000 for the freehold subject to an old lease held by Morgan & Ball, Hosiers, with over 20 years still to run at an annual ground rent of only £1,000 although even then the building was worth over £6,000 a year. No-one could understand why Littman was satisfied with only about 1½% fixed for 20 years. But, as usual, Joe knew exactly what he was doing without a calculator or training in higher mathematics. Rent reviews were unknown and immediately after signing the auction contract, Joe resold to the Legal & General at the price he paid without profit but conditional on a lease being granted back to him for 150 years at a rent of £2,500 a year subject to the underlease to Morgan & Ball for 20 years at a ground rent of £1,000. Joe, therefore, made an annual loss of £1,500 but as a property dealer, he was able to off-set this against his taxable income and the Legal & General had secured a perfectly safe investment. Consequently, after the underlease to Morgan & Ball expired, Joe or his heirs could enjoy a profit for a great many years without any cost. As a negotiator, he was brilliant. If telephoned by an agent with a low offer for a shop, he would sing a song on the other end of the phone, indicating that he would not accept the terms and that he was undismayed. Unlike some owners who reprimanded their agents for failing to find a tenant quickly, Joe would just say, casually: 'Take your time, don't worry – we shall get our terms.' This usually had the desired effect.

I remember going to Gloucester with him to see the Mayor and local council to lease a market site. Littman sat back, impassively confident, and allowed me to do the talking. The council members were accommodating and agreed a ground rent very much lower than the figure Joe had mentioned he was willing to pay during the train journey. Having virtually pre-let the proposed new building, it was difficult for him to contain his pleasure. Favourable terms agreed, he started to kick me under the table. I was slightly embarrassed facing the Mayor and council members and I asked permission to withdraw from the Council Chamber to consult my client. In the next room, Joe grinned and asked me if I had the nerve to request a peppercorn rent free period for a year. I could hardly believe it when the Town Clerk announced: 'There will be the usual peppercorn period of 18 months.' To create the right impression, I replied that I had been expecting two years' rent free during rebuilding and Joe stepped in to say that as we were doing a friendly deal, he would accept the terms. We went home in the train delighted with the day's work. Littman's innate shrewdness overcame his limited education. I shall also never forget the occasion when Frederick Szarvasy, a sophisticated international banker, happened to be present in Isaac Wolfson's flat when I called with Joe regarding Drages' Oxford Street building. Szarvasy probably expected Littman to be more impressive and articulate. He adjusted his monocle and said: 'Littman, do you ever have a flutter on the Stock Exchange?' Far from being overwhelmed, Joe answered in his usual relaxed monotone in parable form: 'I once went to my physician who said I don't deal in Consols – only Tonsils.' This completely silenced Szarvasy. Subsequently, Isaac Wolfson remarked: 'Littman, we shall do a lot of deals together.' Joe, cheerfully accepting several refills of neat whisky from the butler as if it were water, replied: 'We haven't done this one yet.' Unfortunately, Joe died in the early 1950's, but he is well remembered in the property world as a man who always kept his word and inspired confidence. He was a rugged individualist with innate ability.

Through Joe, I came across two famous London restaurateurs, the late Armand Belli and G.D. Rossi. Joe acquired the freehold, as a going concern, of the Café Anglais in Leicester Square, managed by Armand Belli. Armand was a great character, much loved by those who worked for him, and his reputation extended from the George V in Paris to other leading restaurants and clubs in London. At his Café Anglais, Harry Roy's Band often provided the dance music and Joe's wife, Evelyn, was proud to dance there on special occasions. Joe Littman acquired another Leicester Square property, part of which was occupied by the 400 Club. Then an exclusive night club, the 400 was patronised by many well-known celebrities and socialites. Patrons could only dine and dance there in black tie and dinner jacket. Like the Café Anglais, the club was run by a famous international character – 'GD' Rossi, always known as 'GD'.

He originated from a middle-class, professional family and was the youngest of seven children. At seven he was orphaned and spent a childhood being bounced from one aunt to another. He ran away several times – on one occasion to North Africa – and volunteered with the Garibaldi Brigade to fight in France in the Argonne, celebrating his 17th birthday in vicious hand-to-hand fighting in the Forest. When Italy entered the First World War, GD joined the Italian Army and served in the artillery in the Austrian Alps. An ardent republican, he refused to take an oath of allegiance and, consequently, a commission. For the same reason GD refused the patronage of a childless uncle – a professor of engineering – who wished to make him his sole heir and send him to university or to the Italian equivalent of Sandhurst. On demobilisation as a serjeant-major at the age of 19, GD returned to his home town and organised ex-soldiers in resistance to both the Communist and Fascist movements that were growing at that time. His activities attracted violent attention to his family home, so he was quietly smuggled out of the country to join an older brother in London. Once here, he founded a newspaper – the *Echo d'Italia*, – started the UK branch of an Italian ex-servicemen's Club and ran an import/export business. When Mussolini came to power he was forced to resign from his newspaper and ex-service work. At about the same time a strike in France mined a trainload of foodstuffs GD had contracted to import to this country, so, like many Italian immigrants of his generation, he was forced into the catering business to make his living. He worked in the Kit-Kat, Savoy and at Quaglinos before opening a small restaurant of his own. This came to grief in the depression of the early 1930's. GD's next venture was the 400, which established his international reputation as a restaurateur. He mellowed in later years, losing his republican, anti-clerical and rebellious views. Politically, the French railway strike brought disillusionment with socialism and Mussolini's Abyssinian adventure compelled him to renounce his Italian citizenship and to become a British subject. An interesting coincidence is that the sons of GD Rossi of the 400 Club and Armand Belli of the Café Anglais, both became distinguished professional men. Hugh Rossi is a solicitor and well known Conservative MP; the son of Armand Belli, now known as John Bell, is a senior partner of Robson Rhodes, the City accountants.

*

The late Joseph Fenston – often called Fatty Fenston – was an interesting character of particularly generous proportions, probably weighing about 20 stone. Although he carried out a number of property deals, he made his name as an impresario acting for many well-known actors, actresses and artistes and, as such, travelled to many parts of the world. He also had an interest in a wholesale cigar company based in Cuba with a London office in Princes Street, Hanover Square. In addition, he was reputed to have been involved in the pearl trade in Hong Kong. Joe Fenston was known to nearly everyone in the musical and theatrical world. He sponsored many famous artists and produced many shows, one of the most famous being Chu Chin Chow. He was not averse to treading the boards himself. He once joined Oscar Asche, the 30-stone actor, on stage – which, with their combined weight of 50 stone, collapsed, pitching Joe and Oscar into the orchestra pit.

After the 1939 war, Joe had acquired a site in Bexley Heath in which Associated British Cinemas (ABC), under the chairmanship of John Maxwell, expressed an interest. ABC employed on a part-time basis an astute negotiator known as Sam Eidenow. All Sam's deals were done verbally and I do not remember ever seeing or receiving a letter from him. I duly arranged for Joe, Sam and I to visit the Bexley Heath site by car – with Joe doing the driving. At first, I was a little apprehensive as the car was quite small and Joe's huge frame was barely able to get into the driver's seat. But all went well and, having seen the site and after some negotiation, Joe and Sam agreed the price and shook hands. Expansive, jovial Joe decided he was in a good mood and invited Sam and I to lunch with him at the Hungarian Restaurant in Lower Regent Street. I well remember this lunch; Joe was a renowned gourmet and very fond of his food, and Sam was quite partial towards drink. The latter was also quite well built and I as the agent must have appeared a somewhat skeletal figure beside the pair of them as we entered the restaurant. Joe ordered caviar and vodka for the three of us and then asked to see a selection of fish for a first course. The chef, who obviously knew Joe well, appeared, chattering volubly in a foreign language and carrying a rod on which were strung several fish of different kinds. Joe selected no less than three specimens and, having eaten his way through these, followed them with an entrée and several other dishes. Joe and Sam were still eating and drinking vigorously at 3.30 p.m., but I was obliged to stop abruptly at about 2.30 as I had reached the limit of my capacity and I was unaccustomed to such a volume of rich food. At the time, I was a rather ambitious young agent and the main thought in my mind was to conclude the transaction and to earn my fee. On each occasion they toasted each other, 'Even if this deal does not materialise we shall always be friends,' I anxiously reminded them they had agreed the price.

Joseph Fenston was a warm and kindly man who, during the latter part of his life, suffered from heart trouble. It fascinated people to see him walk round with a small hot water bottle clutched to the left side of his chest outside his jacket. Pamela, my young wife, was quite overawed by this huge man as one of her first dinner guests after we were married and devoted an entire seven days to ordering an exotic and extensive menu. On my bookshelf, I have two signed copied of books by Joe – *Victory Cavalcade*, written after the end of World War II, and *Never Say Die*.

Joe's son, the late Felix Fenston, was a most unusual character. When I first met him many years ago he lived with his father in a modest flat in Maida Vale. Due to his father's theatrical connections, they led a somewhat Bohemian life and I remember visiting them late after a show when Joe, the gourmet and expert cook, knocked up some fried eggs which we proceeded to eat informally in the kitchen. Felix was the victim of a motorcycle accident in the Army as a result of which he was fitted with an artificial leg. This was seldom noticeable and was never the subject of comment. Although he was a talented pianist and fond of the arts, he did not follow his father into the music world, but joined John D. Wood the surveyors to deal with investments and valuation. He eventually left the profession to carry out some property deals like his father. With pluck and a readiness to take risks, he speedily produced some spectacular transactions, became wealthy and moved in society circles. I believe he had inherited some of his father's flair as an impresario. For instance, when undertaking large transactions and inviting other participants to invest large sums of money, he usually set the scene in flamboyant style in his magnificent Mayfair house – at 19 Hill Street, full of antiques and with a butler in attendance. A keen big-game hunter, he went on safari every year and his lovely London home, once owned by the Duke of Devonshire, was full of hunting trophies. One of Felix's friends was the late Prince Stanislas Radziwill – husband of Jackie Kennedy's sister, Lee. The office building in the City known as Lee House was named after her. Felix was one of the private developers who contributed to the redevelopment of bombed sites after the last war. In 1963 he converted his holdings into a public property company called Metropolitan & Provincial Properties Limited. Prince Radziwill, and Lord Ashcombe, the then chairman of Holland Hannen & Cubitts Ltd, the contractors, were members of the board. It was always fascinating to visit Felix at Hill Street where, among other possessions, he had a splendid library. Interested in antiquity, the classics and the arts, he combined the qualities of an intellectual with those of a tough businessman. He acquired Braboeuf, near Guildford – a manor house mentioned in the Domesday Book. I remember him telling me with relish that it was the early custom of the Lord of the Manor to try out any bride on the estate, before giving formal consent to her marriage. He was a practical joker par excellence. His weekend guests were usually presented with a bill for their stay. And once, when Pamela and I were invited to stay with them at Braboeuf for the weekend, we were provided with a bedroom in the west wing which I am sure had not been occupied for years. I was up almost the entire night swatting huge moths and a bat which appeared in the rafters!

One of the practical jokes I shall never forget was in connection with a site Felix had acquired for development in York Road, Westminster, on which there were some disused buildings due to be demolished. When I was extremely busy in the office one afternoon I received a telephone call from a gentleman who purported to be 'Professor Low' of London University. Although engaged at the time, I reluctantly accepted the call. A strange, foreign voice at the other end of the telephone said: 'Good afternoon, Mr Erdman. This is Professor Low of London University speaking. You have a notice board on a building in York Road. I am carrying out research on the death watch beetle and I have observed a particularly splendid specimen in one of the old buildings on your site. May I have your permission to remove it to my laboratory in the university?' I was somewhat amazed by this conversation. But, knowing that the buildings were to be demolished anyway and not being the slightest bit interested in the death watch beetle, I said: 'Certainly, Professor Low, you have my permission to remove any wood you require.' The voice thanked me and rang off. Busy, I hastily banged down the receiver. The following morning, I was interrupted again by Professor Low. I accepted the call – again reluctantly – and heard that the beetle removed from the site was a 'most exciting and successful specimen.' He then proceeded to thank me profusely but, as I was involved in other business matters, I was anxious to terminate the conversation at the earliest possible moment. The next day, I received yet another telephone call from Professor Low. Exasperated, I still did not wish to appear discourteous so accepted the call: 'Good morning, Mr Erdman. I would very much like you to visit me in my laboratory to see for yourself this superb specimen of death watch beetle.' It was only at this point that it occurred to me that Felix – owner of the site – was playing a joke on me in the full knowledge that I was extremely busy. To put my suspicions to the test, I told Professor Low I would visit his laboratory because I was, myself, extremely interested in the sexual habits of the death watch beetle. Whereupon Felix, at the other end of the telephone, burst with laughter which disclosed his identity.

At times, he would go to considerable trouble to perpetrate a practical joke. On one occasion, he invited the late Eric Taylor, then a senior partner of Jones Lang Wootton, to Hill Street to meet a Persian prince who had large oil interests and was seeking 50,000 sq.ft. of offices in London. In those pre-oil boom days, this was a rarity and Middle Eastern dignitaries were seldom seen in London. Eric Taylor told me how this joke was inflicted on him. Apparently, when he arrived in Felix's room at Hill Street, the only occupant was a young man, obviously English but down-at-heel in appearance – wearing a black jacket and striped trousers. He was sitting on the edge of an armchair with a briefcase on his knees and introduced himself to Eric as the 'Prince's private secretary.' Shortly afterwards Felix himself arrived, desultory conversation ensued until, with a flourish the door was opened by the butler who announced: His Royal Highness Prince so and so of Persia. Then entered a distinguished looking, sallow-skinned gentleman, dressed exactly like Lawrence of Arabia. Up to this point, Eric had no inkling that this was a practical joke. However, his suspicions mounted as the discussion continued. The denouement came when Felix said: 'By the way, Eric, apart from his Royal Highness's interest in oil, he is considering building a fish canning factory on the shores of the Caspian Sea and I wonder whether you would be prepared to go out there and survey the site?' It was clear that this took the 'Prince' by surprise as much as it did Eric. Eric later met the actor who had played the part of the prince – a German who had been elaborately made up for the occasion. But Felix was never prepared to admit that the episode was a leg-pull and Eric heard that a repeat performance had been attempted on someone else.

Felix, who was quite tough and had strong nerves, told me once of a flying experience. The late Lord Melchett, who in his young days was on the board of Hill Samuel, the bankers, had his own plane and always returned to his country house by air. An enthusiastic pilot, he had purchased a new machine and invited Felix to join him on a flight. When they reached their destination, Lord Melchett started to fight with the controls and to circle round the landing strip. He then exclaimed to Felix: 'Damn it, I can't get the under-carriage down.' Felix was understandably uneasy, was anticipating a crash landing at least, and beads of perspiration appeared on his brow. Suddenly, Lord Melchett announced that all was well and the plane landed safely. Felix thanked him warmly for the excellent flight – but made a mental note never to fly with him again. On a personal note, I always found it disconcerting to hear Felix playing classical music vigorously on the piano, giving vent to his feelings when I was waiting in suspense to submit an offer to him for one of his buildings.

*

Lord Rayne, known to me as Max, is a great entrepreneur. He achieved overwhelming success as a young man within a comparatively short time, without capital or special training. He was one of the pioneers who built a number of large office blocks in the centre of London after the last war. After serving in the RAF, he joined his father in the family textile business. His early success seems to have spawned from some brilliant business moves allied with shrewd judgement and an outstanding ability to inspire confidence in others to finance his ideas on a profit-sharing basis. He was thus able to build up a large public company known as London Merchant Securities Limited. After completing a successful property deal for the family textile company, he left the business to concentrate on property. With the help of his bank manager, he carried out one or two small deals which provided him with a limited amount of capital. He then built a relationship with the Portman Estate which owned properties in Portman Square and Baker Street and obtained finance to build office blocks on the site. He eventually formed a joint development company with Lord Portman. Next, Max boldly tendered for a building lease on a large island site in Wigmore Street at the rear of Selfridges. He won the tender in direct competition with several other leading, well-established developers – despite the current ban on office building and the added complication of Treasury restrictions on borrowing. With a list of prospective tenants to encourage him, Max undertook to finance and build on the site. Later, the prospective tenants changed their minds, but Max persuaded Claude Leigh, then chairman of MEPC, to provide the finance to erect the building on a share basis with Max's company. It was eventually let at a favourable rent. He then became the first developer to approach the Church Commissioners directly with a joint development proposal. A group of dilapidated houses in Eastbourne Terrace, close to Paddington Station, were an embarrassment to the Commissioners because the properties had become notorious for prostitution. Max stepped in to convince the Commissioners that, instead of selling the site, they should participate in the development profit by financing the building of an office block in partnership with Max's company. They agreed and the block was built and let. It gave the Church Commissioners their first taste of participating in direct development and Max seized the opportunity to arrange a similar joint development on another estate he had acquired off Tottenham Court Road.

Many years later, when Max Rayne's company had formed an American subsidiary, he met the famous American developer, Bill Zeckendorf. He was a big man with big ideas – an enthusiastic super-salesman, full of inspiration to rebuild the whole of the United States if necessary. Once, when Zeckendorf was seeking finance, Max Rayne acquired from him an interest in the Savoy Plaza Hotel in Fifth Avenue, New York. The hotel was unprofitable and Max prepared plans to convert it into an office block. Some time later Zeckendorf changed his mind and offered to buy back the hotel from Max as he had discovered that General Motors were prospective tenants of the proposed office block. Zeckendorf agreed to accept a commission for the introduction of General Motors, but as he was still in debt to Max's company, he agreed to forego the debt in lieu of the commission. Max arranged a joint company with General Motors, who became tenants of a substantial proportion of the space in the new 40-storey building. London Merchant Securities is now a large and powerful company which has diversified its activities into industry and investment, including North Sea oil and gas exploration, a whisky distillery and a printing company which has pioneered the application of computer typesetting. A soft-voiced and cultured man, Max enjoys family life with his second wife, the former Jane Vane-Tempest-Stewart.

Recently he has devoted a great deal of time to charitable causes and the arts and for this and his public service, he was created a Life Peer in 1976.

*

My own family was not without its share of misfortune. Shortly after the death of my mother's wealthy uncle, Reuben Gliksten – the old man who had founded an immensely successful timber business – his eldest and youngest sons died leaving the middle son, Stanley Gliksten, no choice other than to become chairman of the family firm. A great sportsman, Stanley was one of the founder members of the Aero Club and his hobbies were flying and motor racing. Already the salesman and world traveller of the international firm which J. Gliksten & Sons had become, he hated administration; but he felt obliged to assume responsibility for the company's future.

The Gliksten family owned a large amount of property in the West End, but as I was somewhat overawed by them in my younger days I kept well away as I did not like the idea of being employed as an agent merely because I was distantly related. Fate, however, played a strange hand, and in 1946, not long after I had restarted my practice, my firm sold a factory at Wembley. The surveyor acting for the purchasers happened to be the son-in-law of William, Stanley Gliksten's chauffeur. Knowing that there was a distant family connection between myself and the Glikstens, the surveyor casually mentioned the deal to William. William repeated the story when driving Stanley Gliksten home. The next morning Stanley Gliksten telephoned me and said he had heard I had sold a factory in Wembley and that perhaps I could deal with a factory for him in Coventry. He owned the property through a property company he had set up with Charles Band, a Coventry solicitor. I inspected the large factory, known as Rudge Works, which was occupied by GEC, paying a rent equivalent to about 3d a square foot. Strangely, even though it was peacetime, I discovered that half of the building was still under requisition to the Ministry of Supply. After making a few enquiries, I decided that the factory must be worth a rent of about 1/6d a square foot. And, when I got back to London, I told Stanley that I felt there was justification for terminating immediately the requisition on half of the factory which had probably been overlooked. I well remember my first meeting in London with Stanley's co-director, Charles Band. He told Stanley that as I had just returned from the Army – unlike him – I was completely unacquainted with the property market in Coventry. He said that if notice to terminate the requisition was served, GEC would probably vacate the entire building, leaving him and Stanley with a depreciating, rambling, old factory on their hands. I knew that if GEC decided to vacate, in practice it would take them several years to do so due to the large amount of plant and machinery installed in the factory.

Stanley – whom I had already briefed – embarrassed me somewhat by saying: 'Band, you are a bloody old fool. Coventry does not dictate terms to London, but London dictates terms to Coventry. I am the major shareholder in our company and I intend to get Eddie to serve this notice and I am ready to back his judgement.' On the following Friday I enjoyed writing a formal letter to the Ministry of Supply requesting them to terminate the requisition and to deliver the keys to me at noon on the following Monday, knowing that this would be physically impossible. I received a reply by special delivery confirming the Ministry would terminate the requisition forthwith and that they would instruct GEC to move into the other half of the works which they held on short lease. The local solicitor for GEC in Coventry informed me that the company would be terminating their tenancy on the whole building. I therefore circulated details of the factory quoting a rent of 1/6d per square foot. The Dunlop Rubber Company expressed interest and, unknown to me, the chairman of Dunlop telephoned the GEC chairman to ask him unofficially when they would be moving. Things then happened swiftly. The managing director of GEC in London asked me to call and told me to disregard the statement made in Coventry. GEC would surrender its short-term lease and enter into a long lease at 1/6d per square foot. After the letting was concluded, I arranged a sale of the shares of the property company which owned the works to Joe Littman. And, as a result of this exercise, my office was entrusted to handle all future business of J. Gliksten & Sons.

Stanley Gliksten eventually became chairman of Charlton Athletic Football Club and, among my more unusual tasks was the negotiation and purchase of houses close to the football ground for occupation by members of the team. I was always amused by the antics of Stanley's son, Michael, who at that time was a large, tall, copper-headed youth who went to Marlborough School. Apparently, Swindon was out of bounds to the boys and, when Charlton Athletic played Swindon Town, the chairman of Swindon Town said he knew Michael Gliksten very well. Stanley was amazed to hear this, but discovered that Michael – who was soccer-mad – cycled regularly to the Swindon Town ground, against the school rules and unknown to his father. There he introduced himself as Stanley's son to the chairman of the club and regularly received a free seat in the stand. When his father died, Michael became chairman of Charlton Athletic and he was honoured at quite a young age by being elected a member of the Football Association. Apart from football, his interests are antiques and art and he lives in the country. Neither he, nor his late brother, David, followed their father into the business. The firm eventually became the International Timber Corporation. It is a pity that Reuben Gliksten was not there to see sales in 1980 exceed £216 million.

*

The first man I invited to join me in partnership in 1947 was Edward Mowle. He was a man of great integrity and loyalty and a sound valuer and negotiator with both feet planted firmly on the ground. He was a modest, retiring person which sometimes caused others to underrate his ability. One of his great assets was that, unlike me, he was a perfectionist in dealing with office routine and the records he maintained were always impeccable. Papers were seldom to be seen on his desk. Implicit trust in Eddy helped me to initiate business and expand the practice speedily in the early days. The feeling of mutual trust enabled us to work together for a lifetime. Indeed, when I decided to retire, Eddy elected to do likewise but, as consultants to our former firm, we still maintain close association and friendship.

A keen and consistent golfer, Eddy became president of EGS – the Estates Golfing Society – in 1969. It was customary for the president to wear a fez at the annual dinner and I can well remember the uncharacteristic sight of Eddy wearing his oriental presidential headgear at the top table. The guest speaker was the late Arthur Dixon Wright, the famous surgeon. Eddy put me next to him and asked me privately to ensure that he was offered plenty to drink so that he would be in a good mood to speak when the time came. I may say that I had no difficulty in executing this task. Arthur Dixon Wright stood up and brought the house down with his opening remark: 'Gentlemen, I am honoured to be invited to this distinguished company of property swindlers. You have a comparatively easy time in your profession as if a client does not take your advice, you can tell him in impolite language to sheer off. In my profession, I am governed by the strict rules of the British Medical Association and I have to be extremely careful what I do and what I say. Only last evening, an attractive lady patient of mine suddenly said: "Doctor, kiss me", and I declined and said: "I have to be careful to abide by the strict disciplinary practices of the BMA and, in fact, I should not be in bed with you now!"'
The Estates Golfing Society emerged almost by accident. The late Lewis Hammerson, founder of the Hammerson Group of Companies, gave a Christmas party in 1956 at his offices in Park Lane to which he invited guests from the property world. Jack Hughes, now Sir Jack Hughes of Jones Lang Wootton, Joe Levy of Stock Conversion, Robert Van Hee of the Friends Provident & Century Life Company and Henry Joel, the estate agent, were happily discussing golf in the early hours of the morning. Somewhat bemused by the evening's entertainment, they suggested playing a four-ball match at Sunningdale on New Year's Day. Each was amazed when they all remembered to arrive at the club on the morning of 1 January, clad in arctic clothing. But none of them was a member of the club and they were embarrassed to find that, without an introduction, no golf could be played. After a frantic search of the clubhouse, they discovered Sir Charles Forte talking to a friend. When he learned of their

plight, he agreed to be sponsor. They managed to play two enjoyable but scarcely skilful rounds and, during earnest discussion in the bar, the suggestion was made to form a new golfing society of which they would be the founder members. They decided that an appropriate name would be the 'Estates Golfing Society' (EGS) with a motif of an egg on the Society tie. Each then approached friends in and connected with the property industry – since when the Society has gone from strength to strength. If they had not met that enthusiastic personality, Sir Charles Forte, the Estates Golfing Society might never have been formed. Sir Charles has had an amazing career as head of Trust House Forte; his chain of hotels have made an enormous contribution to the tourist industry and he has been honoured in 1982 with a life peerage in the New Year's Honours List. Jack Hughes has also since been knighted for public services during a continuing, distinguished career. Chairman of Bracknell New Town and a board member of other public bodies and companies, he is also an adviser on commercial property to the Department of Environment.

*

Around 1946, during the restrictions on office development, the Ministry of Works found that office space was urgently needed by Government Departments and the Ministry was unable to supply it. A system was formulated to ease the problem. The Ministry granted licences to build in cases where a developer who owned a suitable site was willing to contract to erect a tailor-made office building, designed to the exact requirements of the Government Department concerned. In the interest of economy, the building had to be erected in strict accordance with the official pamphlet on Utility Buildings and a full disclosure of costs had to be declared by the developer to ensure that the rent payable by the Ministry upon completion was fair and reasonable. These arrangements were known as Building Lessor Schemes and they gave developers opportunities to build during the period of restriction. Probably the first man to seize such an opportunity was the late Emanuel Curtis, known as Manny, who practised as Vickers & Stanley. He was a bright young man with ginger hair and a keen eye for a deal. Manny secured an inexpensive site in a fringe position for offices in Theobalds Road, just off Southampton Row, and agreed tentative terms with the Ministry to rent the proposed building on lease, based on plans and specifications subject to Building Lessor Scheme conditions. Manny himself could not provide substantial finance to back the scheme, but he formed a syndicate with several others and was eventually able to sell the finished building – known as Adastral House – to Lord Samuel's company at a substantial profit. I also recollect acting for Harry Neal, the contractors, in connection with another Building Lessor Scheme now occupied by the British Council in Davies Street, almost adjoining the recently erected 'West One' shopping concourse in Oxford Street with Bond Street Underground Station.

Alfred Esdaile was another developer who carried out Building Lessor Scheme developments. A former Music Hall trouper in his young days, he was an entertaining character with a great sense of humour. His partner was Arnold Klausner, an intellectual individual with a law degree and a very kindly disposition. I could never imagine two people less suited to be partners than Alfred, the extrovert, and Arnold, the reticent. Alfred acquired and converted the Royal Court Theatre some years ago. Eventually, he sold his property company, and due to failing health, lived in the south of France until his death. In his later years, despite indisposition, he was still full of fun. During the holiday season, nothing gave him more pleasure than meeting English friends and handing them his visiting card, specially engraved: 'Alfred Esdaile. No Business. No Telephone. No Address'.

9

THE SOLUTION WHICH STUCK

*

During 1948, I plunged into the problems of large-scale residential management, somewhat against the recommendation of my young partners at that time. I had become friendly with Harry Massey, an enthusiastic man who had made a fortune in the ladies' gown trade. From a manufacturing business in Aldgate, he moved to the West End and his business flourished and expanded. Harry also started Simon Massey, an exclusive couturier business which was later run by Leslie, one of his sons. His commercial success caused him to seek other sources of investment and he became interested in property. He met Louis Scott, a quick-thinking agent and property entrepreneur who always had an eye for a deal. Harry seldom concluded any business transaction without James Clement, the shrewd City accountant, now senior partner of Robson Rhodes, at his side. Louis Scott and Harry jointly acquired a large block of flats called Grove Hall Court in St John's Wood containing 210 flats, a club restaurant in the basement and a number of shops and garages. They had also bought another modern block of flats – Bentinck Close – facing Regents Park and an office building in Victoria Street let in a number of suites. Differences of opinion between the two of them resulted in James Clement the accountant arranging for each to go their separate ways – Harry retaining the two blocks of flats and Louis Scott the Victoria Street office building. Harry then asked me to manage the two blocks of flats. They produced a strain on my office because our management department was comparatively small. We were accustomed to dealing with commercial property management – less personal and demanding than residential.

I had to devote a considerable amount of my own time to the job. There was a variety of mixed tenancies, some furnished, some unfurnished – the unfurnished flats providing the tenants with security of tenure under the Rent Restrictions Act. Problems and complaints abounded and, in the case of indiscriminate parking by tenants on the approach road and forecourt, I decided to take rather unorthodox steps to eliminate this nuisance. Sincere efforts by the Tenants Association and Harry Massey's lawyers had failed to solve the problem. There are several entrances to the Grove Hall Court flats and, at about 2.00 a.m., I visited the block and handed each entrance porter a pot of glue and some large posters with the words: 'You have been reported to the Managing Agents'. I told them to use as much glue as possible to stick the posters across every offending windscreen parked on the forecourt. It was a dastardly trick, but an effective one – executed in the best interests of the majority of the tenants.

In 1951, a Conservative Government removed certain provisions of the Rent Restrictions Act to enable flats of this calibre to be restored to their full rental value. After consultation with my management department, we decided that a dramatic rise in rent might cause some of the tenants undue hardship. We therefore formed our own plan to grant new leases at the full rent but to give a letter of undertaking to existing tenants. The letter confirmed that as long as they personally remained in occupation, a rent rebate would be given over the next five years on a progressive scale, reverting to the full rent in 1956. If they assigned their leases, the full rent would become payable. Our plan was a success. But, some time later, I heard from Sir Wavell Wakefield, then MP for St Marylebone and legendary rugby captain for England. He had received letters from six aggrieved tenants in the block who complained that we had not granted them leases. They had also alleged that we wished to demand a premium. I saw Sir Wavell and told him that the six people in question were not desirable tenants. Some had criminal records and one of them had been involved in a serious offence. Sir Wavell accepted the position immediately. Several years later, walking round the office, I had noticed that the manager of the flats was absent from his desk on an unusually large number of occasions. I then received a telephone call from the Police stating that Mr X, the manager in question, had been reported missing by his wife. A taxi took me straight away to Grove Hall Court as I suspected that Mr X was unlawfully residing somewhere in the block. Deciding to give the impression to the head porter that I was fully aware of the situation, I told him I had forgotten the number of Mr X's flat. Without hesitation he gave me the number. When I rang the bell, the door was opened by a voluptuous blonde and, looking through the hall, there was our property manager – Mr X – in trousers and vest, lathering his face with the help of a shaving mirror hung on the door handle. I gave the couple several hours in which to vacate the property. Harry Massey sold his interest in these blocks of flats many years ago and, although the practice still manages them on behalf of the present owners – The Freshwater Group – the flats are being sold off rather than rented, but still under the experienced supervision of my former partners Brian Harding and John Lamming.

Not long ago, I met Herty Massey, Harry's widow, who had flown over from Cannes to attend an anniversary party of June and John Pearson at Claridges. They are well known in social circles in London and the Riviera. June is a charming and attractive hostess. John is a successful Whisky exporter but never drinks it. I had been a friend of both Harry and Herty, but my relations with Herty became strained when she felt I was unnecessarily stringent in carrying out my duties as joint executor of her late husband's will. Herty is fashionable and sophisticated and, despite some disparaging remarks she passed about me, I decided to take a broad view and to greet her affectionately. I was extremely amused when she introduced me to her French gentleman friend at the party as the 'executioner' of her husband's will!

Louis Scott is a man whom I have encountered many times in the course of my career. Due to his flair as an entrepreneur, he has promoted over the years dozens of property transactions with well-known investors and developers – often on the basis that they purchased the property jointly with him. As a result, it is not widely known that he had initiated the transaction. Many years ago, when I called at his office – then in Berkeley Street – I saw a young man who had joined him as an assistant straight from university after taking a degree in economics. He was none other than Arnold Weinstock, now Lord Weinstock. Arnold left Louis to join his father-in-law, Sir Michael Sobell's company which later merged with GEC and many other companies. Since then, Lord Weinstock has proved himself to be one of the most astute and successful industrialists in the country. He is still managing director of GEC, which employs more than 150,000 people in the UK.

*

I first met Leslie Marler when he was in practice as an estate agent in Maddox Street with Basil Atkinson. One of the early pioneers of the successful public property development company, he has made a considerable impact on the property industry. An ambitious, bold and restless character manifested itself from his youngest days. At the outbreak of the 1914–18 war, he assumed the age of 19 instead of 16 and joined the Horse Artillery Section of the Honourable Artillery Company. He was later commissioned in the Royal Artillery. Leslie did not relish joining the family firm of surveyors of Marler & Marler in Knightsbridge as he felt it was not sufficiently progressive. Instead, he obtained a post at Hamptons as a junior clerk. When Hamptons refused him time off to attend annual Territorial Camp, he defiantly gave in his notice. He was then introduced to Hillier Parker May & Rowden and was interviewed by Tom Parker, one of the then senior partners, at the door of his office. Parker asked him: 'If you were writing to confirm acceptance of an offer, what would you put in a letter?' Leslie's answer of 'subject to contract' apparently secured him the job. He quickly gained experience, worked for a time with Edward Lotery, the developer, and, once he had procured a limited amount of capital, started in practice on his own account as Atkinson & Marler in Maddox Street. The partnership broke up just before the outbreak of the last war. As a Territorial, Leslie was recalled to serve in the Army until 1945. On his return, he bought the shares of Capital & Counties Property

Company – a quoted public company which had not paid a dividend for 17 years – securing control in 1952. In 15 years, Capital & Counties became one of the largest property companies. I believe the cost of the original acquisition was about £50,000 and, as Leslie sold one property which had been overlooked in the books for exactly the same sum, it seemed quite a good deal! On his retirement, the company was worth about £140 million.

Leslie's grandfather sold part of the Knightsbridge Estate in 1909 to a Mr Goddard who, in turn, had left it to his son who was faced with a bill for death duty of about £25,000. Leslie solved the Goddard family's problem by buying the Estate, which included properties in Knightsbridge, Brompton Road, Sloane Street, Basil Street, Hans Crescent, Hans Road and Pavilion Road. Many other properties were quickly added, including the prominent triangular site at the corner of Brompton Road and Knightsbridge, at present occupied by the Scotch House. Highly respected by the property world, Leslie was one of the first developers to arrange close links with insurance companies, encouraging them to take up shares in the borrower's company at the same time as providing debenture funds. His first approaches were to the Norwich Union, whose Board he subsequently joined. One of Capital & Counties' take-overs was Greenhaven Estates. An unusual company, it was floated by the late Mr Rind and Mrs Sylvia Rind without sponsorship or underwriting by a merchant bank. Mrs Rind, an attractive and capable business woman, helped her late husband to build up Greenhaven, but his sudden death forced her to sell a parcel of shares to meet Estate Duty. Control of the company was therefore acquired by the Union Corporation of South Africa. Leslie flew to South Africa and agreed a deal with the Union Corporation in exchange for Capital & Counties shares. As a result Union Corporation and Mrs Rind became large shareholders in Capital & Counties. This enthusiastic lady has since not only succeeded in salvaging her diminished fortune, but has increased it.

Among Capital & Counties' more spectacular developments is Arundel Great Court, containing nearly 350,000 sq.ft. of office space in the Strand. An attractive development, it includes an acre of lawns and footpaths between the Strand and the Thames, and at the rear is the Howard Hotel. The scheme was funded by Legal & General. The site, owned by the Duke of Norfolk, was to be submitted for sale by auction. Leslie called upon Jack King of Matthews & Goodman, the auctioneers, who informed him that the auction particulars were not yet available. As Leslie was leaving on holiday for Monte Carlo, he asked Jack King to forward the particulars to him at the Hotel de Paris. Intrigued by the development possibilities Leslie made up his mind to buy. When the particulars arrived in Monte Carlo he was pleased to see that many of the important people in the property world who might be competitive bidders were also on holiday there. So the day after the auction details arrived he returned to London, met his son, Richard, and they agreed the valuation together. Leslie saw Jack King and the deal was done prior to the auction. Richard Marler died tragically in a shooting accident in 1962.

Another of Leslie's more important transactions I describe as the 'hole-in-the-ground' project. Leslie acquired from British Rail the old Victoria Station at Nottingham and some adjacent land. Literally a hole in the ground, the site was in a cutting much below street level. At that time, as a potential shopping development, it showed little promise, but Leslie and his colleagues had the foresight and courage to develop it as a 1,000,000 square foot shopping centre. They were confident that the centre's size and the right tenant-mix would bring success. One special feature is a unique clock, 20 foot high, with a water fountain designed by Rowland Emmett and visible from both shopping levels to provide a focal point. Another work of art by the ingenious and imaginative mind of Rowland Emmett, the title being 'The Featherstone Kite Openwork Basket-Weave Mark Two Gentleman's Flying Machine', which is an attraction to shoppers in the Merrion Centre, Leeds, was built by Arnold Ziff's Town Centre Securities. At the Victoria Centre topping-out ceremony, I found myself seated next to the Sheriff of Nottingham, who was wearing full civic dress, including lace ruffled sleeves. I asked him his occupation and was told he was an engine driver. I then introduced him as 'a colleague' to the late Fred Howe, one of the directors of the British Rail Property Board, who was also present. Fred shook him warmly by the hand and could not understand why they had not met previously at Executive board meetings.

Leslie Marler retired as chairman of Capital & Counties in 1971. He always said that, had it not been for his outside activities, he would have been a multi-millionaire. His interests included rugby, cricket, golf, parish council activities and fox hunting. In addition, he was a director of the Norwich Union Group, the chairman of three other public companies, held life membership of the Court of the City University and of the Court of the Corporation of the Sons of the Clergy, and was a past Master of the Worshipful Company of Merchant Tailors. He was High Sheriff of Buckinghamshire, founded the Bolebec House Stud and the Wavendon herd of Dairy Shorthorns and was honoured for public service. He lived in semi-retirement high up on the Chilterns in a delightful Carolean house which included a fascinating library of first editions and where he was constantly visited by his son, daughter and six grandchildren. Even in his later years, he was a fine, upright figure of military bearing and he passed away in his 81st year in 1981. Dennis Marler, Leslie's cousin, is the present managing director of Capital & Counties. He joined the board in 1962. Ian Northen, another member of the Capital & Counties board, has made a study of shopping centre development. In recent years the company built the Eldon Square shopping centre at Newcastle-upon-Tyne, one of the largest covered shopping centres in the UK. In 1972, as a result of the property crisis, Capital & Counties found itself in difficulty. To Dennis Marler's credit, he has been able to pilot the company through the storm by selling the Australian and Canadian properties in 1976, the Knightsbridge Estate in 1977 to BP Pension Fund and the Victoria Centre, Nottingham, on a sale and leaseback basis.

10

FROM NEWS VENDOR TO EMPIRE

*

Many of the multiple shop and distributive trades provide good examples of achievement through personal endeavours of individuals. Not long ago, I was a guest with Terence Goodman, a partner in my former practice, at the head office of W.H. Smith & Son. Sir Charles Troughton, Peter Bennett and Hugh McNearnie were stimulating and attentive hosts and I learned with interest of their policy decision to open new superstores. Little Grosvenor Street, renamed Broadbent Street, almost an alley – across the road from our offices in Grosvenor Street, was the origin of the W.H. Smith empire. It was here in 1792 that Henry Walton Smith and his wife Anna opened a small newsvendor's shop. Their sons, Henry Edward and William Henry, succeeded to the business. William Henry proved to be a vigorous businessman and the firm became known as W.H. Smith. He wanted to provide the fastest newspaper delivery service in the country so he built up a fleet of small carts and fast horses. He was later to use the new railways for transportation and, although still adventurous, it was left to his son, also William Henry, to realise the full potential of travel in future years. When William Henry Jnr was 21 he was taken into partnership and the firm became known as W.H. Smith & Son. When the railway network advertised bookstall rights on its stations, young W.H. Smith seized the opportunity, signed a contract and opened the first bookstall at Euston in 1848, to be followed by many others. These early bookstalls were an example of enterprise, providing not only newspapers but books, candles to read by and rugs to keep readers warm. In 1935, W.H. Smith operated 1,115 bookstalls. The firm spread overseas and one of the novelties of Paris is its shop in the Rue de Rivoli. It became famous for the sale of English books and, on several occasions while I was in the French capital, I have felt back in England when taking tea in the tea room there. I was secretly proud of the fact that in the 1930's, before the war, I purchased from W.H. Smith an American machine known as the auto-typist. The only other user at the time was the accounts department at Selfridges. The machine worked on the pianola principle and was the most modern piece of typing equipment of its time. Nowadays, of course, the wordplex machine is its modern equivalent – quicker, faster and better. W.H. Smith & Son is now a huge organisation with a turnover of more than £500 million and 340 branches in the UK with a book section in the United States.

During the course of my career, a revolutionary change has taken place in the men's tailoring business. In the 1920's, the wealthy used to have their suits made by well-known tailors in Savile Row. Many tailors refused to make a suit for an unknown customer unless he was well introduced, and it was the boast of aristocratic young men that they never settled their tailor's account within six months. Even middle-class families had their clothes made by small working tailors in their local area. The ready-made tailoring business, previously frowned upon, started to grow. At one time Leeds, at the centre of the Yorkshire wool industry, was the source of a large volume of mass-produced suits. The outstanding figure of the ready-made industry was the late Sir Montague Burton – a remarkable man who set up a tailoring manufacturing plant in 1921 at Hudson Road Mills, Leeds, to supply his fast-growing retail chain. He undoubtedly led the huge growth of multiple tailoring shops during the 1920's and 1930's. Apart from his talent to provide suits for the masses at reasonable prices, he had an extraordinary flair for property. First known as 'Montague Burton – the Tailor of Taste', his company subsequently became 'Montague Burton Limited' and is nowadays known as the Burton Group. Hudson Road Mills now covers about 40 acres and the Burton Group has its own transport fleet delivering an estimated 70,000 garments a day to its branches. About 80 years ago, as a young man, Sir Montague started a menswear shop in Chesterfield. There was a tailoring workroom over this shop which prospered and Sir Montague married and opened other shops. In 1931 the *Daily Mail* revealed that Montague Burton had carried out a record £1-million deal in cloth which would give employment to 100,000 people, including those already employed in the firm's factory.

I have clear recollections of my early contacts with the company when Archie Wansbrough, the property director, came to see me from Leeds. Polite, efficient and tactful, he was always proud of his modest Montague Burton suit. He usually arrived in the same yellow taxi cab on Thursdays which, in most cases, was early-closing day for local shopkeepers. Archie liked to inspect shops in various London suburbs on early-closing day by arrangement with owners, who could talk freely during the absence of their staff. He was more subtle and discreet than other prospective purchasers, who felt the price might drop if they pointed out every possible defect they could find; this was not the case with Wansbrough from whom I learnt much about the art of negotiation. I can still visualise scenes of shop owners, often husband and wife, sitting in their dining room above their extensive premises waiting for Archie to complete his inspection. After this they would expect to invite him to have a drink and discuss price. But all Archie would do was compliment them on their excellent shop and upper premises and, without uttering a single word about money, politely shake hands and apologise for having to leave. This left the owners without any inkling of whether Montague Burton wished to purchase their premises or at what cost. About two days later, we would normally receive a concise, effective letter, signed by R.J. Pearson, the secretary of Montague Burton, from its head office at Hudson Road Mills, Leeds. The heading usually comprised nearly all the letter giving the frontage, depth, accommodation, whether freehold or leasehold and other essential information about the property. Underneath that, above the signature of the secretary, would be typed 'If you can offer us this building at a named price, we are willing to recommend it to the board for consideration.' Montague Burton was thus able to acquire many of the finest corner sites in shopping centres throughout the UK and, when Sir Montague died in 1952, there were about 600 shops trading, many with extensive window frontages in prominent positions. Large first-floor premises above Montague Burton shops were often let to the Lucania or the Temperance Billiard Saloons patronised by potential customers. In more recent years, when fashions changed, many of these upper floors were let to dancing clubs. In the early days Montague Burton bought many freehold properties in the name of one of their companies, Key Estates – an appropriate name for a company with shops in such prominent positions. Where freeholds could not be acquired, company policy was to take 999-year leases. Today the total value of Burton Group properties may be estimated at about £200 million or more.

I did not make a habit of meeting my clients socially, but Aubrey Orchard-Lisle, my good friend and brother agent, knew Sir Montague Burton. He tells me that, although Sir Montague spoke with a slight European accent, he was a fluent writer and scholar, a member of the Pen Club of Authors and he published several books, notably on travel and industry. I am told that while Sir Montague seldom, if ever, negotiated personally to acquire branches, he virtually acted as the company's estates manager. He possessed a photographic memory of all the shopping centres in the UK and frequently inspected his properties without disclosing his identity. This sometimes led to embarrassing situations. Aubrey recollects the time about 30 years ago when a caretaker of a potential Burton shop in Westminster Bridge Road, opposite the House of Commons, locked Sir Montague in a room, thinking he was a prowler.

There was a similar incident when I was involved in the sale of a prominent corner property in High Road, Kilburn, occupied by W. Southon, the gents' outfitters. My office at that time was acting with the ebullient estate agent, Douglas Tovey. Mr Southon was extremely sensitive concerning possible disclosure of the private sale of the property and insisted that no inspections should take place without prior appointment with him which was to be arranged after closing time. One afternoon, I received an indignant call from Mr Southon, who told me that a strange man calling himself Mr Morris, a shopfitter, was walking round his shop. The man had arrived without prior appointment and, subject to my agreement, Southon proposed to throw him out. I telephone Douglas Tovey whose reaction was: 'For heavens sake, try to satisfy Mr Southon as the so-called Mr Morris is Sir Montague himself.' Reminiscing one day with Raymond Burton, he told me that his father, Sir Montague, was an enthusiastic – if eccentric and unorthodox – bridge player. On one occasion, he raised his partner's opening 'No Trump' to 'Three No Trumps' but, with a slim point count. When his partner went down heavily, he remarked cuttingly to Sir Montague: 'I'm afraid that all your suits aren't worth double.' Sir Montague Burton died aged 67 and his eldest son, Raymond Burton persuaded the company to go into ladies' wear when Peter Robinson, the great Oxford Street store, was acquired with the intention of putting the Burton name on the finest corner shop in the country. The company then expanded its ladies' fashions interests, which now include Top Shop, Evans Outsize and Dorothy Perkins, with a new and virile management.

*

Another unforgettable character in the tailoring trade in Leeds was the late Sir Henry Price. He was a shrewd Yorkshireman and, although his organisation was not as powerful as that of Montague Burton, he built up an empire of tailoring shops in a comparatively short time. He was, perhaps, a rival of Montague Burton, but his policy was different to Sir Montague's. He tended to rely upon street plans and could not devote the time to carry out personal inspections when his company was expanding. One of his first actions, when a shop was offered to him, was to look at the relevant street plan and ask us to pinpoint the position of Burton's. This helped him to form an opinion. He would come to London and interview agents in connection with property in his branch on the south side of Oxford Street. He spoke with a pronounced Yorkshire accent and, when he looked at the key plan of a town centre, he would say: 'Where are these 'ere Burtons?' When he traded as Price's Tailors and had comparatively few shops, suits cost about £5 each. He waged a cut-price war on the market by converting his shop in the Moor, Sheffield, into a 50/– Tailors. Apparently the opening of this new shop was on a Saturday and I am told that he and his wife got a tram to visit the branch in question. Unable to stand the tension, he got off the tram and walked. The shop looked as though a football crowd had descended upon it and Sir Henry Price relates how he turned to his wife and said: 'I shall be a millionaire in no time – I have struck gold.'

In later years, as a result of his experience with shop property, Sir Henry became interested in property investment and he built up a large, valuable family trust. Aubrey Orchard-Lisle became adviser to the trust and he tells how he travelled down to Wakehurst Place, Sir Henry's country estate in Sussex, on a Friday evening with Sir Brian Mountain and Jock Collier, then chairman and managing director of United Drapery Stores. Wakehurst Place contained many valuable antiques and paintings and, as a prelude to discussing the takeover of Price Tailors, Sir Henry showed everyone round. Sir Brian Mountain took immense pains to comment on the paintings and *objets d'art*. But Jock Collier – a tough businessman who started his early career with shops in New Kent Road at the Elephant & Castle – became increasingly impatient and whispered to Aubrey: 'Can't we cut out the bloody culture and get down to brass tacks?' The deal was done on a shake of hands some half an hour afterwards and the 50/– Tailors shops are now known as John Collier and have become part of United Drapery Stores.

Leeds has been a flourishing part of the country for business success and two other well-known personalities who started business there are the brothers, Bernard and Jack Lyons. They commenced a chain of tailoring shops known as Alexandres, which was also subsequently taken over by United Drapery Stores, and in 1972 Bernard Lyons became the chairman of the entire Group. His brother, now Sir Jack Lyons, is a director and was knighted for his contribution to music and the arts; Bernard has been honoured by the CBE for his public service.

*

I shall never forget my meetings with the late Lord Marks, known to my generation as Simon Marks. The remarkable success of Marks & Spencer seems to stem from close family bonds allied with rigid maintenance of moral principles and high standards. The origin of the firm makes romantic reading. Simon Mark's father, Michael Marks, the founder of the firm, was a Polish immigrant whose family had suffered great hardship. He settled in Leeds as a young man and started his working life as a pedlar. Stark necessity and the hardships endured by his family inspired him with a fervent desire to prove himself. Honesty and fair dealing enabled him to obtain credit and open several market stalls and these were followed within a few years by a number of Penny Bazaars in Yorkshire and Lancashire. His sales centred on a fixed price of 1d giving maximum value. After some success, Michael married. The birth of Simon, the eldest son, was followed by that of Rebecca. A friend of Simon's Israel Sieff, became Rebecca's husband and, a few years afterwards, Simon married Miriam, Israel Sieff's sister. This closely united the Marks and Sieff families and in later years the late Lord Sieff became vice chairman and chairman of the company. One of Rebecca's younger sisters married Harry Sacher – who also became a director – which has stamped the Marks & Spencer board with an indelible family hallmark. As the Penny Bazaars developed, Michael Marks needed help with accounts and administration, so he teamed up with Thomas Spencer – hence the company name. Marks & Spencer was founded, in fact, only ten years after Michael Marks started as a pedlar. As a schoolboy, I remember visiting Penny Bazaars with open fronts and wooden floors in High Street, Stoke Newington, High Street, Kingsland and Brixton Road.

My first dealings with them were with director Alexander Isaacs, who dealt with the acquisition of new stores. More recently it has been with successive property managers, Douglas Green, Arthur Giffard – who eventually became a director – John White and the present manager, John Upton-Prowse. Marks & Spencer are almost fanatical in ensuring that the goods they sell are of the highest quality and, by coincidence, my niece married Lewis Goodman, a former Marks & Spencer director. A trained expert in textiles, Lewis told me at dinner one evening how he had received a rebuke from Lord Marks when he referred to a line of clothing as being 'cheap'. Lord Marks immediately corrected him by pointing out that the company sold nothing cheap – but suggested that perhaps Lewis had meant to say 'inexpensive'.

Lord Marks was a champion of the abolition of unnecessary paper work which prevents essential personal contact between individuals. He abolished a costly department at head office dealing with stock records on the grounds that the cost of compiling these was greater than any loss that might be incurred. And he also spoke in the House of Lords suggesting the abolition of unnecessary paper work in Government Departments to cut costs and, eventually, taxation. I shall never forget the hilarious meeting which took place following a direct confrontation between Lord Marks and Isaac Wolfson concerning a building in Market Street, Manchester. As the agent concerned, I was asked to call upon Lord Marks at his head office in Baker Street, and at that time two of the other directors and Arthur Giffard were present. Lord Marks was a highly respected important man who dominated the decisions of his board by having been chairman for over 40 years and I sat down waiting for him to open the conversation. He gave me a penetrating look and said: 'Your client, Isaac Wolfson, is a most remarkable man, he rushed up the stairs, two at a time, dashed into my office unannounced and said: "Simon, will you put me in touch with someone in your organisation who is able to make a decision."' I found it difficult not to roar with laughter but I realised at the time that these direct negotiations between two illustrious tycoons had been conducted on too high a level to materialise. Ultimately, Lord Marks built a much larger modern store at the other end of Market Street. Under the strong leadership of the present chairman, Lord Sieff, the company has had outstanding success and the present group turnover is well over £1¾ billion including substantial exports. The angelic countenance and self sacrifice of the founder, Michael Marks, no doubt prompted the 'St Michael' trademark; it is a pity that he is not here to witness the growth of the firm which stemmed from his early labours.

*

Mervyn Orchard-Lisle, like his brother, Aubrey, was a surveyor who often crossed my path. We both concentrated on multiple shop property, particularly during the time when chain stores were expanding. We often dealt with the same firms – sometimes on opposite sides – but this did not prevent our being friendly as brother agents. I always found him to be a man of principle who upheld the strict ethics of the profession.

He mentioned to me the story of Malcolm Cooper, former chairman of Allied Suppliers who controlled Liptons, Home & Colonial Stores, Maypole Dairies, Shepherds Dairy and many other shops with branches throughout the UK. They were regarded as one of the leading and strongest multiple firms in the country. Before the advent of the supermarket, grocery shops were mostly small single units, the majority being freeholds owned by the company. In my school days I enjoyed looking into some of their shops to watch skilled assistants in spotless white overalls handling large wooden butter pats. It was fascinating to see them grasp between the pats a large mound of butter, transfer it to the marble topped counter, cut it up into small portions to be weighed in greaseproof paper, packed and handed to the customer in a matter of seconds. Malcolm Cooper – whose nickname was Breeze, in recognition of his dual talents as an extrovert and sportsman – says he became chairman of Allied Suppliers because of a 'White Shield Worthington'. This, to the uninitiated, is a bottled ale made by Worthington, originally known as IPA (Indian Pale Ale). It had a white label to signify it was a sediment beer. As a young man, Breeze worked for his father, a solicitor. In due course, Breeze passed his final Law Society examination and was given the day off to celebrate. He went up to Chorley Wood Golf Club looking for a game and found in the bar someone who seemed to him to be an old boy – called Bamford. 'Old' Bamford asked Breeze if he would like a drink. Breeze's request for a 'White Shield' immediately met the approval of his host. Over this Breeze explained why he wasn't working that day and Bamford asked him how much he was earning from his father. On being told the modest sum, Bamford said he would double it if Breeze worked for him and, after due consultation at home, the offer was accepted. J.H. Bamford & Son were solicitors to the whole of the Allied Suppliers Group. At that time an Act had been passed on the de-rating of industrial property and Breeze was given the job at Bamfords of sorting out the position of Allied Suppliers in relation to the new legislation. As a result, Malcolm Cooper's name often appeared in memoranda before the parent board.

One day the chairman of Pearks Dairies rose to make a speech, suddenly collapsed and died – and a replacement had to be found. The general manager became chairman, but he, too, had to be replaced. One of the parent board directors said: 'What about this young fellow, Cooper – he seems an able chap?' So Breeze was appointed (after protesting that he was a lawyer and not a grocer). From chairman of Pearks Dairies, he then went on the parent board, to become number one to Sir Lancelot Royle and finally, chairman of the whole group – all, as he used to say, due to a 'White Shield Worthington'. Allied Suppliers are still a powerful supermarket concern now owned as a subsidiary of Sir James Goldsmith's Générale Occidentale SA Paris.

*

An interesting character was the late Lord Fraser, a successful financier, master draper and tycoon. As chairman of the House of Fraser, he controlled a large number of leading departmental stores throughout the UK. He befriended Douglas Tovey, a former partner of Healey & Baker, who became his property adviser and was successful in many takeover bids – the most sensational of which was Harrods. Many of Lord Fraser's acquisitions and subsequent sale and leaseback deals were achieved with Tovey's assistance. He recalls that his Lordship was a natural property valuer and whenever he was planning a takeover he would visit the stores personally. Once inside, he would quietly go by lift to the top floors, quickly descend by the main stairs, taking a hasty glance floor by floor, and walk out of the front door before he could be identified. His Lordship would then scribble on the back of his cigarette packet the approximate area and stock value of each floor – plus the capital value of the freehold. According to Tovey's reckoning, Lord Fraser was seldom more than ten per cent wrong.

Hugh Fraser was happiest when entertaining friends. Each Hogmanay, he gave a big party at the Drummond Arms near Loch Lomond. Two years before his death, at a New Year's Eve party, he rose from the table at the stroke of midnight and said: 'I want you all to rise and drink to my dear wife, Katy, who is now Lady Fraser.' This was the first inkling he gave his family and friends that he had been awarded a knighthood. Just over a year later, Sir Hugh became Lord Fraser of Allander. An excellent host, he ensured his guests wanted for nothing. His own tastes, however, were simple. His usual main course was what he called a 'jumbo' sandwich – a jambon sandwich which he washed down with coca-cola. Lord Fraser was a chain smoker of more than 100 cigarettes a day. His donations to charity were considerable and before his untimely death at the early age of 62 he established a charitable foundation under the direction of his son, the present Sir Hugh Fraser. If the late Lord Fraser had a weakness, it was smypathy for any human being in trouble. He realised himself that he was an easy touch and could never turn down a plea for help. I am told that when the House of Fraser went public, strict company policy of discharge and prosecution applied to any member of staff caught pilfering. When this happened, it greatly distressed Lord Fraser and, more often than not, without the knowledge of his fellow directors, he would secretly visit the homes of these unfortunate people and put them on his personal payroll until they found another job. Douglas Tovey was present on one occasion in Monte Carlo at the height of the summer when everyone was sunbathing. Lord Fraser, dressed in a smart summer lounge suit, smoking the inevitable cigarette and carrying a brief case containing confidential papers including a list of the weekly cash takings from each of his stores, quite unabashed, announced in a loud voice: 'I am going to take a wee paddle'. Rolling up his trousers, he then proceeded to do so, oblivious to the amused and shocked glances of his onlookers. He was a man of no inhibitions. One of his favourite relaxations was an annual January visit to St Moritz. Here he enjoyed the Scottish game of curling, at which he was a recognised expert, and he skippered his team to numerous successes against other teams led by Sir Gordon Richards and Lord and Lady Gluckstein.

I have always enjoyed meeting Douglas Tovey, who is a forthright, extrovert character. He is also a super-salesman who has promoted sensational deals in his time. At the age of 16, thanks to the influence of the Free Masons, he became a junior on the staff of the Great Western Railway at Paddington Station. He eventually became the right-hand man of Reginald Scarsbrook, the Assistant Chief Surveyor, to whom Tovey says he owes everything. In 1938, Scarsbrook advised Douglas to leave as he had reached the maximum salary – £250 a year – for his grade and it would be some years before he could expect a rise. He briefly joined Edward Lotery of Greater London Properties and then, two weeks after the outbreak of war in 1939, Aubrey Orchard-Lisle offered him a job at Healey & Baker at £4 a week. Douglas tells me he jumped at the offer. Shortly after 1945 he entered the partnership directly with Arthur Hemens and Aubrey and Mervyn Orchard-Lisle. When Sir Charles Clore proposed to float City and Central Investments Limited, he asked Leonard Sainer – his colleague and solicitor – and Douglas to go to America to acquire the biggest New York skyscraper they could find. They purchased 40 Wall Street, then the third tallest building in the city, from Bill Zeckendorf Senior. Bill Zeckendorf was a New York property developer with grand ideas and visions for the future. He eventually over-traded and lost his property empire. Douglas tells me that he introduced to Sir Charles the idea of taking over the True Form shoe chain and later, the firms of Saxone, Lilley & Skinner, Phillips and Curtis Shoes. Owned and managed by Harry Levison, these companies formed the backbone of the British Shoe Corporation which later became part of Clore's Sears Group. Sir Charles used to say in later years that the acquisition of Harry Levison was his greatest bargain.

Archie Sherman was another property man who worked closely with Douglas Tovey. A member of the Sherman football pool family of Cardiff, Archie practised as a chartered surveyor and was recognised as one of the leading experts on shop valuations. He had worked throughout the war at Bath in the Lands Department of the Royal Navy and later ran his own property companies. Preferring to work as an individual rather than run a public property company, he cleverly financed all his transactions and experienced no financial problems when the property crisis swept away many of his contemporaries. For reasons of health, he now lives abroad and devotes his time to charitable causes.

*

J. Sainsbury, the provision merchants, are an example of another empire which started modestly in 1869 and grew to be successful through high standards and the principles of an exceptional family. The original John James Sainsbury, the founder, was born in London and, after marrying, he opened his first shop in Drury Lane. With the help of his wife – a dairyman's daughter – he converted the shop into a dairy. They were a hard-working and devoted couple with six sons and five daughters. The family resolved to expand the business and its earliest branches were established at Kentish Town, Stepney and Croydon. The family also built up a good relationship with suppliers, including the Dutch firm, Van den Berghs – margarine manufacturers. Trade was cemented when J.B. Sainsbury, eldest son of the founder, married Mabel Van den Bergh. Subsequently, his son, Alan John Sainsbury, now Lord Sainsbury, became chairman and eventually President. In turn, he was followed by his eldest son, the Hon John Sainsbury and Sir Robert Sainsbury and the Hon Timothy Sainsbury are also directors. By 1901, there were 56 Sainsbury branches and just over 50 years later, the company became a quoted public concern. From small beginnings, Sainsburys is now a vigorous and progressive concern with over 200 supermarkets. And their property directors, Charles Burdsey and Geoffrey Haynes, are still actively negotiating for additional sites.

II

THE INDUSTRIAL WIZARD

*

I was fortunate in the early days of my practice to meet a client of the calibre of Sir Isaac Wolfson – popularly known in business circles as IW. I am sure he will not object if I now refer to him as IW. He possesses all the attributes of a broad Scot and is the natural leader of his clan. IW has always been devoted to his wife, the late Lady Edith Wolfson, a charming person who had been a great help to him in his social life and particularly in assisting charitable causes. He was a non-smoker, a non-drinker and a strong family man. He had a dynamic personality and was such an enthusiastic businessman that his vitality affected everyone around him. I often found myself almost rushing out of his office in eagerness to do the next deal. We first met in the Wolfson family business of S. Wolfson & Sons at Old Street in the City of London. Shortly afterwards he was running Great Universal Stores Ltd and beginning to transform a mediocre company of little significance into one of the largest and most powerful concerns in the country. Like many other successful tycoons, he was in his office at 7.30 every morning. Whenever I offered him a property investment, his answer was always: 'Why should I buy a property to yield about six per cent when I am quite comfortably able to earn more than double this in my own business?' Never a property man at heart, he was an industrialist with enormous faith in his ability to earn profits. However, during the years when GUS took over many diverse companies, IW built up property assets worth several million pounds. GUS now has its own property development company. It may well be that my quiet professional style suited Isaac Wolfson. Perhaps it provided a suitable foil for the vociferous and dominant negotiations he conducted with opposing directors when settling terms to take over their companies. I must admit that, in his early days, IW was tough on the payment of fees to my firm. But I always took a broad view as this was compensated for by his stimulating personality and the possibility of a large volume of future business.

I have the greatest admiration for the capacity, energy, natural ability and brilliance of IW. He has demonstrated his prowess as salesman, judge of merchandise and wizard of accountancy, balance sheets, corporate law, real estate, administration and management. He had a photographic memory for figures, could glance through a balance sheet, memorise it and repeat it days afterwards. I frequently called upon him at 9.30 a.m. after he had seen many other callers and had already done two hours work. His desk would be clear, with the exception of four or five letters which he had just received from me. His ability to make quick decisions and his retentive memory – a human filing system – enabled him to adopt the habit of returning my original letters addressed to him with his answer and verbal instructions on each. I prided myself a little on my literary efforts and found it somewhat disconcerting to receive back from him the carefully worded letters which I had composed with a great deal of thought only the night before. When I left his office with my own letters under my arm, his desk was perfectly clear. He never needed a filing clerk. He could rely upon his memory – and heaven help me if I overlooked taking action on any of IW's verbal instructions. In his early days, I found it fascinating to watch him exercising charm, aggression, humour, optimism, pessimism or whatever attitude was most effective at the time. He was always prepared to take the gloves off if necessary when negotiating with many powerful and important business men. I recollect many exciting moments as a result of the businesses he acquired in which I was indirectly involved. Prior to making an acceptable offer for shares, full details of the properties were usually unobtainable. It was IW's habit to give me a long list of the addresses of the branches of a firm, sometimes divided into freeholds and leaseholds. My job was to give a snap forecast of the total value. Values were more stable at that time and, although my figures may have been high on some shops and low on others, if the firm had a large number of branches on an average basis, the total figure was seldom far out. After IW acquired the business, my next exercise to recoup the capital was to prove the value by selling each property as an investment on the basis of granting back a lease to GUS.

Great Universal Stores is perhaps the most extensive commercial empire amassed by one man. Its early foundation was a hugh mail-order division – probably one of the largest in the UK – followed by shops, factories and companies including banking, travel, real estate, retail, overseas manufacturing and export divisions. The meteoric early expansion of GUS and the fact that IW was too busy to give interviews to the Press or to bother about his public image, caused the company to be criticised years ago as unstable. Its covenant had a low rating, too. The Norwich Union was, however, the first insurance company to have the foresight to measure GUS's worth by purchasing from them as an investment a freehold shop property in Southend, subject to a leaseback to GUS. Many transactions with other insurance companies and pension funds followed because, at that time, GUS needed the capital for expansion. The tables have now turned and GUS have been able to plough capital into the business to buy back many of these freeholds. When my practice carried out its first GUS valuation in 1955, it was a momentous task. We had a limited staff then and, although my lifelong colleague, Eddy Mowle, and I, both retired in 1973, neither of us ever forgot the time in 1955, the day after our valuation had been finally vetted by us and had been completed. The chairman of GUS, IW, personally visited our office at 9.30 a.m. and left at 5.30 p.m., without a break for lunch – except a bar of chocolate and an apple. IW considered the figure placed on every single property as he turned over the large loose-leaf page on which we had prepared each individual item. Where he agreed with our figure, he turned the page quickly with a hum hum but, in cases where he considered we had been conservative, he yelled at me: 'You are not a valuer, you are a butcher.' I did not flinch as when IW bellowed, I was satisfied that my figure was safe but when he thumbed the pages with a hum hum, I was a little concerned that I had over-valued. After these many outbursts, I was amazed when IW slapped me on the shoulder and said: 'Ah, well, I think you have done a good job.'

At that time George Bourner became chairman of the Conservative Industrial Association whose function was to raise funds for the Conservative Party. It was customary for the Association to hold occasional luncheons in one of the dining rooms at the House of Commons and to invite about 24 business people. I often attended and George Bourner asked me to try and persuade Isaac Wolfson to come. IW was not involved in politics and, in any case, was far too busy building up the GUS empire to devote much time to lunches. However, on this occasion I was able to entice him to the House of Commons. It was usual for a Cabinet Minister to be present who, following lunch, would be introduced to the guests, give an off-the-record address on policy and then answer questions. The Cabinet Minister attending this particular lunch was Peter Thorneycroft (now Lord Thorneycroft), who was then President of the Board of Trade. IW asked me what he could talk about. I suggested Treasury restrictions as a topic, as it was necessary at that time to obtain sanction of the Capital Issued Committee to borrow more than £10,000. The guest speaker, Peter Thorneycroft, had not yet been introduced to the guests by the Chairman, George Bourner, when the enthusiastic IW uninvited and without any complexes whatsoever, gave an entertaining and hilarious discourse on Government restrictions and world trade in general. He finished on a more personal note about GUS and their takeover of a Leeds-based concern known as Town Tailors with its trademark of Weaver to Wearer – pointing out that anyone round the table unable to afford a new suit could get credit on deferred terms. There was no time for Peter Thorneycroft to be introduced or to give his speech but, as a quick aside, he asked IW if he could get a suit on deferred terms. The quick reply in a broad Scottish accent was: 'We do not allow credit to Members of Parliament.'

Among other purchases, IW acquired for GUS the famous, old-established, wholesale drapery concern of Rylands, which had a valuable freehold building in one of the premier shopping positions in Manchester. It occupied extensive upper floors, the whole of the ground floor and

CHAIRMEN OF THE THREE LARGEST PROPERTY COMPANIES

67. Lord Samuel: Chairman, Land Securites Investment Trust

68. Sir Gerald Thorley: Chairman, MEPC Limited

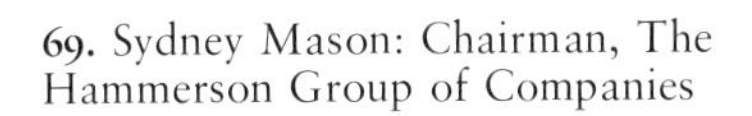

69. Sydney Mason: Chairman, The Hammerson Group of Companies

AUCTIONEERS WITH RECORD SINGLE BIDS

70. Ben Allsop

71. Arthur Hemens

72. Edward Stringer

73. David Yorke

74. Herbert Burnige

MEN WHO REBUILT BOMBED CITIES

75. Louis Freedman

76. Fred Maynard

77, 78. Ravenseft Properties, Exeter: before and after

TWO PROMINENT MEN

79. Lord Ashdown

80. Col. John Trevor

SERGEANT ENLISTS FORMER GENERAL

81. Walter Flack Field Marshal Sir Claude Auchinleck Alan Wright

TWO MEN WITH FLAIR

82. Sam Chippindale

83. John Ritblat

THE SHAREHOLDER'S CHAMPION

84. Sir Charles Clore

A LIKEABLE PROPERTY MAN

85. Jack Cotton

AN EMPIRE BUILDER

86. Sir Maxwell Joseph

A SHREWD LAWYER

87. Leonard Sainer

A FORTHRIGHT CONTRACTOR

88. Bernard Sunley

89. John Sunley

'DOING A HASLEMERE'

90.

91. Fred Cleary

GUESTS AT THE SAME TABLE

92. Richard Peskin, Basil Samuel, The Author, Kenneth Eyles, Walter Philp

A TALENTED FAMILY

93. Harold Wingate

94. Roger Wingate

A CHESTERFIELD DEVELOPMENT

95. Chestergate House, Victoria

A CITY COMPANY

96. Samuel Sebba

97. Max Sebba

A WARNFORD LANDMARK

98. Salisbury House, Finsbury Circus

99, 100. Park Tower Hotel, designed by Richard Seifert

101, 102. Fifteen-storey office and bank, Abu Dhabi designed by Fitzroy Robinson

103. Nigel Mobbs

104. Harry Axton

105. Ron Diggins

106. Percy Bilton

107. Ronald Lyon

108. The late Duke of Westminster

109. The present Duke and Duchess of Westminster

110. George Ridley, former Trustee and Adviser

111. Jimmy James, Trustee and former President of the Royal Institute of Chartered Surveyors

112. Stanley Coggan, Estate Surveyor

113. Kenneth Eyles, formerly of Grosvenor Estate Commercial Developments

114. Councillor (Sandy) Sandford

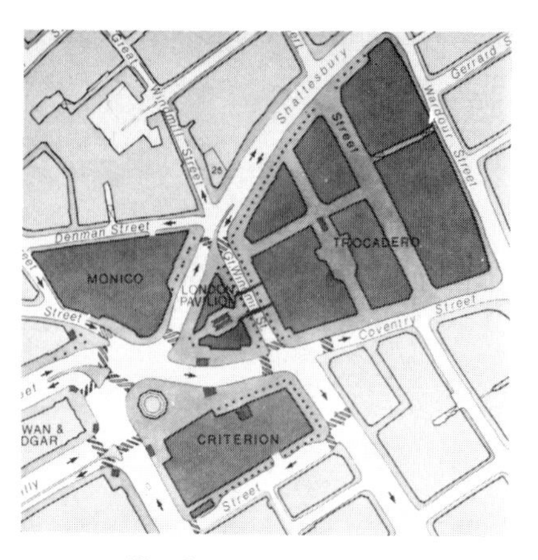

115. Traffic plan

116. Sir Horace Cutler former leader, GLC — The Author — Charles Williams, the well-known surveyor

LONDON WEEKEND TELEVISION

117. London Weekend Television complex

118. The Hon. David Montagu

THE SENIOR PARTNERS OF MY FORMER PRACTICE

119. John Cook

120. Colin Kerr

121. The book title with a hint

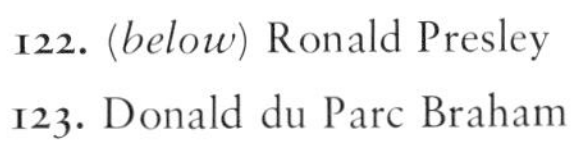

122. (*below*) Ronald Presley

123. Donald du Parc Braham

HOMES FOR THE NEEDY

EVENING STAR, Saturday, May 16, 1981

• *Some of those who attended the official opening of the WPHT development at Stoke Park, Ipswich, were, left to right, Ipswich MP Mr. Ken Weetch, Mr. P. Grimwade, Mr. Edward Erdman, the Mayor and Mayoress of Ipswich, Mr. and Mrs. Syd Mason, Mr.Hugh Cubitt, and Mr. and Mrs. D. M.Cato.*

400 homes for Ipswich

A HOUSING development which cost nearly £7 million was opened yesterday, providing Ipswich with 416 new homes.

The development, Oaklee, Downside Close, Whitland Close and Alderlee, in the Stoke Park area, was built by the WPHT housing association — a registered charity.

It includes 32 bed-sitting rooms, 108 one-bedroomed flats, 206 two-bedroomed flats and 70 three-bedroomed houses.

It was officially opened by Mr. Hugh Cubitt, chairman of the housing corporation. He said that the development looked "absolutely marvellous".

He said, "I wish we could see a lot more of this type of development, but I do not think we will at the moment."

Funds for this type of project were short at present, he said.

The first phase of the development, Oaklee, which was financed by the local authority, was finished in 1977. The other three parts of the scheme were funded by the housing corporation.

Half the properties are let to people on the WPHT waiting list and the remainder are let to people nominated by Ipswich Council.

124.

A LECTURE TO ENCOURAGE FUTURE STUDENTS

125. The Author addressing careers masters at Manchester with Clifford Tippett, past President, and Michael Thomas, past Chairman of the Membership Committee of the Incorporated Society of Valuers and Auctioneers

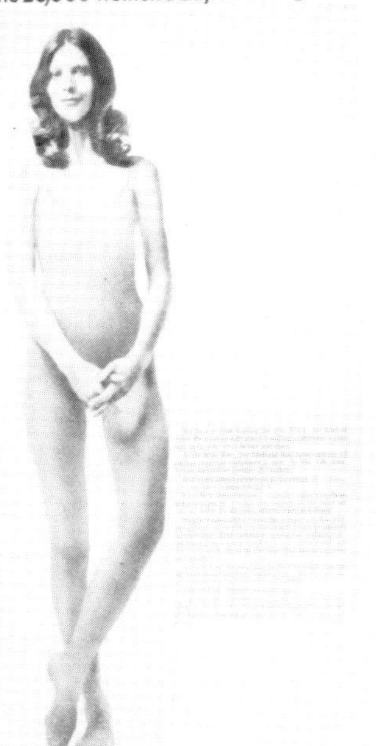

126. (*above*) Approach to the escalators and the station

127. Advertisement in the *Financial Times*

128. The attaché case which was distributed

TOPPING OUT EUSTON STATION DEVELOPMENT ON BEHALF OF BRITISH RAIL

129. John Cook — Lord McAlpine — Robert Lawrence — Bobby Dashwood — Sir Peter Parker

TWO YOUNG TYCOONS

130. Gerald Ronson of the Heron Group

131. Sir Don Gosling of National Car Parks

CARDIFF CENTRAL AREA SHOPPING CENTRE CELEBRATION

132. Tony Royle of the Heron Corporation — Colin Kerr — Hugh Jenkins of the Coal Industry Nominees — John Eyles of the Cardiff City Corporation

basement with prominent frontage to Market Street being divided and let to multiple firms, including Horne Bros, Wallis Fashions, Dolcis Shoes, Wilsons Brewery, Marks & Spencer and others. I have vivid recollections of meeting Jack Cotton in Isaac Wolfson's offices. Jack was then famous for many important deals he had carried out, a large number of which he had transacted on his own account in Birmingham and elsewhere. But at times he still enjoyed functioning as an agent where a spectacular transaction was concerned. He had written to IW making a conditional offer for Rylands Buildings on behalf of investor clients of his based in Manchester, subject to GUS taking back a lease. Rylands Buildings at that time was one of the finest properties in Manchester and Jack's judgement was absolutely right. If he had had the finance available, I have the feeling he would have purchased the property himself. As an agent, Jack had to rely on the decision of his clients. IW, with his usual shrewdness, decided that this might have been a tentative approach and asked me to contact Jack Cotton to confirm that the purchasers could proceed. I telephoned Jack and, exercising his friendly and lavish hospitality, he invited me to see him during the weekend at his country home, Thames Lawn at Marlow, and to bring my wife. I was very impressed with the house and its opulent atmosphere. Jack was his usual charming self and could not do enough to make Pamela and me welcome and happy. But I found that IW's assessment was correct. Jack Cotton, with his nose for a good deal, had recommended his clients to proceed. However, they were unable to invest as much as £5 million. IW instructed me to arrange a sale-and-leaseback to GUS and, as it was a large property, I decided that the best price would be obtained by selling it in two stages as unlike today, pension funds and insurance companies were not overloaded with cash. I arranged the sale of the freehold to the Royal Liver, subject to a leaseback for 999 years at a ground rent and sold the resultant leasehold interest to the Norwich Union subject to GUS taking back a lease.

When Isaac Wolfson was in his hey-day, he acquired the International Fur Stores, known as Jays, on the corner of Regent Street and Oxford Circus. IW was never interested in having impressive headquarters of his own. Often, he set up his office in the premises of a firm he had taken over – partly to knock it into shape. Jays was a case in point. I once called on him with George Bourner, who was acting for the Royal Liver, to discuss final terms for the sale of the freehold ground rent on Rylands Buildings in Manchester. Jays' former staff and organisation were still functioning and suddenly a pale, undernourished-looking waiter appeared, wearing an old, soiled dinner jacket with a drooping black tie. Carrying a tray with three cups of coffee and a plate of biscuits, he was spotted by IW who exclaimed: 'Who told you to bring biscuits? These people are not customers, they are only agents. Take the biscuits away.' We enjoyed the joke and terms were agreed.

Our Practice used to hold all-male Christmas cocktail parties to which most of our clients, other agents and professional advisers were invited. Apart from chairmen, managing directors and important industrialists, we made a point of inviting property managers who were our day-to-day contacts in some of these large companies. IW disliked cocktail parties but, one year, I persuaded him to come to the Ballroom at the London Hilton. During the course of the evening a deputy estates manager of one of our client companies drank rather too much champagne, lit a cigar and, seeing IW was in a rather flamboyant mood, walked up to him, gave him a slap on the back and asked: 'How's business?' Although Isaac Wolfson is a good mixer, I felt I should intervene to avoid an unhappy incident. I therefore tapped the estate manager on the shoulder and told him a friend of his at the other end of the ballroom was looking for him. Before he knew where he was, I had rushed him to the other end of the crowded room. Travelling with IW was also an entertaining and exciting business. I remember being on a corridor train going to Manchester from Euston. Half the people walking past our compartment appeared to be managers of one or other of his subsidiary companies. As each one went by, he would call them into the compartment and ask for their trading figures. At frequent intervals during the journey he would relax into a deep sleep, snoring loudly; like Sir Winston Churchill, he was able to sleep at a moment's notice, wake up completely refreshed full of energy and then discuss the next business project. At the Midland Hotel, Manchester, GUS kept a permanent suite of rooms for executive use. It was customary for Isaac Wolfson to breakfast at 7.30 a.m. and I and all his senior executives were obliged to be down at breakfast at the same time. An expert merchandise man, he would point straight to a shelf containing some dead or incorrectly marked stock which was wrongly located in one of his stores. This caused the local managers great embarrassment.

When IW was approaching 80, he agreed to address my fellow partners on the art of salesmanship. He duly arrived in our conference room with Captain Myers, his aide-de-camp, and Philip Gould, the GUS property manager. He then gave an inspiring address recounting his early days as a commercial traveller leading up to his present position. The young members of the practice were thrilled to hear him. It was obvious that he still retained his old fire and retentive memory. On his 80th birthday, Pamela and I presented him with a linen scroll engraved in colour with a birthday greeting and inscribed with the names of every company he had taken over. Born in Glasgow, IW came from a close-knit family and the death of his wife, Edith, in 1980 was a great blow to him. Only one of his two brothers, the late Charles Wolfson, joined him at GUS as a co-director. Charles was a kind individual – more cautious and less ambitious than Isaac – who was forced to retire prematurely through ill-health. To follow a man like IW is an almost superhuman task, but one that has been achieved with distinction by his son, Sir Leonard. He possesses the ability not only to manage a vast concern but also to modernise and improve it. I remember seeing a youthful Leonard learning the business and, like many others at the time, I wondered whether he would have the ability to take over the reins. IW is still consulted about GUS affairs, but as he now devotes the greater part of his time to charitable activities, it is Leonard's responsibility to make decisions. He takes after his father in his shrewdness, quick wit, strength of character and forceful decision-making. Indeed, since he took over GUS, no chink has appeared in the armour of the organisation. The empire has remained intact with particular growth in the mail order and export business. In addition to controlling GUS, Leonard is interested in history, economics and literature and, like his father, takes an active part in charitable work and the Wolfson Foundation. His attractive wife, Ruth, is a great asset to him and they have three daughters.

*

The late Sir John Cohen, Founder of Tesco Stores, known to everyone as Jack, was one of my early clients and friends and I let him some of his first shops in Walthamstow and Edmonton. His father was a tailor in Hackney. Jack served in the Royal Flying Corps in the first World War and was demobolised with a small gratuity in 1919. He started with a barrow in an East London market and his ability and sales patter would quickly draw a crowd. He finished his career as the founder of the fabulous Tesco Stores supermarket empire with many hundreds of branches throughout the UK. He was well loved for his human understanding and sympathy for others. Despite overwhelming success, his personality and approach to people of all classes never changed. He was a bold and amusing character, was married at 24, and gave many millions of pounds to charity. Remarkable salesmanship which he operated in his supermarkets sparked a succession of High Street 'price wars'. At one stage of his career, at the age of 60, Jack Cohen had an internal operation which was so severe that it would probably have finished the active life of most people. Jack was a lion-hearted man and seeing his lifestyle and vigour, nobody would have believed he had overcome such a disability. Pamela and I were guests of Jack and Cissie Cohen at the celebration of his 70th birthday at the Dorchester. The property industry was well represented at this function and the family arranged with the Master of Ceremonies to surprise the guest of honour with a programme on the same lines as TV's 'This is Your Life'. As each stage of Jack's career was announced, the person actually connected with it was asked to come up to the platform and say a few words. The surgeon who had performed his operation was present and called to the stage. He announced jocularly: 'When we opened up Jack and looked inside, all we could see were Green Shield Stamps!' This brought the house down.

Jack's philosophy was that anyone can make a fortune in the retail trade if he is willing to work hard and sell cheaply, and if the turnover is large enough. Mervyn Orchard-Lisle mentioned to me some time ago that he used to travel on the same ship as Jack from time to time when they were both *en route* to South Africa. He recalls Jack telling him one night how he had been sitting on the deck talking to a friend of his. Inevitably, they got round to the subject of merchandise. Jack's friend, by way of illustration, took off one of his very nice shoes and passed it to Jack, asking him to guess how old it was. When the other chap announced they were 13 years old, Jack promptly threw the shoe overboard. 'My god, what did you do that for?' screamed his friend. 'Because you ought to be ashamed of yourself for wearing things that long and keeping people unemployed', was Jack's reply. Tesco Stores opened a supermarket in the Grosvenor Estate's shopping centre in Chester forming an extension to the ancient city Rows. The nearness of Eaton Hall, the country seat of the Dukes of Westminsters, caused Anne, Duchess of Westminster, to take a special interest in Chester and to visit the new development. The Duchess was appalled to see bill-posters on the windows of the newly opened Tesco and her views were made known to the Trustees of the Grosvenor Estate. These comments were duly conveyed to Jack from the Grosvenor Office in London. Jack was invited to lunch with the Trustees. Some of my colleagues were concerned that Jack's blunt market style might clash disastrously with the aristocratic conservatism of the representatives of the Estate. On the contrary. Jack's human, frank and honest reactions captivated the people at the Grosvenor Office. At a Wembley Cup Final one year, I found myself seated next to Lady Cissie Cohen. A charming and friendly lady, she cannot be described as a soccer expert and, when the teams changed over at half time, I had the feeling that she was not exactly *au fait* with the progress of the game. Some years ago, the financial editor of one of the national newspapers suggested a Monopoly game between Jack Cohen and three young tycoons – Nigel Broackes, Oliver Jessel and Jim Slater. They all accepted the challenge and played at a West End Hotel in front of cameras. I am told that the old campaigner, Jack, outclassed all his young opponents. After carrying out an enormous expansion policy, Jack retired as chairman of Tesco Stores in 1969, handing over the reins to his two sons-in-law. In 1973, Hyman Kreitman was succeeded by Leslie Porter, who is the present chairman. He is continuing the same vigorous policy as Jack, assisted by Francis Krejsa, who is always looking for new sites. In 1979 Jack died at the age of 80. Both his funeral and memorial services were crowded to capacity by the people from all walks of life who loved him.

*

A year or so ago, while sitting in a departure lounge at Heathrow ready to take off for my annual visit to the south of France, a fellow passenger appeared wearing a JR-style stetson. He was none other than Manny Cussins, chairman of Waring & Gillow (the furniture retailers), Leeds United Football Club and other companies. He is another of the group of astute and successful businessmen who hail from Leeds, such as Sir Montague Burton, Sir Henry Price, Hector Fraser, Bernard Lyons, Sir Jack Lyons and Arnold Ziff. Manny has had a full life, enriched by experience of people, property and, in more recent years, professional football. His able son, John, now runs the Waring & Gillow empire. Manny has been closely involved in property development and formerly controlled a Yorkshire housebuilding company with his late brother, Philip. His flair for the property business is matched by his understanding of people. As chairman of Leeds United, he learned a lot about character and once said to me: 'A man can be taught, trained and coached by the finest in the land, but if he lacks the prime instinct and intuition to be a first-class footballer, he can only go so far and no further; this applies to every walk of life and especially to the turbulent world of property.'

A somewhat impulsive individual, Manny was once presented to the Queen. He was a trifle concerned beforehand as to what he should say, but was assured that Her Majesty would take full charge of the situation. From a respectful distance, Ben Pomerance – one of his co-directors – noticed that Manny was completely relaxed and contributing substantially to the conversation. When it was all over, Ben asked Manny what he had said: 'Well,' replied Manny, 'I didn't say very much – it wasn't my place to say anything. Oh, I did say to her that you have to be commercially minded.' Staggered to hear a report of such a seemingly inappropriate remark, Ben told him one was not meant to give that kind of advice to the Queen. A bewildered Manny replied: 'Why on earth not? The Queen entirely agreed with me.'

A very able young man I have met many times is Selim Zhilka of Persian descent who conceived the idea of establishing a chain of shops specialising in baby and maternity wear under the original name of Mothercare. Selim opened the first shop in 1964 and it proved so successful that Mothercare are now an empire with over 400 branches. If the present takeover bid succeeds, Selim Zhilka will have earned quite a fortune in a short time.

12

THE CHIEFTAIN OF MOFFATT

*

Lord McAlpine, formerly Sir (Robert) Edwin McAlpine, known to many of us affectionately in the property industry as Edwin, is an inspiring and influential leader of private enterprise. The family firm, Sir Robert McAlpine & Sons, has been functioning as civil engineers and building contractors for more than a century. Many of its important engineering and building projects have been inspired by Lord McAlpine, a man of warmth, creative ability, keeness and enthusiasm. After building the Dorchester Hotel in Park Lane many years ago for Gordon Hotels, the McAlpine family acquired the hotel and ran it successfully until 1976, when it was sold to Middle East interests. The majority of the hotel's management and personnel remained and its well-established traditions have been allowed to continue. Edwin used to hold magnificent Christmas lunches in the Dorchester Ballroom to which he invited about 1,000 friends and clients of his firm. The perfect host, he ensured that the organisation, food and arrangements were superb. But the lunches were most famous for the calibre of Edwin's friends, including Cabinet Ministers, leaders of industry, Government officials, leading business and professional men and some of the most important people in the country. I think I am right in saying that the only lady ever present was Mrs Margaret Thatcher. Edwin always set the right note with a relaxed, witty and sincere address of welcome to guests and speakers – among whom I remember Harold Macmillan, Ted Heath, Sir Alec Douglas-Home, the late Airey Neave, Margaret Thatcher and Lord Chandos. A newly published book by a prominent figure was usually presented to the guests and, on many occasions, the authors themselves were guest speakers. The luncheon tables were so arranged that at the head of each sat a member of the McAlpine family. Family pride in the business, allied with patriotism as a British company, is the strength of the McAlpine organisation. It has over the years undertaken a number of construction projects of national importance. Between the wars, apart from housing estates and factories, the family firm built the Wembley Stadium and Exhibition Buildings and also some of the largest units comprising Mulberry Harbour for the D-Day landings in France. Among its more spectacular developments are: the National Theatre on the South Bank of the Thames, Odeon cinemas at Marble Arch and Leicester Square, the Hyde Park Cavalry Barracks, the Inn on the Park and the Inter-Continental hotels at Hyde Park Corner, the

Euston Square development for British Rail and the Brent Cross Shopping Centre. It has also built five nuclear power stations and three concrete platforms for off-shore North Sea oil and gas production.

Edwin McAlpine has a long and vivid memory. In 1931, the Dorchester Hotel was topped out – I believe it was the first reinforced concrete building of its type to be built in the UK. Work started in 1930, it was completed within 12 months and furnished ready for opening in 18 months! Specially designed on a huge raft, it was constructed to allow variation of the upper floors above mezzanine level. At the topping out party in the presence of the Press, the late Sir Malcolm McAlpine wished to explain this important innovation when delivering his address to the guests. He had great difficulty in describing in simple, laymen's language the intricate engineering characteristics of the construction in comparison with other buildings. He became so bemused with engineering technology and jargon dealing with modules and cantilevers that, in wild exasperation, he finally exclaimed: 'Only two people have any knowledge of this complicated construction – God above and me – but I am totally incapable of explaining it.'

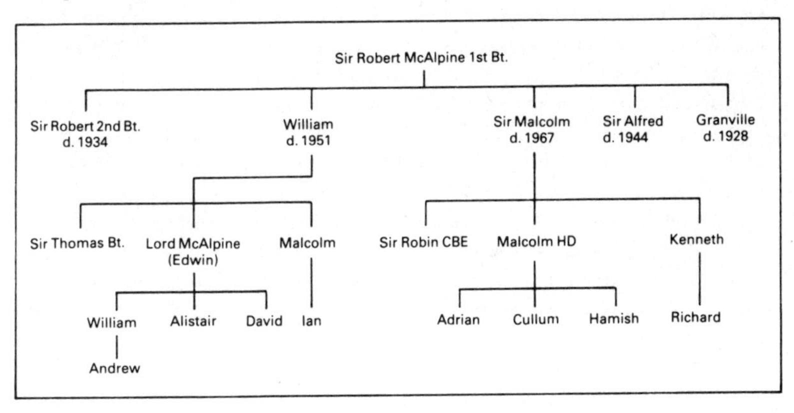

The McAlpine family tree

*

Lewis Hammerson was one of the pioneers of the post-war property industry. As a young man, he worked in the family textile business in north London and, on the outbreak of the last war, joined the Army. Shortly afterwards, however, he was discharged for medical reasons so he set up an office in London. Without any special training, he had decided to follow a career in property for which he possessed a natural flair. After the war, he made some spectacular long-term decisions. One of these was the acquisition of a number of properties in Marylebone Road, close to Baker Street. He needed to plan ahead to secure possession and to obtain town planning consent. His far-sightedness paid off and he eventually built Castrol House on the site and let it to C.C. Wakefield & Co at a rent which, at that time, beat the £1-per-square-foot barrier. It is the massive office building with a tower, since taken over by Marathon International Petroleum and now called Marathon House. He died suddenly only a year later at the young age of 42 and his devoted wife, Sue, founded an elderly persons' home in his memory.

Today, the Hammerson Group of Companies is one of the leading quoted public property companies. It has been fortunate for the Group's investors and shareholders that Lewis Hammerson had an able successor in his team – Sydney Mason – who has piloted the company to outstanding success. Like several other well-managed companies, Hammersons carried out many successful property developments and had no difficulty in weathering the storm of the 1973–74 property crisis. Sydney Mason is a shrewd, down-to-earth character. Before joining Hammersons he was employed by Harold Samuel. Although he is now chairman of the Hammerson Group of Companies, he remembers incidents from his early career. Hard as it is to believe today, it was a young and nervous Sydney Mason who, on arriving at his new job on 1 August 1949, was told by his new boss, Lew Hammerson, to go and negotiate for the purchase of the site at 129 Park Lane, W1. Lew had been thinking of building an office on this prestigious spot for some time and the purchase price was high – £4,500. Lew implied, of course, that Sydney had better get it for less, hadn't he! Our hero did his best and concluded terms at £3,750. Thinking he had carried out a masterful exercise, he then faced the crunch. The leaseholders were friends of his new boss and they told Lew – after the negotiations were concluded but not signed – that one of the conditions of the deal was for all builders' materials on site to be bought by the purchaser. Summoned to the Hammerson inner sanctum, our brave young man was instructed to conduct another mighty negotiation, getting, of course, the very best deal. The day came for Sydney's meeting with the vendors and builders. Into the room went the intrepid young man to face the vendor – the then heavyweight world amateur wrestling champion, Freddie Oberlander – together with 15 henchmen seated round the table. There was no chair for Sydney. With one hand, Freddie lifted a heavy leather seat and motioned him to sit down. Always a wise man, Sydney sat. The negotiations began: 'The price for the materials is £200' said Mr Oberlander. 'The price for the materials is £200' said our hero – and left. Lew was most impressed. He was even more pleased when it was learned that a crane and a concrete mixer had been overlooked and were now consequently included in the price. Sydney was a very happy man. Could this be the beginning of the stories which circulated throughout the industry about the hard-headed chairman of Hammersons getting his own way and the best terms on every deal he does? Further back in the past,

Sydney remembers approaching Harold Samuel, now Lord Samuel, to persuade him to part with a 1939 Hillman Minx, registration number LMG 82, which had been maintained in impeccable condition. Lord Samuel, who proposed buying a new car, said to Sydney: 'You may have my Hillman for £400 (which was less than it was worth at the time) but, rather than buy this car, I recommend that you buy with your £400 shares in Land Securities Investment Trust.' Sydney agrees with some amusement that, if he had bought the shares, they would have been worth millions today.

The Hammerson Group has a large part of its property holdings in Australia and Sydney attributes the Group's successful entry into the Australian property market to a lady, Madeleine Maynard. In 1958, when her husband, Fred Maynard – a director of another development company, Ravenseft Properties – frequently visited Canada, he had an option on a site in Australia and was due to go there to clinch the deal. Fred and Madeleine are happily married and, tired of her husband's many trips to Canada, Madeleine threatened him, perhaps not seriously, that if he now started to make trips to Australia, she would leave him. In consequence, Fred handed over his option to Sydney Mason of the Hammerson Group, free of charge, and the Group has since built up a colossal empire in Australia. Sydney feels that this was due – in part at least – to the affectionate reaction of a lady. One of the outstanding developments in the Hammerson Group is the impressive Brent Cross Shopping Centre in north-west London with its huge car parking facilities.

*

I have had many pleasant meetings with Sir Gerald Glover, an influential solicitor, and from 1959 the chairman of Edger Investments Ltd, a development company closely linked with the Prudential Assurance Company. Formerly chairman of the City of London Real Property Company, he was also concerned with the development of the Inn on the Park and Inter-Continental hotels at Hyde Park Corner. A keen racing man, he has been an active member of the County of London Red Cross and was knighted for public services in 1971.

Another Mayfair solicitor who shares a similar passion is Isidore Kerman. With his charming wife, Blanche, he divides his time between a West End flat and a country estate near East Grinstead, Sussex. Blanche has a reputation as an expert horsewoman and rides side saddle. His legal practice is successful, handling a variety of affairs from divorce to take-overs and he has promoted many successful business ventures. Chairman of Scott's Restaurant of Mount Street, London W1, he is also a director of the British subsidiary of Loew's Hotel group of America – owners of the Churchill Hotel in Portman Square. Isidore's favourite pastime is racing –

he is chairman of Plumpton Racecourse and a director of Fontwell Park Steeplechase Company. Once the owner of a well-known horse called 'Kybo', he watched it romp home the winner of many steeplechases. When I asked him the derivation of the name, he told me with a twinkle in his eye that his mother used to admonish him: 'Keep your bowels open' – hence the inspiration for Kybo. This gelding was one of the most exciting propsects for the 1982 Cheltenham Gold Cup, but had to be put down after a disaster at Lingfield in January 1981.

*

During one of my youthful yachting weekends at Mersey Island, I first met Sir Robert Bellinger. A boyhood friend, known to me as Bob, he is a great sportsman and a down-to-earth, self-made man. From a modest family background and early education at a Church of England school, his strong character, integrity, aptitude for figures and shrewd business sense enabled him to rise from the post of insignificant cost clerk to become chairman of his company. His success was purely on merit, without family influence, major school, university or Army background. Bob's former firm was a successful public company, Kinloch (Provision) Merchants Limited. His policy of bold, speculative bulk buying of grocery provisions in the UK, Australia, Denmark and various other parts of the world contributed to the success of the firm. He also had a flair for property and, in order to reduce overheads in the early days, he acquired disused high-ceilinged buildings, including a riding school, in strategic residential areas. These were suitable for fork-lift stacking of foodstuffs and were comparable with new warehouses. To obtain town planning consent, he would arrange for these food distribution depots to be screened with trees to avoid spoiling the residential environment close by. Kinlochs became the champions of small grocers by giving them credit to carry out improvements, install modern shop fronts and stock up with groceries and provisions. The chain of individual shops which developed in this way became known as the Wavy Line grocers. Bob acquired several other companies including the old-established wholesalers, Charles Arkoll of Maidstone. Apart from valuable goodwill, Sir Robert foresaw the development possibilities of the Arkoll warehouse site in the heart of Maidstone. He therefore commissioned a large modern office building to be erected in two phases which became worth many millions of pounds.

After he retired to undertake public work, Kinlochs and its subsidiaries were taken over by Booker McConnell Limited. His later career resembled that of the former Sir Thomas Lipton, the famous grocer who became Lord Mayor of London. Robert had served on the Common Council of the City of London since 1953 and became an Alderman. In 1962 he was appointed Sheriff and, in the same year, married an attractive young lady, Christiane, after a romantic meeting at the Brussels Exhibition where

Christiane was a hostess. They have a son and a daughter. Knighted in 1964, he was elected Lord Mayor of London in September 1966. Two years later he became Gentleman Usher of the Purple Rod of the OBE. He is a former Governor of the BBC, a director of the Rank Organisation and eventually became chairman of National Savings. He is also a director of Arsenal Football Club. Bob and Christiane live in Buckingham and farm about 3,000 acres in Scotland. In 1966, during Bob's year of office as Lord Mayor, the Labour Government restricted overseas investment in an effort to assist home industry. He therefore decided to promote the 'invisible' earnings of the City, which included income from overseas investment. The Prime Minister, Harold Wilson, intimated that the Lord Mayor's speeches were conflicting with Government policy. The matter was highlighted at the conclusion of a dinner at Buckingham Palace and, as the Prime Minister was leaving, the Lord Mayor bade him farewell. The Prime Minister replied: 'Good Night, Invisible Man; I have you well in observation.' The Government later withdrew its embargo on overseas investment and the Lord Mayor continued to promote the City's invisible earnings.

13

THE RETICENT PERFECTIONIST

*

Lord Samuel, known to his personal friends as Harold, is looked upon as a leader in the property company sector of the Stock Exchange. His Land Securities Investment Trust, of which he is chairman, is one of the largest property groups in the world, owning some of the finest shops and office buildings. Among its many subsidiaries are the City of London Real Property Company Limited, which owns many important office buildings in the City; City Centre Properties Limited, formerly managed by the late Jack Cotton; the late Sir Charles Clore's City & Central Investments; and Ravenseft Properties, initially formed by Louis Freedman and Fred Maynard with financial backing from Land Securities. The running of the Land Securities Investment Trust forms almost a blueprint for the property industry under Harold Samuel's guidance and forward planning. Strong and prompt decisions are taken without wavering. Knighted in 1963, he became a Life Peer in 1972. He is a perfectionist whom I can describe as the 'perfect tycoon'. His timing is always precise, not only in connection with the financial arrangements he has made for his huge company, but also in the context of personal appointments. When you meet him for lunch – if the appointment is fixed for 1.00 p.m. – you will find him ready to receive you five or ten minutes beforehand. I have often arrived at lunch early to see if I could get there before him, but I have never yet succeeded.

Harold qualified as a chartered surveyor and, as a young man, was instructed to solicit instructions for his West End firm. While walking down Kingly Street he smoked a cigarette to ponder and steady his nerves. Before entering the shop from which he was instructed to seek business, he stubbed out the cigarette and placed it in his pocket. After introducing the subject a little nervously to the owner, the latter turned to him and, to Lord Samuel's utter embarrassment and confusion, pointed to his coat pocket and said: 'You seem to be on fire, young man' – I doubt whether this was the start of a good negotiation! After passing his exams, Harold set up in private practice as an estate agent in Baker Street. Then, in order to avoid a conflict of interests when he formed his company, he closed his estate agency firm. Sydney Mason, now chairman of the Hammerson Group of Companies, remembers when, as a young man, he was employed by Land Securities in Westmorland House, Regent Street. Sydney had conducted prospective tenants over a building known as Regent Arcade House at Oxford Circus. Harold asked Sydney the name of the prospective tenants and he replied that their agents had merely stated that the tenants' covenant was as good as the Bank of England. The tenant proved to be the Bank of England. When the 21-year lease was prepared, Harold thought that the Bank could well take over the full length of the 59-year lease, so he wrote in the margin on the draft lease 'or 59 years if preferred.' The Bank of England readily agreed to sign a 59-year lease without rent review. As the transaction was carried out before meteoric inflation took place, it was thought that the long unbroken lease would give an advantage to the landlords. Instead, it proved the opposite!

Although Lord Samuel is almost superhuman in the conduct of his company affairs, he and his wife, Edna, dislike ostentation or publicity and lead a comparatively quiet family life. Many years ago, even before he had received his knighthood, Pamela and I attended a party arranged in a marquee in the garden of his town house. The party was arranged in typically perfect Samuel style, with every detail considered for the comfort of their guests. Immediately in front of us in the queue of guests waiting to be presented to our host and hostess were Mr and Mrs Hubert Cox, formerly of Regional Properties. Unlike the other guests, instead of giving his name to the toastmaster, Hubert Cox produced his invitation card. The toastmaster, a tall, fine-looking man of military bearing – with a strong voice but lacking in observation somewhat – announced to the host and hostess: 'Mr and Mrs Harold Samuel.' There was uproarious laughter from all the guests and much embarrassment for the toastmaster. Lord and Lady Samuel have a fine mansion with extensive grounds in the country. The rhododendron drive, flower beds and greenhouses are maintained with the same care and perfection as Lord Samuel runs the affairs of his company. His garden is an outstanding achievement and is probably one of the finest of its kind in the country.

*

Louis Freedman, together with his partner and colleague, Fred Maynard, has had a most successful career as a shop property developer and is highly regarded by local authorities and leading multiple firms with whom he has had dealings. A shrewd, clear-thinking man, Louis made three momentous decisions which profoundly influenced his life. First, upon his release from the services in 1946, he decided there was more scope to redevelop blitzed sites and neglected central areas in the provinces than in London, where redevelopment activity had already started. Second, he accepted backing for his comparatively small property company from Lord Samuel of Land Securities Investment Trust. To be offered this was a mark of the ability of Louis Freedman as Harold Samuel is selective in his associations and is known generally to dislike joint arrangements with other parties. And third, he entered into parnership with Frederick Maynard, a multiple-shop expert formerly with Healey & Baker, who was accustomed to dealing with shop property outside the central London area. Louis and Fred with their company, Ravenseft Properties Limited, set to work with enormous energy and enthusiasm to carry out central area redevelopment schemes, in participation with local authorities. I have pleasant memories of dealing with them in connection with part of the rebuilt centre of Coventry. The Ravenseft scheme included many shops and the Leofric Hotel facing the Lady Godiva statue. Prior to Coventry, they had already helped rebuild the centres of Plymouth, Exeter and Bristol and carried out other schemes including Hull, Sheffield and Swansea. Louis's straightforward dealings with local authorities and participation exercises with them have become a blueprint for others to follow. I believe his abilities have made a significant contribution to the amenities of many provincial towns and cities and to certain New Town Corporations. After the success of Ravenseft was assured, Harold Samuel arranged for Land Securities to take over the remainder of the shares of Louis's company and he and Fred Maynard were invited to join the board of Land Securities.

Now in active retirement, Louis has become an eminent figure in the racing world and owns a stud farm and a string of well-known horses – one of which is named 'One Fleet Street'. Sired by 'Habitat' out of 'The Creditor', 'One Fleet Street' is the address of a branch of Williams & Glyn's Bank. No doubt this has some special significance. To Louis, like most racehorse owners, his horses are sometimes in good form, but they sometimes go through disappointing periods. Despite occasional lack of success, he retains a particularly good sense of humour. I remember meeting him at a function and perhaps untactfully asking how his horses were doing. His quick reply was: 'Do not remind me of the dead.' In 1971, he was appointed president of the Race Horse Owners' Association and later became a Steward of the Jockey Club. A public-spirited man with a strong social conscience, he served for some time as a member of the Race Relations Board and, from 1975 to 1979, was vice-chairman of the North-East Thames Regional Health Authority. A former governor of the Royal Hospital of St Bartholomew, he has recently undertaken the challenging task of becoming chairman of the Camden and Islington Area Health Authority – an Authority which includes representatives from Camden who did not take kindly in the first instance to a man such as Louis being appointed to control the purse strings. He has been married for 20 years to Valerie who, most of the time, manages to keep him relaxed when he is working hard under pressure. Consequently, they have a happy married life and there is a good understanding between them.

Frederick Maynard, known to me as Fred, is a dapper well-built man, unassuming and, on first acquaintance, likely to be underestimated. Following his release from the Army after the last war, during which he had been promoted to the rank of Lt-Colonel, he joined Ravenseft Properties, formed by Louis and financed by Lord Samuel's Land

Securities. I think I am right in saying that while Louis devoted time at headquarters formulating policy and dealing with finance, Fred concentrated on meeting local authorities in the blitzed and neglected cities in the provinces. As a result of his pre-war professional training as a negotiator, Fred developed a particular grasp of the thinking and methods of municipal authorities and he had considerable success in dealing with them. He also possessed the flair to understand shopping needs relevant to purchasing power in provincial centres. Therefore, many attractive – and viable – shopping areas were built which rid blitzed towns and cities of blight and improved the local environment. Many of Ravenseft's more recent developments were for multi-million, covered shopping centres. During the property crisis of the early 1970's, Lord Samuel took strong decisions to realise some of the cash invested in large shopping developments and many were sold off.

Like Louis Freedman, Fred Maynard has retired from the board of Land Securities. While there, he also served as a voluntary member on several committees of the National Enterprise Development Office, known as NEDDY, including those dealing with retail trading patterns, inner city redevelopment and retail distribution. He is also an active member of the Central Council of WPHT Housing Association, formerly the World of Property Housing Trust and, for some time, was chairman of the Commercial Section of the British Property Federation.

*

I have known John Barnett, secretary and director of the Gestetner organisation for many years. He is an unassuming man with simple tastes who is both courteous and thoughtful. I have always enjoyed acting on behalf of Gestetners. The business was founded by David Gestetner, whose inspiration, enterprise and hard work created a prosperous international organisation with branches throughout the world. Before the invention of duplicating, office clerks had to write out individual copies by hand. I am told that the idea of the stencil process came to David Gestetner when he saw a torn Japanese kite made from long fibred paper. It was from this type of paper that he later made stencils. Initially, the process of stencil duplication was resisted by businessmen as it was thought that it would insult their customers. But the inventor was also a talented salesman and he steadfastly marketed his invention, to overcome prejudice and sell hundreds of machines. David Gestetner was succeeded by his son, Sigmund, who spread the company worldwide. His charming widow, Mrs Henny Gestetner, is still a member of the board – the two joint chairmen also being members of the family. From its Tottenham-based headquarters there is a network of 20 factories and sales and service centres covering 130 countries and employing 17,000 people, nearly 4,000 of whom work in the UK.

I first met Harry Hyams many years ago at the Upper Brook Street offices of the late Felix Fenston. Desmond (known as George) Robinson, a former solicitor, was also present to discuss a building to be erected in York Road, Waterloo, opposite County Hall. The new development, to be known as Petrofina House, was on the site which was allegedly the home of the bogus death watch beetle joke played on me by Felix. I well remember how Harry explained his policy of letting his buildings as a whole to tenants of undoubted financial stability. Already at that time established as a highly successful property developer, he had been previously involved in two quoted companies, Barranquilla Investments and Park Investments, and had been the subject of much press comment. Fairly tall and well dressed, Harry sported a vandyke beard, and I was impressed with his pleasant and relaxed but decisive and confident manner. With experience gained in his teens as a junior with Hampton & Son, the estate agents, he had gradually become a developer on his own account. His career has been incredible, combining the qualities of a clear mind, flair for large-scale development, and very strong nerves to take risks.

It is not surprising that he became such a target for Press criticism. He provoked resentment in some quarters for making a fortune when particularly young; and in addition, the Oldham Estates Company, in which Harry was a large shareholder, built the spectacular and controversial building, Centre Point. Harry acquired the shell of Oldham Estates as a vehicle for his developments, and although there were other shareholders and investors, Harry personally was the person who excited public interest. In my view, Centre Point, the 32-storey building at the corner of New Oxford Street and Charing Cross Road, is aesthetically attractive and designed with considerable skill by Colonel Richard Seifert. It has alleviated the drabness of the surrounding area and made a dramatic contribution to the London skyline. When Centre Point was first completed I am told Harry agreed a provisional letting of the whole building to the newly-formed British Steel Board – only to find, at the eleventh hour, that the prospective tenant withdrew because of Government intervention. Perhaps the building was considered to be too lavish for occupation by a Government body. To make matters worse, Harry refused to compromise with the media which – using him as the target for most accusations about property developers – published several adverse comments about Centre Point. Harry believed that the Press campaign against him caused another firm which had agreed terms for the whole building also to withdraw from the transaction. Harry Hyams has never apologised for creating wealth and making a large amount of money at a young age. He dislikes publicity and is disinclined to co-operate with the media by giving them information. Nor will he bother to refute incorrect statements circulated about Centre Point to the effect that his company deliberately kept the building empty. It was evident that Oldham

Estates were experiencing difficulties in letting the property. Influenced by newspaper comment inferring that an unlet Centre Point was Harry's policy, the local authority – which bears no particular affection for developers – caused an enquiry to be carried out to enable it compulsorily to acquire the residential maisonnettes comprising the upper floors of the building. I recollect reading the formal report made by the Inspector, Peter Boydell QC, several years ago, and I was interested to see that he confirmed my own opinion that the building had not been deliberately kept empty for financial gain. In these days of frequent rent reviews, I do not know of any development company, including Oldham Estates, who could possibly get richer by leaving a building empty! In fact, due to the building being vacant for so long, the cost of maintenance, repairs and redecoration became too great for the developer to bear alone. So in the end Harry Hyams was forced to vary his single-tenant policy in the case of Centre Point. The building has since been let in sections to more than one concern.

Harry leads a happy but secluded private life, enjoying his hobbies of yachting and (until recently) off-shore power-boat racing – pastimes which provided welcome relief from the media criticism and the activities of landlubbers dealing with the intricacies of planning constraints. When I bumped into him recently in a well-known hotel, he told me that he has given up power-boat racing, but still enjoys carrying out property developments for a rapidly expanding public company, Oldham Estates.

*

Auction sales are sometimes exciting and entertaining. They date back to the early days of the market place or mart where chattels and property were knocked down to the highest bidder. Prior to the last war, real estate auctions were confined principally to forced sales on the instructions of a liquidator or receiver to wind up an estate in bankruptcy or by order of mortgagees who had foreclosed through default by the borrower. Many auctions would have been dull if it were not for one of the auction habitués, the late David Galinsky. He was a gentleman of foreign descent who was one of the regular patrons of the London Auction Mart and other salerooms. He had a slightly foreign accent, was quick witted and possessed a sense of humour which often enlivened the proceedings. For instance, he would tantalise the auctioneer by enquiring facetiously if the property contained dry rot or if the roof had been repaired. I remember one occasion when a young auctioneer was struggling hard to obtain a bid for a property for which there did not seem to be a single buyer in the room. He pleaded: 'Gentlemen, give me an opening bid – almost anything to get me started – will someone say £8,000, £7,000, £6,000, £5,000'. There was complete silence and David Galinsky stood up with a twinkle in his eye saying: 'Mr Auctioneer, I will give you a bid. I bid you good day.' He then walked out of the saleroom amid loud laughter from the remainder of the assembly. On another occasion, Galinsky was present at an important auction sale of properties belonging to the Portman Estate. One of the properties submitted was subject to a lease with about 16 years to run. Galinsky was bidding and his seemed to be the last bid when the auctioneer, Edward Poulton, hesitated and had a word with the auction clerk. In a flash, David Galinsky stood up and said: 'Mr Auctioneer: if you do not make up your mind quickly, the lease will have expired.' I remember, too, an auction run by Arthur Hemens, a leading auctioneer. The lot, a freehold property at Leeds, was let to Lloyds Bank. David Galinsky stood up to ask a question. Arthur Hemens was experienced, well acquainted with Galinsky's comments and reluctant to be interrupted: 'Yes, what do you want?' he asked. His questioner then said: 'Mr Auctioneer: Is the stock in the vaults included?'

Over the years, I have been impressed by a few outstanding auctioneers with a particular aptitude to sell properties under the hammer. I have in mind the late Stanley Edgson, a dominating figure usually adorned with a carnation; Colonel Jack Trevor, who had the gift of the gab and thrived on the limelight; Leslie Walton and Arthur Hemens, who have both retired, were extremely experienced and able auctioneers; and Ted Stringer, who had a friendly style and was always anxious to extract a higher bid. Inflation has demolished the records of many proud auctioneers who felt sure his was the highest single bid ever made for a property. In 1962, the late Ben Allsop, a highly respected, monocled, professional auctioneer of good standing, thought he held the record by selling at auction 36–38 Queen Anne's Gate for £1,350,000. He was beaten in 1969 when Arthur Hemens knocked down the Hampstead Garden Suburb in one bid for £2,450,000. He, in turn, was outclassed in 1979 by Edward Stringer of my practice who sold the Carnaby Estate in London's West End to the ill-fated Sir Eric Miller of the Peachey Property Corporation for £3,400,000. Once again, this was overshadowed when David Yorke of Weatheralls secured a single bid of £6 million for an island site in Bloomsbury Square. I think, however, that Herbert Burnige, popularly known as 'Burney', beat them all in 1979 by securing a single bid for a freehold office block, Brent House, Wembley, of no less than £7,600,000. It will be interesting to see whether there will be any advance on this in the future.

*

The late Walter Flack had an exciting career which ended in tragedy. He served in the late war after experience as an estate agent and during the post-war property boom started his own property company, Murrayfield Real Estate, which was the shell of a company quoted on the Scottish Stock Exchange. He managed to enlist as chairman Field-Marshal Sir Claude

Auchinleck, under whom he had served as a sergeant. Other members of the board included Alan Wright, a handsome young negotiator and keen rugger player, and Sir Frank Price, a politician formerly on Birmingham City Council. Murrayfield expanded speedily and carried out large developments in provincial centres including Preston. It acquired Whitehall Court, an established block of service flats close to the Houses of Parliament, the upper floors of which overlooked the Embankment and River. Some of the flats were occupied by MPs and others who were worried that Walter Flack would disturb their tenancies and rebuild. He expanded his company so fast, in fact, that to solve some financial problems he sold a block of Murrayfield shares to Jack Cotton's City Centre Properties. Cotton later obtained control of the company and Walter found himself sharing a boardroom with two 'heavy-weights' – Jack Cotton and Charles Clore. He achieved considerable success, was an exuberant and strong minded man, and probably resented any suggestion of domination by older members of his board. They, in turn, may have secretly resented Walter Flack's outlook. This, combined with the breakup of his marriage, led to dissension and unhappiness and he was eventually found dead in his bath at Whitehall Court.

During his hey-day, Walter and other members of the Murrayfield board enjoyed themselves – particularly in pursuit of sporting interests. Walter, the super-optimist, was keen on cricket and horse racing and, in 1961, co-owned a colt named 'Winged Pharoah'. A stewards' enquiry was called after a race at Bath in which Winged Pharoah had ostensibly finished third. Walter's jockey objected to both the first and second horses for pushing him out of the race. As a result, the stewards disqualified the first horse, pronouncing the second horse the winner but, after ten minutes, they examined the objection lodged by Walter's jockey and placed Winged Pharoah first. Walter had, of course, telephoned his office at five minute intervals whilst this was taking place and all the staff received a blow-by-blow account of the race.

*

A man who made a name for himself building shopping centres is Sam Chippindale, an enthusiastic and forceful estate agent. Originally from Bradford, Yorkshire, he is said to be directly related to the furniture Chippendales. He made a study of covered shopping centres in North America and set up a company with Arnold Hagenbach, a multiple baker, known as the Arndale Property Trust – derived from the prefix and suffix of the two names. Sam has a strong personality, a pronounced Yorkshire accent, and he became well-known with multiple firms and local authorities for his forthright opinions. He was uncompromising in his criticism of old-fashioned shopping methods and this impressed many local authorities, particularly in the north of England. Gradually, he built up a large empire and developed more than 20 covered Arndale shopping Centres in various parts of the UK. At the peak of Arndale's success he merged with Town & City Properties, as a result of which he became a substantial shareholder. After the crash, like many others, Sam found his fortune on paper had almost disappeared. Undaunted, he decided to start again and he is now promoting new schemes with the backing of Taylor Woodrow, Legal & General and other large companies. Sam can expound fluently – and almost indefinitely – on covered shopping centres without taking a breath. I have enjoyed introducing him jocularly in public as 'the undercover agent who has defected'. He is very proud of the Arndale Centres and, as one time consultant to Town & City Properties, he sent me a piece of poetry by a Luton shopper applauding the new Arndale Centre there. I think it is true to say, however, that Sam is much more interested in covered shopping centres than poetry.

*

Some years ago my former employer, the late Dudley Samuel, said he would like me to see a young nephew of his, John Ritblat, who had done well at school and whom he thought would prove a first-class prospect for my office. When he called, I was very impressed with his manner and enthusiasm, but I had misgivings as I thought he would be far too ambitious to settle down patiently to the disciplines and rigours of a professional career. However, with reassurance from Dudley Samuel concerning John's professional background – his father was a dentist in Hampstead – I agreed to engage his services and he quickly became a persuasive and successful negotiator. As I had anticipated he was not prepared to stay the course with my practice, preferring to set up his own firm with Neville Conrad as Conrad Ritblat & Co. Apart from agency, they initiated some profitable deals on their own account. Later, their partnership split – John retaining the agency practice of Conrad Ritblat & Co and Neville, who gives the impression of being less extrovert than John, ceased estate agency, becoming a shareholder and chief executive of the public property company, Regional Properties Limited. When Peter King, chairman and principal shareholder of that company, died Neville took over. He is supported by Victor Lucas, who has been with the company for many years and who is well known for his public and social work. John Ritblat established himself as an entrepreneur and is now chairman and managing director of the British Land group of companies which also controls his agency practice. Under his enthusiastic direction, British Land built up an extensive property portfolio in the UK, Australia, Belgium, Eire, France, Holland and the USA. In addition, the company established an industrial division and acquired the Dorothy Perkins chain of ladies' shops which were later re-sold at a profit to Montague Burton.

When his company was hit by the property crash in 1973, John showed optimism and courage. It was whispered in City circles that British Land was bound to fail, so its shares crashed. Many people felt that John Ritblat was exaggerating when he averred that the company would survive. It is said that the test of a good captain is when the ship is sinking. John is a hard worker and has revitalised the company. Though John takes an optimistic view of business and life, he is a steely realist. During the difficult days of the 1970's one of British Land's bankers tried to alarm him by presenting what he thought was an extremely pessimistic view of the company's prospects. When he had finished, he asked John if he agreed. 'Oh, no,' said John, 'Our position is much worse than that and yours is even more so.' He is a pleasant man socially and, not surprisingly, he can be persistent and forceful in business matters. When selling the Classic cinema chain a few years ago, he pursued another well-known entrepreneur, Laurie Marsh, onto the airport bus at Heathrow to clinch the final details of the deal. He is an enthusiastic skier and his staff are said to dread the day when someone devises a method of telephoning from the piste.

*

It has always been my policy not to mix my business and private lives, but Prince and Nora Littler became an exception to the rule. One of the reasons was because I had a small dairy farm – Catsfold – in Henfield, Sussex, close to Chestham Park, the Littlers' large country estate. Everyone knew everyone in Henfield, indeed, almost adjoining our farm and farmhouse – parts of which were more than 500 years old – was the home of Keith Wickenden and his family. I have a high regard for Keith, formerly an accountant, not yet 50 but already a leading industrialist, chairman of European Ferries and a host of other shipping and dock companies including a large scale property development company. He is Conservative MP for Dorking and a director of the Brighton and Hove Albion Football Club.

Prince and Nora Littler were a delightful couple and charming hosts who lived in style at Chestham Park and observed all its best customs. Like those of his brother, Sir Emile Littler, Prince's roots were in the live theatre. So, too, were Nora's – her stage name was Nora Delany and, in her young days, she played the part of principal boy in pantomines. Prince's eldest sister, Blanche Littler, married George Robey, the famous comedian. And the Littler parents owned a theatre in Woolwich many years ago known as the Royal Artillery Theatre – hence Prince's name.

I had the greatest admiration for Prince when I first met him in offices adjacent to the London Hippodrome, now the Talk of the Town. His obviously loyal staff gave the impression that they had worked for him for many years and I was impressed with his personal ability, his knowledge of property throughout the country and his aptitude to make clear-cut decisions. Most of all I liked that atmosphere and the pleasant courtesies he extended to everyone, so lacking in today's business world. At that first meeting many years ago I had the feeling that mutual trust had been established between us. In the future I was to carry out many transactions for the companies then controlled by Prince – Stoll Theatres Corporation, Associated Theatres and Moss Empires which owned, at that time, probably the largest circuit of London theatres including the Palladium, the Coliseum, the Hippodrome, Theatre Royal, Drury Lane, Apollo, Her Majesty's, Aldwych, Lyric, Globe, Queens, the Victoria Palace and 17 Empire Theatres in the suburbs and provinces. I was brought to assist the defence of an unsuccessful takeover bid by Jack Cotton and Charles Clore. And it was in Prince Littler's offices that I met Toby Rowland, a dedicated theatre man who hailed from the States, but who settled in the UK and became a naturalised British citizen. Toby, assisted by Jack Barham, became Prince's right-hand man and was able to take over the reins at the time when Prince's health was failing. Toby then became managing director of the theatre empire following Prince's death in 1973. (Control is now vested in Lord Grade's vast empire, Associated Communications Corporation which owns ATV and one of the largest cinema chains in the country.)

Prince and Nora were reserved and shunned publicity in their private life at Chestham Park, where most of their guests were famous actors and actresses – the Press or photographers were never admitted. I well remember the Littlers' summer parties when Prince, smoking a cigar in the picturesque loggia, would quietly watch many of his famous guests strolling on the extensive lawns adjacent to the house. Pamela and I were often invited to dine there. It was a rule of the establishment that black ties should be worn and, on such occasions, I had to change from my farm clothes into a dinner jacket. After a perfectly served dinner, Prince, Nora, Toby Rowland and his wife, Millie, two other guests, Pamela and I would form two tables for an enthusiastic and competitive game of canasta – despite the stakes of 3d a 100 points. On the first occasion, I remember Pamela saying to Prince: 'How boring to play for only 3d a 100.' He replied with a charming smile that it was a rule of the house that he never liked to see his guests lose money. It was only after Prince's death that I learned he had been incurably ill for two years. Typically, he did not disclose this, was very brave, showed no signs of distress and made all his business decisions on a long-term basis. His remarkable career started from humble beginnings when he managed his parents' theatre in Woolwich. Then, while still young, he went on the road as a showman, touring the country and working 18 hours a day. He met and fell in love with Nora, who was acting in one of his shows and, after they married, with strong support from his bank, he acquired theatre after theatre until he became the largest and most respected proprietor of the theatrical world. At one time he acquired the Britannia Pier at Great Yarmouth, the West Pier and the Palace Pier at Brighton. He was a perfectionist and, despite his medical report, took a great interest in his garden and farms and won many prizes for his pedigree Guernsey and Sussex cattle.

For a time, Prince Littler was chairman of the newly-formed Associated Television, followed for a short time by Lord Renwick and then by Lord Grade. Some time ago I had an entertaining meeting with Lord Grade, known as Lew. He is an irrepressible character and a shrewd and outstanding example of an entrepreneur who, by hard work and ability, has become a leading figure in the commercial world. He came to this country as a child refugee from Russia, was connected with the entertainment industry and, in his young days, was reputed to be a Charleston champion. Later, with his brother, Leslie Grade, he established one of the largest variety agencies. Lord Grade was clever enough to take a stake in commercial television immediately after the Act of Parliament discontinued the BBC monopoly. He entered the television industry when Associated Television was formed and he has since turned the company into a vast enterprise with diversified interests in various parts of the world. His holding company, now called Associated Communications Corporation, ATV Network, and his other subsidiary companies produce and distribute films and television programmes for both the UK and overseas markets. In addition to this, after the death of Prince Littler, Lord Grade became Chairman of Stoll Moss Theatres Limited, which owns most of the leading theatres in London. He recently arranged the acquisition of the Classic Cinema Group with its huge cinema chain. Lord Grade, a super salesman, made a great contribution to the British Film Industry but recently incurred serious losses. He could not contemplate failure and may have been influenced by the big screen with its bottomless purse. His chief executive, Jack Gill, resigned and Bill Michael and Ellis Birk, the shrewd solicitor, may not have always agreed with their irrepressible boss. Lord Grade's brother is Lord Delfont, who began his theatrical life as a theatre manager. He later owned theatres and presented West End theatrical shows throughout the country and on television. He built up and became a director of EMI Limited which was recently merged with Thorn Electric.

*

The life of the late Sir Charles Clore is the story of a young man of humble background and education whose personal ability and drive brought him a vast fortune. He also made an impact on the whole outlook of City institutions towards quoted companies and their directors' duties to shareholders. He was a robust man with a blunt, down-to-earth manner and very dry sense of humour. Always quick to make decisions, he practised economy of words at board meetings. One of the most significant incidents in his career, to my mind, was the takeover of J. Sears, the footwear firm trading as the Trueform Boot Company, and Freeman Hardy & Willis, which owned about 900 shops, many of them freehold. Charles Clore made the daring decision to go over the heads of the Sears board of directors by circulating the shareholders direct. At the time, the City establishment criticised him as ruthless and unprincipled. But Clore's action represented a breakthrough, although it was not until sometime afterwards that it was acknowledged and recognised as such. Clore, by taking courageous action, had performed a great service to shareholders of public companies. As a result, complacent boards of directors have been sacked or forced to work in the best interests of all company shareholders.

After skating as a young boy at the Cricklewood Roller Skating Rink, he acquired the building at the age of 22 and, instead of paying for admission, collected the proceeds himself. At the age of 25, he purchased the Prince of Wales Theatre in Leicester Square, managing to secure and re-sell some of the film rights of the World Heavyweight Boxing Championship between Jack Dempsey and Gene Tunney. Then, after the last war, by shrewd dealing in South African gold mining and other shares, he accumulated considerable capital. He used this to acquire a large shareholding in Investment Registry, an issuing house dealing in shares which gave Clore a vantage point from which to seek public companies ripe for takeover. In addition to acquiring J. Sears, Clore bought a host of other important companies. These included, among others, Dolcis, Lilley & Skinner, Saxone and Mansfield, now known as the British Shoe Corporation; also Bentley Engineering Company, Furness Shipbuilding Company, Scottish Motor Traction, Mappin & Webb and Garrards, the jewellers, and Lewis's Investment Trust with its group of department stores and bookmakers, the William Hill organisation. Apart from his enormous and diversified trading operations, Clore had a flair for property investment and development. He built up City & Central Investments, which he floated as a public property company. Years later he merged this with City Centre Properties after a favourable share exchange with Jack Cotton. Undoubtedly a brilliant industrialist, he possessed a shrewd 'sixth sense' for acquiring businesses and improving their productivity. The famous Oxford Street store of Selfridge may be a good example. His right-hand man – always at his elbow – was Leonard Sainer, an able and clear-minded solicitor who served Sir Charles so well that it was fitting that he followed as chairman of Sears Holdings. It is difficult to gauge to what extent the sound advice and judgement of Leonard Sainer contributed to the success of Charles Clore. Clore also became interested in farming and acquired a large agricultural estate of more than 1,600 acres as an investment. It was recently resold to the Prudential Assurance Company for about £20 million.

I have vivid recollections of calling some years ago at his town house at 95 Park Street. Douglas Tovey was acting on his behalf and I had introduced the possible takeover of Scottish Motor Traction, known as SMT, a powerful public company with extensive motorcar showrooms, pumps and agencies throughout Scotland and with a strong Balance Sheet. The possibilities of takeover were not readily seen by other clients of mine, but Clore quickly decided to proceed. When the bid was announced there was some opposition in Scotland to the fact that voting control would be in the hands of Sassenachs. The late Hugh Fraser made a counter bid, but Clore won the day and I remember seeing the headlines in one of the morning papers: 'Bonnie Prince Charlie comes to Scotland'. The meeting at 95 Park Street remains in my memory as Clore, usually so robust, on that occasion had temporary back trouble and was confined to bed on a board. Gathered in his bedroom with the representatives from Scotland, therefore, were Douglas Tovey, Clore's accountant, Jack Gardiner, and I. There was also an attractive nurse in attendance and I was impressed on my way up to his room by the large number of paintings and other valuable works of art on display. Clore had an outstanding ability to delegate and quickly gave instructions from his bed. It seemed, however, ironic that although he was in pain he was interrupted incessantly by telephone calls during our meeting which he had no alternative but to answer himself. They were obviously from his stockbroker and no-one else in the room could be entrusted to discuss Charles Clore's shareholdings. Each time he answered the phone, he was obliged to give an abrupt 'yes' or 'no' to a question. This is one of the penalties of being wealthy.

Clore was also involved in a number of important property developments including the Stoll Theatre building in Kingsway, Charles House, Kensington and also the London Hilton Hotel in Park Lane. His favourite architect was Sidney Kaye of the Sidney Kaye Firmin Partnership. The Hilton development presented many problems, including difficulties in obtaining vacant possession and then achieving town planning consent. Welton Beckett, the famous United States architect, was brought in to design a 1930's-type skyscraper. This was deemed totally unacceptable to the London County Council due to the height of the building facing the royal park and overlooking Buckingham Palace. Sidney Kaye was able to find a solution and the design drawings were eventually agreed. Charles Clore's development company then entered into an agreement with Hilton International Inc. for the hotel to be built, but limited to an outlay of £4 million, the specification to be decided by Hilton International within a specified time limit. Sidney Kaye found himself in the odious position of not having a single working drawing prepared when building work started and receiving instructions from Clore to make variations whilst piling was in progress. However, fate was kind and the hotel was built in just over two years at a cost of £4½ million. To Sidney Kaye's amazement, this figure was accepted. Today, such a building might cost £25 million to build and probably take three years to erect. The Hilton site was believed to be one of the first to be surrounded by bored piles – a construction technique which produced substantial savings in the vast dig for the four basements required beneath the 30-storey tower. A further interesting point is that the weight of earth excavated was nearly equal to the weight of the tower under construction and fossils of snails were discovered that I am told were extinct before the early Middle Ages.

Prior to his knighthood, Clore bought Stype Grange, Hungerford from the Rootes motorcar family. The main house overlooked some beautiful man-made scenery, but Clore had moved temporarily into some converted cottages with a view of the Wiltshire hills. Contrary to his normal, instant decision-making, he prevaricated on this personal issue of whether to build a new house and, if so, overlooking which view. Sidney Kaye recommended a contemporary single-storey house in stone and timber to blend with the rural surroundings. Not unnaturally, while Sidney was keen to produce the house he had designed, he was nervous of attempting to impose his personal taste on a client of the strong character of Charles Clore. It is easy to lose a valued client over such a personal matter as a home. In view of this, Sidney decided to be open minded, accept an invitation to a private lunch at the Penthouse of the Carlton Tower Hotel to meet Clore, Lord Bessborough and an architect recommended by the latter who specialised in design of country houses. The second architect drew up plans. Sidney then called upon Clore in company with Dim Gran, staff architect to the Hilton Organisation, to discuss certain details of works regarding the hotel. Dim Gran was an elderly Russian experienced in hotels and luxury home design. Across Sir Charles's desk were plans prepared by Lord Bessborough's architect of the suggested new house to be erected at Stype Grange. Clore thrust the plans in front of Dim Gran and Sidney and asked for their opinion. Without examining them, Sidney thought it discreet to say first class, but Dim Gran was so outspoken and scathing in his comments that Clore did not go ahead with either home and stayed in coverted and enlarged country cottages. Sidney built a stud for him instead, designed with a round arch and clock tower.

Moor House, London Wall, was a building in the City erected by Sir Charles Clore's company. In this instance, Sidney Kaye set aside a sum out of the building costs for a low-relief sculpture to be put adjacent to the entrance. To avoid becoming involved in possible controversy concerning the sculpture, he concealed the work with a hoarding and discreetly unveiled it when Clore was away on one of his many visits to the United States. Frederick Ellis, the journalist, contacted Sidney to find out why the semi-abstract sculpture had been unveiled in such a discreet fashion. Sidney told him, off the record, that a sculpture of this type was so much a question of personal taste that he did not wish to delay completion. A week later, he found a write-up about Moor House in the *Daily Express* Midlands edition with the bold headline: 'What happens when the boss is away' above a photograph of the sculpture.

Like most great empire builders, Charles Clore had a genius for retaining control of his organisation, remembering the smallest detail but entrusting the execution of his wishes to his top executives headed by Leonard Sainer. He was assisted by Geoffrey Maitland Smith, Aubrey Hawkins and Isaac Levison, and Sainer's sisters were also loyal members of the Clore team. Charles Clore was knighted in 1971 for outstanding donations to charitable causes. In his later years, Clore acquired a magnificent apartment in Monte Carlo, but he became too ill to enjoy the benefit of this and passed away at the age of 74 in July 1979. It is sad that his private life was not as successful and happy as his outstanding commercial career. His former wife, Francine, won the Croix de Guerre for heroism for her part with the French Resistance in the last war, but their marriage was dissolved in 1957. He left a son and daughter.

14

THE DORCHESTER SUITE

*

Every time I pass the Ballroom entrance of the Dorchester, I think of that exuberant character, the late Jack Cotton, affectionately known to everyone in the property world as Jack. I can see him now, wearing his bow tie, with his customary warmth, friendliness and penetrating gaze. He was seldom alone as he liked people around him. As a young man he set up as an estate agent in Birmingham, quickly became prominent and carried out a number of land deals to create housing between the wars and built blocks of flats and other buildings. When I met him just after the war he was already a well-known personality and, in addition to establishing Jack Cotton & Partners in Birmingham, he had also set up a London office in Regent Street with Samuel Messer and Barry East – although the latter, at that time, was working with him as a young negotiator.

Jack also created his own architectural practice known as Cotton Ballard & Blow. He carried out many spectacular transactions in Birmingham, including an extensive site in New Street, formerly occupied by the King Edward School. This was a sentimental deal for Jack who was educated there prior to Cheltenham College. Jack saw enormous possibilities in large-scale development and he had the courage to divorce himself completely from his practice. He engaged a permanent suite at the Dorchester in London and, although he remained in contact, he passed the reins of Jack Cotton & Partners of Birmingham, to his son, Derek. This enabled him to plan and to execute a policy of expansion without day-to-day interruptions from clients and staff. He took a broad view and dealt with most of the larger firms of estate agents in London and elsewhere. His financial adviser was David Finnie of Finnie Ross & Co, the City accountants. David Finnie, a shrewd, pleasant Scot, helped Jack to secure control of Central Commercial Properties, a quoted public property company with a large portfolio of multiple shops formerly controlled by the late Stanley Edgson and his family. Jack converted this company into City Centre Properties Limited and carried out some fabulous deals. Always ambitious, Jack foresaw the necessity of using pension fund and insurance company money to finance large-scale development. He therefore set up a large number of joint companies and his captivating personality and successful development policy enabled him to cultivate close relations with Pearl Assurance. He also formed a joint company with Ravenseft Properties in order to carry out the huge shop development known as 'The Big Top' in Birmingham.

I asked my friend, Eric Rutherford Young, how he became Jack's chief surveyor. Formerly with the Coal Board Pension Fund, Eric was invited to Thames Lawn, Marlow – Jack's country residence – one Sunday with the late David Finnie. There, Eric found himself being interviewed for the job. At the end of the interview, Eric agreed to join the company and Jack then said, shaking him by the hand: 'We are going to have fun, aren't we? If not, I don't bloody well want you to join the firm.' Eric tells me he will never regret serving Jack Cotton and his company for more than four exciting years. Just after starting his new job, Eric was left in a room with Charles Hambro of Hambros Bank. Jack was answering the telephone in an adjoining room and handed Charles a copy of the Report & Accounts of City Centre Properties. When Jack returned, Hambro said: 'Jack, the thing I like about you is that you always leave something for the other man' – a direct allusion to Jack's partnership agreements with other institutions. It was always interesting to call at Jack's Dorchester suite. He had a great sense of fun and once, when he was being interviewed in his flat by Frederick Ellis, the journalist, he enjoyed a joke at Ellis's expense. When his secretary announced that William Hickey was in the outer office and wished to see him, Jack arranged for Ellis, the financial editor of the *Daily Express* to see the Hickey representative of the same newspaper, in the outer office on his behalf. Jack fought for several years to get planning permission from the then London County Council to reconstruct the Monico Building at the corner of Piccadilly Circus. Not unnaturally, he was very proud of himself when he eventually achieved planning consent and, in his suite at the Dorchester, he enjoyed showing off the Monico model by switching on the lights inside it.

Apart from overseas transactions in South Africa, Jack Cotton made one of his most spectacular moves by amalgamating his property company with that of Charles Clore – City & Central Investments – and reaching agreement with Erwin Wolfson of New York in connection with the development of the Pan Am building. This was reputed to be one of the largest office buildings in the world and had been erected above Grand Central Station in New York. Flamboyant Jack decided to celebrate the deal with a lunch at the Dorchester and he arranged for a model of the Pan Am building to be displayed in the centre of the dining room. With his great sense of fun, he paused in the middle of his welcoming speech to say: 'We are, to the best of my knowledge, the only UK property company which has its own signature tune.' His surprised guests then heard – exactly on cue – a recording of the tune Grand Central City composed by Lud Gluskin, the musical director of CBC of America. It was amusing to witness the amazed expressions on some of the faces of important City bankers and institutional investors when the tune was broadcast in the middle of the chairman's speech. At about the same time, Jack announced his Monico redevelopment plans to the Press. The disclosure caused enormous opposition as a large number of important groups, including the Civic Trust and the Fine Arts Commission, condemned the plans and Jack's hard-won planning consent was called in by the Minister. Fate never allowed Jack his desire to carry out the Monico development – despite his bringing in, as consultant, the world-famous architect, Professor Gropius.

It was Douglas Tovey who initiated the ill-fated marriage between Jack Cotton's company, City Centre Properties, and Charles Clore's City and Central Investments. Financially, it appeared to be a good deal for Clore's company, but it brought home the lesson once again that two dominant tycoons in the same boardroom produce a temperamentally explosive combination. When he agreed the merger, Jack Cotton stipulated he should remain chairman of the enlarged company. Charles Clore's reaction was that the financial terms were such that he did not object to becoming what he called: 'Jack Cotton's office boy.' Jack's company contained his life work, whereas the resultant merger represented only a small part of Charles Clore's empire. Clore's main company was Sears Holdings which included, among many other companies, the British Shoe Corporation. Jack was essentially an individualist. After the merger, his health started to fail and he resented the encroachment on his personal authority. He was accustomed to sitting in his suite at the Dorchester and making his own decisions without attending too many board meetings. Eventually, Jack and his family trusts sold their shares in the merged company to Sir Isaac Wolfson and Sir Kenneth Keith. Jack became president and went to the Bahamas to recover his health. Unfortunately, he did not return. In order to protect the vast sums invested in the company, a strong new board was formed including the late George Bridge, formerly of Legal & General, Sir Charles Clore, Leonard Sainer, Sir Kenneth Keith, Sir Isaac Wolfson, Edward Plumridge of Pearl Assurance, Archie Sherman, Peter Folliss and Alan Wright, Edward Footring becoming managing director. After Jack Cotton's untimely death, Lord Samuel finally absorbed the company within Land Securities. Jack Cotton made a large number of donations to charity, including the Royal College of Surgeons and the London Zoo. He left a widow, three sons and a daughter; two of his sons, Derek and Gordon, have remained in the property world, while the third, Jeremy, qualified as a solicitor and then became a stockbroker in the City of London.

Apart from being a friendly and disarming host, even after he became a famous tycoon, Jack was never arrogant or demanding. He always had time to talk to everyone. His death produced something of a void in the property industry. The late Arthur Dixon Wright, the surgeon, was nearly always willing to speak at a function for friends prepared to make a donation to his favourite charity – Cancer Research. I remember him giving a brilliant speech at a City Centre Properties luncheon at the Dorchester. Prior to operating on any tycoon and just before administering the anaesthetic, Dixon Wright would whisper in his patient's ear: 'Will you give me a tip for some good shares?' His speech went on: 'Last night, I had an amazing dream. I dreamt I saw Jack Cotton on a trapeze at the Olympia. He was travelling through the air at an enormous speed, first with two hands on the bar, secondly with one hand, then he did a somersault, turning upside down and holding on with two feet. My heart was thumping in suspense as, at any moment, I felt he was likely to fall. Just before I woke up, I was relieved to see underneath him a huge net inscribed with the names of Pearl Assurance and Legal & General.' At that time, Jack was in his hey-day, investing millions in various projects in the UK and overseas.

I have vivid memories of a dinner party at the miniature town house where we lived in 1960 at Wilton Row, a cul-de-sac mews off Wilton Crescent in London's West End. Our guests included Mr and Mrs Michael Richards and the illustrious Jack Cotton. Michael Richards, a somewhat blunt Yorkshireman and qualified lawyer, had become a banker and financier. During the course of dinner, Jack with a twinkle in his eye, complained of the prima donna tantrums of many directors of the various companies he had taken over. We all enjoyed Michael Richard's quick retort: 'Jack, you are the biggest prima donna of them all.'

After 1945, it became increasingly difficult for people to afford large town houses in the capital and many were converted into flats or offices. Mews houses became fashionable in the West End, indeed their cobblestones and individual conversions help create quiet havens of almost continental charm in the heart of town. There was also a trace or two of mock modesty in some social circles to mention casually at cocktail parties that one lived in a simple mews house. Most of the houses in Wilton Row, like many other mews in Belgravia, were conversions from stables once attached to large town houses, in this case of Wilton Crescent on one side and Grosvenor Crescent on the other. Part of Wilton Row was charmingly picturesque, opening out into a large courtyard with a street lamp in the centre. It was known as the Piazza and some residents held open-air parties there during the summer. Entering Wilton Row from Wilton Crescent, the first three houses formed a terrace of three bijou town houses, built in 1935 in neo-Georgian style. They were well constructed but were tall, narrow and small – each with basement and three upper floors. Number 1 was occupied by Alan Morris, a banker, and Number 3, on the other side of us, was the home of Sir John Charles, an eminent City solicitor. Number 2 appealed to me as a surveyor because it was purpose-built, the structure was sound and, more important, the purchase price was reasonable. But our bijou town house on several floors proved difficult to run. It had staff quarters, a large kitchen and a butler's pantry in the basement with a service lift to the upper floors. Due to the layout of the house, we felt obliged to employ a married couple – a manservant and his wife as cook. They were an eccentric pair who had worked for a nobleman's family in a large manor house on a country estate. We led a comparatively simple life in London and were unaccustomed to being served by a butler of this kind, who was something of an anachronism in such a small house. It proved, however, next to impossible to change the habits of our major-domo, who persisted in devoting a great deal of time to changing clothes – a grey alpaca jacket to sweep the four front steps, a blue and white striped jacket to serve breakfast, a white jacket to serve lunch, a chef's cap and chiffon scarf to bake a cake, and black tie to serve dinner. My wife was not pleased when he insisted upon serving me at the table before her – on the grounds that it was correct for the master of the house to be served first. It also caused considerable amusement in our small drawing room when he served drinks and then walked out of the room backwards. When we were entertaining, we were terrified that he might trip over the furniture. We had some good times at Wilton Row, but, as is often the case in London, we did not become friendly with many of our neighbours. To keep my car under cover, I rented a lock-up garage lower down the mews next to the Grenadier pub adjoining Old Barrack Yard, where Wellington's troops are said to have massed in the past. With its distinctive sentry-box outside, the pub was a favourite meeting place for youthful motorists and students. They would drive down the mews at breakneck speed, park their cars indiscriminately and lock them, blocking residents in.

One day I received a call from two neighbours whom I had not met before, Colonel Fox of H.A. Fox, the Rolls Royce agents, and George Pollitzer of Beck & Pollitzer. Knowing I was an estate agent, they asked me to help eliminate from Wilton Row the intolerable nuisance of parking by patrons of the Grenadier. I said I would and invited all the residents to a meeting. My wife was very much opposed to this and warned me that if I promoted an anti-pub campaign, I might be hit on the head with a bottle one dark night by an angry Grenadier customer. Undeterred, I wrote to all the leaseholders in Wilton Row, registered the Wilton Row Tenants Association as a corporate body and arranged for all the occupiers to withhold paying ground rent to the Grosvenor Estate, the freeholders, on the grounds that we were being deprived of free access. The Grenadier publican was unsympathetic and the Grosvenor Estate eventually met Watneys Brewery, the head leaseholders, in the High Court in order to protect the rights of their tenants. I attended the hearing and the Court ruled that a gate should be erected at the entrance to the mews and manned by the Estate during licensing hours to refuse access to non-residents' cars. It was ironic that both the Grosvenor Estate and Watneys were clients and friends of mine. In fact, the Estate has adopted similar precautions in several other Belgravia mews.

Many years ago Stanley Hattrell, the Coventry architect, introduced me to the late Sir William Lyons. Popularly known as Bill Lyons, he masterminded the success of the Jaguar Car Company, prior to its takeover by British Leyland. I became friendly with Bill as a result of negotiating with the Government on his behalf to lease a Daimler Shadow factory in Coventry. At that time new cars were not readily available and there was a long waiting list of buyers for Jaguars. I urgently wanted one and Bill put in a word for me direct with Bert Henley of Henley Motors, the main distributors. I got my new Jaguar. New cars were so hard to come by that many people were prepared to pay a substantial premium over the purchase price to secure one. The Board of Trade in those days required a purchaser to sign a legal undertaking not to resell a car within a specified period. After collecting my brand new car, I dined with friends at the Embassy Club in Old Bond Street. Suddenly, the head waiter appeared with a note on the back of a menu which said: 'Are you prepared to flog your new Jaguar for £200 profit?' It was signed Bert. I looked up, over to the other side of the Club, and saw Sir William Lyons and Bert Henley, two of the leading figures in the motor industry at that time, rocking with laughter and thoroughly enjoying the joke.

15

A RUMBUSTIOUS CHARACTER

*

In the latter part of 1960, I met Bernard Sunley, founder of the Bernard Sunley Investment Trust – a group controlling a number of property companies and the large building construction firm. I received a sudden telephone call in which he said: 'Is that you, Edward Erdman? It's about time we met – come round and see me and have lunch.' I duly visited him at his impressive offices in Berkeley Square. There was a powdered footman present in full regalia and I noticed a line up of bottles of crystal champagne. He asked me what I would have to drink. I was on the water wagon and told him so. Bernard exclaimed: 'How the bloody hell do you do any business?' My reply was that I didn't do much business as my practice was in its infancy. This slightly defiant remark intrigued him as he asked what I thought of his business. When I told him he was ingenious, I was told to explain myself. Here is my reply: 'You have managed to carry out a successful public issue of your company during the Stock Exchange boom, based on low yields from your investment properties but including the more speculative profits from your contracting business on the same basis.' His reaction was to stand up and, on the internal telephone, to invite his directors to come in. We were joined by Bill Shapland and Bernard's son, John, to whom he remarked: 'This man, Erdman, thinks we are ingenious.' Following this, we became friends.

Bernard Sunley was a rumbustious character. Blunt and with little regard for convention, he decided on one occasion to join my wife and me at a somewhat formal black-tie dinner party. He appeared, large as life, in a grey lounge suit with a particularly large blue silk tie. Despite the remonstrations of the head waiter and others attempting to bar his passage, he walked straight into the function with a huge smile on his face. My wife managed to appease the organisers by inducing Bernard to substitute his large tie for a borrowed bow. An amusing incident took place at the opening ceremony of the Piccadilly Plaza Hotel at Manchester. During the course of the luncheon, attended by all the local dignitaries when the paint was hardly dry, some plaster fell from the ceiling – much to the consternation of some of the guests. Bernard Sunley, however, was undeterred.

A big man in every way, Bernard enjoyed himself, had few complexes and some humility. In the late hours, he would often tell you about his early days of hardship, relating how he helped his father to gather muck with a pony and cart for a comparative pittance per load. On another occasion I was summoned to his office and, when I arrived, he was in shirt sleeves in company with the rest of his board. Immediately upon my arrival, he stood up and commanded his co-directors to do likewise. He then said, to my complete astonishment: 'I hereby award Edward Erdman first prize for letting our office building at Empire Way, Wembley.' Then he handed me a cheque for £5,000. The negotiations had been handled by John Cook of my firm and I was unacquainted with the precise details of the letting or the commission due to the practice. I said to Bernard: 'Has the office sent you an account?' He was annoyed and said: 'If you don't want the bloody cheque, give it back.' I did so and he tore it into shreds. When I returned to the office, John Cook told me that the letting was to Centrovincial Estates and the commission due to us was £7,000. Our account was subsequently submitted and Bernard paid it in full without comment. Sometimes he reminded me of a big, likeable schoolboy. The building in question overlooks the Wembley Stadium and it was John Sunley's first major property transaction. Sunleys made a handsome profit on the construction and the letting – in addition to erecting a fine building. Apart from John Sunley, Bernard's son, another elder statesman who has been a tower of strength to the company for a great many years is Bill Shapland, a shrewd chartered accountant and businessman. John Sunley sat on the board of the Bernard Sunley Investment Trust from a young age and matured quickly through assuming considerable responsibility when his father died in 1964. A good sportsman, John counts among his daring accomplishments the perilous Cresta Run at St Moritz. His eldest son, James, my godson, is a particularly good cricketer and captained Harrow School Colts. The Eagle Star Insurance Company – for many years the major shareholders in the Bernard Sunley Investment Trust – led by Sir Brian Mountain, followed by his son, Sir Denis later acquired the company, selling back to John Sunley's family the construction company and other assets. The Sunleys have completed a full circle from private company in the early 1930's to public company and now back to private company. I am sure many public company directors and founders are envious.

*

Fred Cleary, chairman of Haslemere Estates, has had enormous success due to his energy and unbounded enthusiasm to preserve and refurbish buildings of beauty and architectural merit. His company is renowned for its attention to detail in restoring both the interiors and exteriors of old properties and reinstating their former grandeur. Unlike some developers who might remove, for example, a damaged marble fireplace and board up the opening, Haslemere would go to untold trouble to replace it with a marble fireplace of the same period. Architraves, cornices, balustrades and even door handles are preserved or replaced with replicas, if this proves necessary, in Haslemere buildings. Fred's concentration on fine, old, empty and neglected buildings in the City and West End of London caused several other developers to follow suit. Nowadays, when a building is refurbished and restored to its former glory, the professionals term the project 'Doing a Haslemere.' After leaving school, Fred qualified as a chartered surveyor. In his earliest days, when living within the Borough of Hornsey, his interest was aroused in the environment and the appearance of houses and their gardens after the bomb damage of the last war. In addition to promoting the business success of Haslemere Estates – now a public company – Fred was always socially minded. Many years ago, he served on the Hornsey Borough Council, becoming chairman of the Town Planning Committee and then Deputy Mayor. He later turned his attention to the City of London and became a prominent member of the Court of Common Council. He is a past president of the City Livery Club and the Worshipful Company of Gardeners and has been awarded the CBE for his public services. His great interest is open spaces, gardens, flowers and shrubs. In aid of charity, he produced a book, *The Flowering City*, and has been an active supporter of the Gardeners' Royal Benevolent Home in Henfield, Sussex.

Fred, an entertaining after-dinner speaker, has been known to produce exactly the right quotation at the right time. I remember one of them in particular, from after a business lunch some years ago: 'I am like the American who said when it comes to humility, I am just the tops.' I was privileged to be one of his guests at his 75th birthday party, given by David Pickford and other directors of Haslemere Estates. It was held in the traditional and impressive atmosphere of the ancient Armourers' and Braisiers' Hall in Coleman Street, embellished with authentic suits of armour, pikes and other weapons. Members of Fred's family were present, in addition to life-long friends who have served with him on the Common Council of the City of London. I was seated next to Victor Wood, a Noble Lowndes actuary. During the course of the luncheon, Victor commented: 'Some people have "green fingers" and are able to foster the growth of plants. Also beyond the skills of professional valuers and mathematicians, "green finger" qualities are possessed by some who have a special flair for picking out property with special growth potential.' He was right.

David Pickford, Haslemere's managing director, was formerly a surveyor with Hillier Parker May & Rowden and joined Fred Cleary in 1949 to become his right-hand man. Both men have probably done more than any other company to preserve our architectural heritage by restoring old buildings and adapting them to modern use. David tells of an amusing incident which occurred sometime in 1960 when John Cook, the partner in my firm then dealing with central London business premises, had just married Cari, a former fashion model. Apart from being friends socially, David and John were doing business together as Haslemere were important clients of my firm. Cari had not had that much experience of housekeeping in those early days although she now runs, extremely capably, a large household at Sunningdale. John Cook decided to invite Betty and David Pickford for dinner as their first important business guests. This was a very special occasion and a detailed discussion took place regarding the menu. After much deliberation, it was decided that duck would be the main course. John recalls the fateful dinner party which took place on a Friday evening. When he arrived home just after 7.00 p.m., he found their Chelsea house absolutely immaculate; flowers everywhere, the dining room table beautifully laid and everything in perfect order to receive their first VIP guests. Cari asked John to question her to ensure that she had not forgotten anything. The question and answer session went very well until it came to the principal item of the evening – the duck. It was then 7.45, the Pickfords were due at 8.00 p.m. and the duck was still in the fridge. Something near panic ensued until, with some misgivings, John suggested a taxi to take the duck to a local restaurant in Sloane Square which he knew had an infra-red grill. Cari hastily departed, clutching the duck – missing the Pickfords who arrived seconds later. John was naturally feeling a little tense and the overall position was not exactly helped by the fact that neither David nor Betty were heavy drinkers. David tells me that when they got to their fourth gin and tonic, they were trying to make it last a long time because they wondered if they were ever going to eat. A few minutes later, Cari arrived, made her excuses for not being present to receive her guests and – somewhat suspiciously – invited John into the kitchen. Apparently all was well as the duck was being dealt with on the infra-red grill and arrangements had been made with the restaurant manager for it to be returned by taxi immediately it had been cooked. Something like 30 minutes later, the front door bell rang and Cari and John decided it would be discreet to express great surprise as to who might possibly be calling. Cari went to the door and there was a taxi-driver holding, somewhat delicately, a box which contained the duck. In the excitement of the moment, Cari had left the drawing room door open and David and Betty overheard the conversation at the front door. Just before John could reach the door to close it, he heard the taxi driver say loudly: 'Whatever might be in that box is ruddy hot.' The duck was quickly deposited in the Cooks' oven and the day was saved. It was not until three or four years later that John plucked up enough courage to tell David the story. I believe they all had a good laugh.

David is president of the London District of the Boys Brigade, which has 17,000 members. He owns a farm in Kent which is utilised as a residential Christian Youth Centre. Another bright young director on the Haslemere Board is Gerald Powell who has a pleasant, witty personality and must be an asset when it comes to negotiating the letting of buildings.

On several occasions, I have had the opportunity of dealing with Lord Goodman, a brilliant negotiator and shrewd and experienced lawyer. During his professional career he has conducted negotiations for the Government, acted for many leading personalities of both political parties and helped settle complex union disputes within the printing industry. I enjoyed dealing with him when he acted for the Arts Council in connection with the fine building, 105 Piccadilly, restored to its former elegance by Haslemere Estates. Lord Goodman also acted for Sadlers Wells, who leased the Coliseum Theatre from the late Prince Littler of the Stoll Moss Theatres Corporation.

Lord Goodman telephoned me a while ago and made a personal request for an option for a few weeks on a flat in Victoria. He said the flat was required for a well-known personality whose name he was unable to disclose. I could not grant an option, but I gave Lord Goodman my personal assurance that, if an active approach was made for the flat by prospective tenants within the next few days, I would immediately advise him. His reference to a well-known personality puzzled me somewhat and I wrongly assumed that he was acting for Lord Snowdon. I was completely wrong, as his client proved to be Sir Harold Wilson, who acquired the flat on the sale of his house in Westminster.

*

Max Keyworth, who originally qualified as a chartered accountant, was an experienced property man and managing director of Covent Garden Properties. It had close associations with the Eagle Star Insurance Company, whose chairman, Sir Brian Mountain, was also its chairman. Since my 'retirement', on my way home from the office I often see Max's tall, athletic figure striding across Berkeley Square. Covent Garden Properties was a prominent public company for many years and due to its sharing the same name, it retained a box in the Covent Garden Opera House. In addition to owning a large number of properties in the UK, the company had substantial interests in the United States and in the Trizec Corporation of Canada which owned, among other buildings, the famous Place Ville Marie complex in Montreal. Max managed Covent Garden Properties successfully for many years, but he eventually found himself catapulted into the huge amalgamation of companies known as Star (Great Britain) Holdings. By coincidence, we crossed paths during the war for a short time when we were both officer cadets. Perhaps the battle inoculation course which we were obliged to undertake enabled Max to cope with equanimity with board changes due to policy differences and pressures of the 1973 property crisis which forced the company to sell off many of its investments in order to repay loans.

Robert Potel was the energetic and ambitious man who sowed the seed which started the huge Star property empire. Robert was formerly a solicitor and he began his career by forming a comparatively small property company known as Star (Great Britain) Holdings Limited. He wished Star – one of the smallest quoted property companies in 1960 – to become a large, international concern. His first move was to merge with David Llewellyn's company known as Real & Leasehold Estate Investment Society. Expansive Robert Potel and the shrewd, accountant-trained David Llewellyn formed a formidable combination and proceeded to take over a large number of other companies, mostly on the basis of issuing shares or loan stock. First they acquired the late Felix Fenston's former public company, Metropolitan & Provincial Properties, with its large and important portfolio of income-producing properties, including recently erected office buildings in the City of London and the West End. The following year Robert and David were able to arrange for the company to take over another property company known as the Rodwell Group and they then acquired the Watney Mann Property Company which owned a large group of properties purchased from the well-known brewers. The chairman of this company was Douglas Crossman, and Stanley Honeyman was also on the board. Douglas Crossman subsequently resigned and the likeable Stanley Honeyman, with his keen sense of humour, was invited to join the parent board. The next acquisition was Second Covent Garden Property Company, following which the late Sir Brian Mountain became Chairman of the main Group. Second Covent Garden's managing director, Max Keyworth, was also invited to join the main board. All these substantial mergers were carried out within the space of three years but, in 1971, Robert Potel resigned as executive chairman and was succeeded as chief executive by David Llewellyn. Since retirement, Robert seems to have changed his life style, living in a delightful, small country house on the outskirts of London where he concentrates on music and cultural pursuits, one of his hobbies being chess.

David is well respected in the property world and is a former president of the British Property Federation. I have often thought that he bore a slight resemblance to Michael Caine, the actor. The name of Star (Great Britain) Holdings Limited was changed in 1973 to the English Property Corporation and, at the time of the property crisis, David Llewellyn as chief executive had to face the formidable task of selling off large blocks of property to reduce the company's huge borrowings and solve problems in connection with several difficult overseas developments. The company survived this critical period and was able to weather the storm. In 1978 David resigned from these pressures and returned to run his own company and Stanley Honeyman replaced him as chief executive. Although there were many board changes, top management continued during the boom and the slump and Sir Brian Mountain remained as chairman until his death in 1977. His son, Sir Denis Mountain, then became chairman with

Philip Shelbourne, a Midland Bank director, as deputy chairman. They both resigned in 1979 when the company was acquired by Olympia and York Developments of Toronto, controlled by the Reichmann family. Stanley Honeyman as chief executive and Max Keyworth as one of the directors, remained as the old faithfuls and, incidentally, my good friend and former partner, Stanley Behrens, has been appointed part-time consultant to the company.

*

When Claud Goddard, that great Victorian character, died in 1944, Alec Brownfield Pope became senior partner of Goddard & Smith, followed by George Bourner. Alec Brownfield Pope was a highly skilled professional valuer and an expert on the Rent Restrictions Act, while George Bourner – a close personal friend of mine – was a promoter of business and a man of enormous energy and ability. He introduced a large number of development transactions for his special clients and in particular, carried out many deals for the Second Covent Garden Property Company. George initiated many central-area development projects with local authorities and built up a reputation for this type of work. He created a large management team for rent collections within his office and had a flair for selling groups of properties from one client of his to another and retaining the management of the buildings. With many friends and clients as shareholders, he promoted the early expansion of the British Land Company which was formerly an inactive tea company. George's favourite method of developing British Land was to acquire properties, but instead of paying cash for them he would satisfy the purchase price by the issue of shares. George Bourner's Trust, consisting of many of his friends, were large shareholders, but control of British Land passed into other hands and it is now a larger public company chaired by John Ritblat.

After a successful career, George became the owner of Bassetts Manor, Hartfield, a famous house on the borders of Sussex and Kent. One of the events of the year was his annual cricket match – his guests against his own eleven – held in the grounds of Bassetts Manor – to which many prominent members of the property industry were invited. Apart from the fact that many of the guests had not played cricket for years, the lavish hospitality of a super lunch with a continuous flow of drinks prevented some of them from being able to see the ball. The game usually turned out to be hilarious. George came from a middle class, fairly humble background. He was educated at Wilson's Grammar School at Camberwell and eventually was appointed chairman of the Governors. It was always amusing to me that, in order to raise funds for the school, George would present his friends with certificates nominating them as Old Wilsonians although they had never attended the school. He served as chairman of the Conservative Industrial Fund by arrangement with Lord Chelmer, the former Sir Eric Edwards, and received the OBE for his service. He relinquished the chair in favour of his friend and client, Lord Ashdown, formerly Sir Arnold Silverstone. He and his wife, Lillian, were close personal friends of mine. Although Arnold qualified as a barrister, he became interested in property development and carried out a number of important transactions. The most significant was a huge, modern development close to Victoria Station in Victoria Street which he built in conjunction with the Church Commissioners. A prominent feature of this extensive block is an open piazza between two sections of the building, giving the public an unrestricted view of Westminster Cathedral. One of the blocks – Ashdown House – is occupied by the Department of the Environment and the other is BP House. More recently, Lord and Lady Ashdown devoted their time to politics and public service. Lady Ashdown for some time was on the Westminster City Council and Arnold became a Life Peer. His ready wit during meetings enlivened everyone and his untimely death was a sad loss.

16

AN INSATIABLE DESIRE FOR SUCCESS

*

Meeting Maxwell Joseph socially for the first time – a slim, soft-voiced courteous man with a friendly smile and a sensitive disposition – it is hard to believe that he is the mastermind who has knit together one of the largest commercial organisations in the country, the Grand Metropolitan Group. He and his wife, Eileen, have a unique and fascinating town house in the centre of London with a terraced forecourt, garden and an interesting library. A casual remark made many years ago when I met Max at the Empress Club in Berkeley Street has remained in my memory. We touched upon the subject of books and I complained of not having enough time to read. He told me that, in order to appease his impulsive disposition, he would start reading half a dozen or more books at once and keep them all going by delving into each in turn. Eileen is unassuming and seldom mentions her practical approach to the layout of her husband's many restaurants and hotels. She also personally participates in redesigning colour schemes and decor, for which she has a particular flair. Max and I first met when we were both employed in the West End Estate Office of Dudley Samuel & Harrison. It is characteristic of Max that he has not forgotten his early, more humble life and old friends in the property world. Only recently he undertook to be host to the newly formed 'Old Guards' Luncheon Club which I was privileged to attend with a few selected members of the property industry. The lunch was held in the impressive and historic pillared dining room of Trumans Brewery in Brick Lane – no longer a salubrious part of the East End of London.

Max's early career illustrates that doting parents need not despair if their children show no scholastic promise. Max failed the Regent Street Polytechnic entrance examination and, despite private tutoring, learnt nothing until his father, in sheer desperation, sent him to Pitman's Business School. There, he passed shorthand, typing and book-keeping exams with flying colours. These skills enabled him to secure a job at 30/- a week, working ten hours a day in the estate agent office of Ernest Owers in West Hampstead. Owers was a wealthy, elderly man, but not over-generous with his staff. There was no commission for selling houses, but 2/6d per week for four weeks for putting up the firm's 'For Sale' or 'Sold By' boards. Max confesses that he made little effort to sell houses but only to get boards displayed. Consequently, nearly every garage and mews in the area had a board outside it – with or without the owner's permission.

The popular Charles Williams succeeded Ernest Owers and in 1981, celebrated his fiftieth year as senior partner. Max then worked for Ernest Durbridge in Thayer Street, Manchester Square, and later for Dudley Samuel & Harrison. He was sacked from the latter after a short period because Dudley Samuel expected quick results. Dudley Samuel had also received a letter from Mr Puddicombe, a Leytonstone draper, who complained that a small boy had been sent to canvass his business. This episode and other unsuccessful attempts to produce business caused Dudley Samuel to give Max a week's salary in lieu of notice.

At the age of 19 Max found jobs difficult to obtain so, with £500 given to him by his father, he set up his own estate agency, known as Connaught Hooper, in Bayswater and a small, private property company. His agency was successful from the start and business grew and prospered. When war was declared in 1939 Max owed William Deacons Bank more than £40,000. Max says he has never forgotten the Bank's sympathetic attitude in not pressing for a reduction of the debt until after the war. Today he is still closely connected with the Bank. He also tells me that Fred Cleary saved him from bankruptcy by signing a contract for the Aberdeen Park Estate, Highbury, on the day of the Munich crisis. Max did not feel suited temperamentally for an army career during the war, but his application for a commission in the RAF was rejected and he remained in the army until released in 1946. He has always been amused by his army reference: 'This man *might* be able to assume some responsibility in civilian life.' They were right!

Having had some experience as a clerk managing service chambers in the St James's area, Max became besotted with the hotel industry and started to buy small hotels in Kensington such as the Milestone, moving westwards to buy the Mandeville, off Wigmore Street, and a number of other hotels in the West End. One of the banks criticised him once for overtrading because he had an overdraft of £25,000. But Max did not look back, carrying out one sensational deal after another until he became a legendary figure in City financial circles. He is the man who took over Watneys Brewery – the then largest takeover transaction involving £400 million – which is recorded in the Guinness Book of Records. I am told that Sigmund Warburg of S.G. Warburg, the merchant bankers, adopted the practice of analysing hand-writing. Upon seeing the results of Max's test, he exclaimed: 'You will never succeed in getting control of Watneys.' He was wrong. Max Joseph has also catered for those who prefer milk to beer by acquiring the Express Dairy Company. During the course of his activities, he has taken over Mecca, a bank, a Scottish cemetery company, Bertram Mills Circus and the Pall Mall Safe Deposit Company. Within his Grand Metropolitan Group are many hotels in the UK and abroad, including the world-famous Carlton at Cannes. Apart from possessing financial flair, he is obviously a master of organisation and delegation of duties. I have never heard Max raise his voice while dealing with problems of the day, large or small, in his private office. He takes personal pride in the service given in his hotels but, on rare occasions, an enraged customer suffering from severe tension decides to write to the chairman. One day, Max was sent a beautifully packed parcel containing a sausage and fried egg – at least three days old – with the message: 'You will never get anywhere in the hotel business if this is a sample of your breakfasts.' I am quite sure he dealt speedily and efficiently with the complaint. It is significant that the activities of one man can still make an impact on the creation of wealth; his companies employ a staff of 118,000.

The workforce is bound to grow as, apart from the acquisition of the U.S. Liggett Group for around £175 million, it was announced in the Press in August 1981 that the incredible Max Joseph had planned the acquisition of the Pan-Am Hotel Group for £267 million. Arrangements were made for his talented takeover team, led by Stanley Grinstead, the managing director, accompanied by Clifford Smith and Michael Orr, to steal a march on their competitors by flying to a Pan-Am board meeting in the States to agree terms. In these days of recession and strikes I hope that the courage and enterprise of Max Joseph will be rewarded in the long term by increased exports and profits. In the New Year's Honours List in 1980, Max received a well deserved Knighthood.

*

Basil Samuel FRICS, like his cousin, Lord Samuel, is a highly respected member of the property industry. He received his early training at J. Trevor & Sons and started his own practice in 1934 in partnership with his late brother, Howard, as Basil & Howard Samuel, Estate Agents and Surveyors. When their company, Great Portland Estates Limited, came into being, their estate agency practice ceased with the exception of its management activities. This continued so that the brothers could instruct other agents to act for them without conflict. Basil served in the army during the war and rose to the rank of captain. On his return he and his brother carried out a large number of transactions in the City and Great Portland Street area and built up close ties with the Church Commissioners and Northern Assurance. Howard died tragically in 1961, but Basil has continued to run and expand the company with great success.

Unassuming to meet socially, Basil is a single-minded individual who never suffers fools gladly. He has positive opinions about people he meets and to him pomposity and 'yes' men are an anathema. In recent years, Richard Peskin, a lawyer, joined him and became joint managing director. Although he is a younger man, Basil does not appear to resent his unrestrained criticism of projects under discussion. They have an excellent rapport which results in a pleasant atmosphere engendering correct and speedy decisions. Basil is something of a gourmet and during a recent lunch with him at Claridge's, I noticed his requirements were treated with studied deference. His favourite dishes seem to be smoked eel, jugged hare and lobster thermador. I am fond of Claridge's. Under the direction of Sir Hugh Wontner, it has retained old-world courtesies and traditions – including its string orchestra. One of its quaint customs assures regular patrons of the same table and, when two regulars dine together, the discerning can spot who is paying the bill by seeing the table they occupy. A Governor of the London Hospital, Basil has taken a prominent and active interest in other charitable causes. He is reticent regarding his private life, has a charming wife, Coral, and a large family and is keen on racing. He owns a stud farm and breeds horses – an interest shared by Richard Peskin.

*

In 1959 I met the late Harold Wingate – a man of diverse interests including chemistry, law, art and the theatre in addition to the more commercial pursuits of finance, commerce and real-estate development. Harry, as he was known affectionately to his friends, was an impulsive character with many talents who changed both his career and his homes at frequent intervals. Having obtained a scholarship, he gained a degree in chemistry, worked for a time at Lever Brothers as an analytical chemist, then studied for the Bar, becoming a practising Barrister at Law and an expert on patent. At one time he financed a firm of optical manufacturers. Then he became involved in the arts by acquiring the Comedy Theatre in Panton Street and the Curzon Cinema, which showed specialist continental films. He was also once the owner of a number of cinemas. When living at Blackwell Hall, Chesham, in Buckinghamshire, he became interested in the acquisition and development of commercial property. He had acquired a number of investments when we met through his solicitor, Edward Footring, then at Harris Chetham & Co. So I started to help Harold increase his portfolio of commercial investments, culminating in the public flotation of Chesterfield Properties in 1960. With his enquiring mind, he enjoyed becoming personally involved with architects on planning matters and with the solicitors on legal matters – there were often lively debates. Among Chesterfield's principal buildings in the West End of London are the Curzon Cinema, the Columbia Cinema building in Shaftesbury Avenue and Chestergate House in Victoria. Unlike other property companies, Chesterfield has retained the majority of its freeholds instead of creating leasebacks.

A somewhat self-indulgent man, Harry was regarded by some as a difficult character, but this, and an impish sense of humour, was part of his charm. His son, Roger, after obtaining a BSc degree in Estate Management at Reading University, joined the Chesterfield team, became managing director and has run the company successfully ever since. He is an example of an able and shrewd son following a successful father. After living in Blackwell Hall – a delightful Queen Anne mansion – Harry bought a beautiful Georgian property, known as Squires Mount, in Hampstead with fine views across the Heath. But he eventually tired of this and purchased a site in the South of France at Cap Ferrat, adjacent to the late Somerset Maugham's villa La Mauresque. He built La Glorieta – a most attractive villa – out of local rock, with a swimming pool above. A steep, winding path descended from the elevated swimming pool and Harry made the journey many times a day to telephone Roger and his able secretary of many years, Miss Jeffcoat, to scrutinise the actions of the company and to criticise the directors, including me, so that we were all kept on the ball. His zest for development never left him and, in course of time, he tired of Glorieta, sold it and acquired another site in Cap Ferrat on which he built a handsome villa called Shoshana with attractive gardens and orange groves. A sensitive man, Harry was terribly conscious of the slightest noise while trying to sleep. He had been known to change his bedroom three or four times in overseas hotels, much to the consternation of the management. It was ironic that, when his offices were at 8 Chesterfield Street with his town flat above, the house faced the rear of the 21 Club where, during the summer months, a band played on the terrace in the evenings. The owners of the club, Harry and Bertie Meadows, had as many sleepless night as Harry Wingate – coping with the latter's threats and injunctions. His married life was most successful and he spent many happy years abroad with his wife, Minnie. He died in 1979 after making a large donation to charitable funds, to a research centre for the London Hospital, and after setting up trusts for his widow and family.

*

Some years ago on a winter holiday, I bumped into Sir Bernard and Lady Docker on the dance floor of the Palace Hotel in St Moritz. Nora Docker was dancing exuberantly and then, uninvited, decided to do one or two entertaining impromptu impersonations on the orchestra's microphone. We met again en route for the airport and home. The Dockers were sitting in the front seats and my wife and I found two spare seats at the rear of the coach. The extrovert Lady Docker embarrassed us by commenting in what seemed a booming voice: 'Look at them being carried out on stretchers; look at the broken legs – see what skiing can do for you – here comes another one.' Soon afterwards I called on the late Sir Bernard on formal business at Claridge House, Davies Street, in connection with the possible takeover of a public company of which he was chairman. He was a charming man and immediately recognised me. With a knowing smile and a twinkle in his eye – no doubt reminiscing on our recent meeting on the dance floor – he said: 'I am not a social snob but, before I discuss anything, you must disclose the name of your clients as I always make a point of being a business snob.' The transaction did not materialise, but I was impressed with Sir Bernard's statement.

*

Since my school days, I have known Samuel Sebba, founder of the property company, Warnford Investments Limited. We had mutual friends, often met at teenage parties and little realised at the time that we were to become closely associated commercially and professionally in later life. As a young man, Sam – the son of a timber merchant – was tall and good looking. Educated well, he graduated in law at London University. He then set up as a solicitor in Great Winchester Street in the City. He is a quick-thinking intellectual and is interested in chess and music. Because he handled the legal formalities on behalf of property-investor clients, Sam was tempted to speculate himself. After a while he found property development more exciting than his legal practice and, although he continued the practice, he formed Warnford Investments, a property company and started to carry out some important deals. He has carried out impressive developments in London's Portman Square and in other towns, but Sam is essentially a City man and his company owns many City properties, including a large office building with shops in London Wall facing Finsbury Circus and Warnford Court in Threadneedle Street facing the Stock Exchange. Sam's meticulous, legal mind and sense of responsibility has rubbed off on the management of his company. He invited me to join the board in an advisory capacity as a part-time director when he floated it as a public company in 1960 and I have remained ever since. Sam's brother Max, who is a qualified engineer, joined the board some years ago and became managing director assisted by Jimmy Andrews, the City accountant.

I do not believe Max has experienced many anxious moments – certainly not to compare with those towards the end of his bachelor days. He was in New York at the time and proposed by airmail letter to Helena, now his wife. For several days he waited agitatedly for her reply, when, to his horror, his letter was returned insufficiently stamped. Already in a turmoil wondering what action to take, he was obliged to fly to Los Angeles on urgent business. He decided to book a telephone call to his loved one – direct dialling was some years ahead. While waiting with some trepidation for his call, several business calls were put through to him. Then after a long time, in final desperation, he telephoned the exchange to ask the reason for the delay. The answer was that, thanks to his business conversations, the telephonist had cut off his personal call. The romance flourished, however, and he is now happily married to Helena.

Sam has since retired as chairman of Warnford and lives abroad. George Ross Goobey, former manager of the Imperial Tobacco Company Pension Fund and a director of other companies, who is highly respected in City circles, has become chairman. One of the most important transactions with which I have been associated was the purchase by Sam Sebba jointly with Maurice Wohl, the founder of United Real, of Bath House, Piccadilly for £375,000. At that time institutional investors were eager to invest life funds, but the penny had not yet dropped concerning the effects of meteoric inflation and their only concern was a regular fixed income and security. On Bath House, a leading insurance company agreed to take over the contract without profit at £375,000, granting back to the vendor's company a 999-year lease without any rent reviews at a ground rent of £15,000 to yield only 4% provided a new building was erected on the site. Sam and his associates were then able to borrow most of the finance required to construct the building known as Reed House, which is now let to Reed International. In today's investment market, with three- or five-year rent reviews as a protection against inflation, it is staggering to look back 33 years to 1948 when deals such as this were possible. Like most other insurance companies and pension funds, it has changed its policy and nowadays would not entertain investing in any project unless there was a short-term rent review.

I think it is true to say that Sam Sebba is a sincere and cautious man with a particular sense of social responsibility. Unlike Max, with his relaxed style, Sam has always spoken quickly, almost like a machine gun, and his brain seems to work with equal speed. At times he therefore gives the impression of abruptness – although he possesses a friendly and kind disposition. Sam shuns publicity and ostentation and is a family man with sons and daughters. I think it amusing that, in his early days of marriage, he rented a large house with a fine garden and swimming pool at Totteridge on a temporary tenancy for six months, but remained in occupation for more than 30 years. He has many hobbies apart from investing in building development. Due to the Sebba family's caution, their company has not over-traded but always has cash reserves.

17

OLD LADY'S INTERVENTION

*

After the property market had boomed during the first few years of the 1970's, the fringe banks, some merchant banks and even the joint-stock banks became over-optimistic and advanced huge sums to property speculators and developers. Many of these companies were over-trading, some were inexperienced and others were taking undue risks, hoping for a favourable town-planning consent or a speedy letting at an inflated rent. Success in the UK property market prompted several development companies to invest overseas. Insufficient knowledge of local conditions abroad led them to invest in unsuccessful developments, supported by bank guarantees secured on their UK assets. When the UK market crashed in 1973, some found themselves in financial difficulty.

Property development is essentially a long-term operation and bank loans are usually short term. Lending rates increased and suddenly the market crashed. Even some of the sound property companies found themselves suffering cash-flow problems. The banks held as security many million pounds worth of property on loans to leading firms of good standing and speculators alike. The amount of money involved was so large that not only the banks but also the UK economy could have been jeopardised if foreclosures and indiscriminate forced sales had been allowed to happen. The latter course could have brought down the market and reduced the value of securities held by the banks with adverse repercussions on shares owned by the public and pensioners. In fact, the Bank of England stepped in and saved the day. Gordon Richardson, the Governor, and the Deputy Governor, Sir Jasper Hollom, are to be congratulated on the prompt, calm and positive action they took to prevent what would have been a disaster. They burnt the midnight oil setting up committees and conducting meetings, resulting in what was called the 'Lifeboat Operation'. The housewives' maxim, 'a stitch in time saves nine', could be applied aptly to the immediate action taken by the 'Old Lady of Threadneedle Street', the fictional name given to the Bank of England. First, the Bank of England issued a directive to the joint-stock banks, merchant banks, liquidators and others to avoid panic and indiscriminate selling, but to reduce loans by gradual, orderly disposals. During the crisis many unsound property dealers known as 'cowboys' in the business were made bankrupt or went into liquidation. Even some of the stable property companies were affected – unable to recover in time from their immediate cash-flow problems – and these, too, were wound up. Strong companies with sound assets reduced their borrowings by selling some of their investments to pension funds and others. Many liquidators were appointed at that time, including Sir Kenneth Cork, who later became Lord Mayor of London.

Real-estate matters are normally handled exclusively by the Department of the Environment on behalf of the Government. During those first difficult months of the crisis, one of its principal advisers was my good friend, Sir Dennis Pilcher, a dedicated property consultant. Because of the seriousness of the situation, the Chancellor of the Exchequer authorised the Treasury to set up a Property Advisory Panel consisting of seven independent, voluntary individuals under the leadership of John Bridgeman, a Treasury Under-Secretary, with Geoffrey Willetts of the Bank of England in attendance. I served on this Panel, which included Arthur Green of Schroder Wagg, the bankers, Hugh Jenkins of the Coal Board Superannuation Fund, John Linbourn of Commercial Union Assurance, David Llewellyn of the English Property Corporation, Professor Michael Stuart of London University and David Watts of the Wimpey Construction Group. I was extremely impressed by the skill and brevity of minutes of meetings which Treasury officials prepared for us. On one occasion, in order to monitor market conditions, the Panel was presented with an extensive analysis of almost every property transaction which had taken place within a given period, based on information supplied by District Valuer's offices throughout the UK. The preparation of this massive document in such a precise form must have entailed a considerable amount of work by many civil servants. I was a little overwhelmed by the size of this document and I could not help admitting that it was far too involved for me to digest in order to express a quick opinion on market trends. I made the mistake of volunteering to prepare a concise proforma on a few sheets of paper, giving a brief summary of comparative figures, easy to analyse and assimilate at a glance. The Panel readily accepted my offer – and I am still arranging for a half-yearly summary to be submitted to the Treasury! Panel meetings continued for a time in case a contingency arose requiring special action. We were finally disbanded when the commercial property market stabilised once more.

*

It is frowned upon for any man to incur debts of £100 million which he is unable to discharge, yet William Stern, the former property man, found himself in this position. He was not a playboy, owned no yachts or racehorses, gave no wild parties but was, instead, a hardworking man with his own strong sense of principle who lived with his wife and six children at Golders Green. Stern, a Harvard graduate, joined his father-in-law in the Freshwater Group around 1960 and then set up on his own account. On his arrival from the United States, he had no experience of the property market in the UK. But as he was able, efficient and intelligent, within a comparatively short time his university training enabled him to grasp quickly the legal, accounting and mathematical aspects of property management and organisation. Despite his ultimate failure, he was found to be a man of his word and also able to make quick decisions. He appeared to have a burning compulsion to expand and he built up a huge property empire like a game of monopoly. Our paths crossed occasionally and I remember calling on him at his office in Kensington Gore. I was struck by his rather impassive, unsmiling manner when he described with cold, mathematical precision his corporate structure. He rattled off, without hesitation, the names of his parent company and other subsidiaries. I believe there were more than 150 of them. My impression was that he was man of considerable ability who lived in a world of figures without taking into account human frailties or possible changes in market conditions. In my experience, most tycoons expect their companies to stand on their own feet and dislike giving personal guarantees. William Stern was the exception. He was so convinced of the success of his property speculations that he gave personal guarantees to the extent of some £100 million. He seemed unconscious of the huge personal risks involved. It will always be a matter for debate whether any one individual on moral or commercial grounds is justified in undertaking personal guarantees as large as these. It is equally a matter for debate whether bankers and lenders should accept such commitments from any one person. In addition to commercial property, Stern's activities also involved several blocks of flats. His bankruptcy caused repercussions for many of his tenants, who were naturally worried about the future security of their homes which created public resentment.

*

The late I.D. Hillman, known as David, had no connection and is not to be confused with the happy-go-lucky butcher, Bert Hillman, who has been mentioned in another chapter. David Hillman – always well dressed, sporting a buttonhole and monocle – secured control of a shell public company known as Calgary & Edmonton Land Company Limited. Essentially an individual entrepreneur, he was perhaps not temperamentally suited to organise and administer a quoted company. I am told that, in private life, he was a sculptor. He appeared unwilling to deviate from his own views and was inclined totally to ignore professional advice. These traits caused him great problems and, in the twilight of his career in the property world, I was sorry to see this man, who refused ever to give in, fighting single-handed against almost impossible odds. He may well have been kind and generous in private life, but in business he was difficult and uncompromising.

Almost 20 years ago, he acquired from the Marylebone Council a freehold building on the corner of Marylebone Road and Seymour Place – formerly the Marylebone Baths. I did not handle the negotiations, but I had the impression that the purchase price was under £40,000 and my first acquaintance with Hillman was through banker clients who sought my advice on whether or not to provide him with finance to complete the purchase of the Marylebone site. I strongly advised my clients not to become involved, but time and again Hillman submitted alternative proposals – all of which I felt obliged to reject. Despite an office consent, he was still unable to complete the purchase. Then, by a stroke of good fortune, which normally seemed to elude his career, the Home Office required the site for a Court. He was asked by the then London County Council (LCC) to hand over his contract for £80,000. This he refused point blank and demanded something like £150,000, although he was still unable to complete the purchase. Hillman came to tell me he had been served with a compulsory purchase order by the LCC and asked me if I would act in a professional capacity on his behalf. I innocently agreed to do so – then ignorant of the background, circumstances and altercations he had already had with Marylebone Borough and London County Councils. The solicitor, Lionel Leighton, and I set to work to endeavour to conclude a sale to LCC to relieve Hillman of his financial pressures. When I called on the late William Webb, then LCC valuer, whom I knew well, he said: 'I thought you would know better than to act for such a difficult client.' He gave me the background of his hostile meetings with Hillman, who could not complete yet who refused to reduce his price to a reasonable figure which would still show him a good profit. But, having undertaken to act for him, I felt I could not withdraw. I tried to reach a private settlement with LCC, which was prepared to pay £80,000 plus costs. I advised acceptance of the offer, but Hillman was adamant and, despite the circumstances, preferred the case to be heard at the Lands Tribunal. So Lionel Leighton, Hillman's loyal solicitor, and I were obliged to prepare a laborious case. I could not produce a comparative undeveloped site, but, after a great deal of research, I was able to cite as evidence other office blocks which had been built and let in Marylebone Road and Euston Road. These, on paper only, may have established a value of about £120,000 for the Marylebone Baths site after deducting the estimated building costs, but I knew that this hypothetical argument might not be accepted. A few days before the hearing Hillman informed me that he had managed to secure the services of a chartered surveyor who would testify that, in his opinion, the site was worth £250,000. I told him that this was absurd – it would ruin his case if two different surveyors on the same side gave evidence quoting different valuation figures. The day of the case arrived. Lionel Leighton had briefed Michael Rowe, QC, to appear on Hillman's behalf and LCC briefed Sir Geoffrey Lawrence, QC. The other valuer was called before me and he told the Tribunal that, after 40 years of experience as a chartered surveyor, he believed the site was worth £250,000. When cross-examined to provide comparative evidence in support of his valuation, he admitted having no supporting evidence. He said his figure was based on his own intuition as a valuer. Then it was my turn. I was asked to give evidence, including my comparative figures. My cross examination by Sir Geoffrey Lawrence took two days, during which time detrimental remarks were made concerning my client which I could not defend. The Tribunal duly gave an award, dismissing the evidence of the other valuer and, as I had anticipated, regarded my valuation as rather high. It awarded compensation of £80,000 or £85,000 – the figure which Hillman could have accepted prior to the hearing. But he faced disaster as he had already borrowed more than £80,000 on the expectation of higher compensation.

It was a similar story in Wokingham, Berkshire, where he had acquired a huge farming estate in the hope of obtaining planning consent for housing. Eventually, after appeal, planning consent was granted, but it was too late for Hillman whose career was sad and unfortunate and it was a great pity that his tenacity could not have been put to better use. The land was ultimately acquired by Jim Slater's company but this also had to be baled out by the Bank of England who were eventually able to recoup the outlay.

*

Charles Gordon is dapper, witty and a charming conversationalist. A Cambridge graduate, he used to be a financial journalist on the *Investors Chronicle*. Through this job, he met the financial heads of many of the leading investment institutions in the City of London. One of them was Charles Clore, who engaged his services in Investment Registry – one of his companies. His task was to spot companies with potential for take-over. Later he worked for Jack Cotton, who took full advantage of Charles's social contacts with pension funds and insurance companies. His next step was to create a company linked with Hambros Bank and then to set up his own company in Old Jewry. Several pension funds put a stake in this company and backed him in his rapid acquisition of properties. But he ran into difficulties during the property crisis and a mutal arrangement was reached for Charles to relinquish his interest. He was married to Nadia Nerina, the famous ballerina who came originally from South Africa but trained with the Bolshoi Ballet Company. It was a loss to the ballet world when Nadia retired from dancing and went to live with her husband in Monte Carlo. Charles Gordon was an ideas man with a flair for promotion. Born into an artistic family, his mother was a successful artist and one brother, Max, is an architect and David, another, is chief executive of *The Economist*. Charles's late father was a frequent visitor to Covent Garden to watch Nadia dance and, as the commissionaire was polite and helpful, it was his father's practice to give him a generous tip to look after the car. On a première evening, his father arrived at the entrance almost simultaneously with the royal car. He never forgot the commissionaire's dilemma – looking each way, first on one foot, then the other, to make the momentous decision as to where his duty lay.

*

Barry East, a man of small stature and softly spoken, built a giant organisation which became difficult to control. We first met in the 1930's when we were both comparatively young. I remember that we visited Colindale to inspect some miserable second-class shop property together. He was then working as an estate agent at Jack Cotton & Partners' offices in Regent Street. In those days I would never have guessed he was destined to become chairman of one of the largest property companies as he was always unassuming and had such simple tastes. When I met him many years later in the chairman's office of Town & City Properties in Carlton Gardens I had the impression – which may have been wrong – that he was a lonely figure at the top of a huge organisation. I thought he would have enjoyed himself more when mixing with executive staff on the shop floor. Around 1956 Barry converted the shell of a defunct rubber company into Town & City. A few years afterwards he reached an understanding with Prudential Assurance which took a small equity stake in the company. The Prudential preferred buying properties to granting debentures and Barry East persuaded it to purchase many freehold sites on the basis that Town & City took back building leases. The company therefore developed very quickly. By early 1960, its development programme involved about £80 million, rising later to more than £200 million. The main area of activity was the UK, but projects were also under way in other parts of the world, including the US, Australia and Holland. Barry arranged several takeovers such as the Eldonwall Group with an excellent portfolio of industrial properties; Sam Chippindale's Arndale Group, with its many shopping centres; Central & District Properties, which was acquired from John Rubins and Barney Shine. Through this takeover, Town & City became the owner of Berkeley Square House. Then Barry acquired Sterling Land Company and Jeffrey Sterling's Sterling Guarantee Trust, with its Gamages site in Holborn, and the Earls Court and Olympia exhibition centres. As these companies were merged, their executives joined the staff of Town & City and several of them held quoted shares in the company.

During the property crash the company experienced serious problems because of high borrowings and interest on outstanding loan capital. Barry therefore handed over the reins to Jeffrey Sterling, in company with Bruce MacPhail – a financial man formerly with Hill Samuel – and Oliver Marriott who wrote *The Property Boom*. As a former amateur footballer and sportsman, Barry raised no complaint when he was dropped from the first team and Jeffrey entered the arena. Jeffrey has had a hard task, but, gradually, through the realisation of assets to the value of about £400 million, he has reduced the loans and brought the company round. Barry volunteered to forget the consultancy fee due to him on retirement until such time as Town & City was in a position to pay dividends again. The 5,000,000 shares he owned were, at one time, worth £3 million, but when he relinquished his position the estimated value had dropped to £800,000. Despite the disappointment he must have felt after reaching such heights, he still retains his sense of humour. A keen football fan, he is now chairman of the Berger Isthmian League. As I am a fellow enthusiast, we usually talk about football rather than real estate when we meet. He told me a story about Sir Stanley Rous, former president of the Football Association, while he was visiting China. During the speeches at a function, a Chinese member of the local team addressed Sir Stanley: 'Sir Stanley Lous, how do you feel now you have reached the age of 85?' He replied: 'When I think of the alternative, I feel bloody marvellous.'

*

Richard Seifert is well known to me both professionally and socially. He is an interesting man and perhaps the most prominent present-day architect. He has designed and supervised many important new buildings erected during the last few decades and, apart from the excitement of dealing with him in connection with the huge office complex adjoining Euston Station which he produced for British Rail, I have been involved with several of his other schemes, including the Associated Television Centre which he designed in Birmingham. After starting his architectural practice in 1934, he served in the army during the war, reaching the rank of Lieutenant-Colonel. He has a flair for original design and, despite financial restraints, has built some extremely attractive buildings such as the Royal Garden Hotel in Kensington, the Park Towers Hotel in Knightsbridge, Centre Point at the corner of Charing Cross Road and Tottenham Court Road, the Wembley Conference Centre, the Sobell Sports Centre at Islington, the London Press Centre and the new headquarters of the National Westminster Bank in Bishopsgate. A man of enormous energy, Richard is woken by his wife every morning at 5.30 a.m. – if my wife disturbed me at that hour, I should be very cross indeed! He also finds the time to be involved in many public affairs, is a JP, has served on the Committee of Management of the Housing Association for Discharged Offenders, is a former member of the RIBA Council and plays chess and the violin in what remains of his leisure hours.

Richard was once invited to see Bernard Sunley at his luxurious Berkeley Square offices to discuss a 'very personal matter'. There, Richard was commissioned to prepare designs for a mausoleum which Bernard

Sunley had decided to build for himself overlooking the playing fields near his country home in Northamptonshire. He and his wife, Josephine, were cordially asked to join Bernard for tea on the following Sunday to view the site. Richard duly drove down to Northamptonshire on a beautiful summer's afternoon and, as they approached the entrance to the Estate they could see the large open terrace where tea was being served. They were greeted by Bernard and his wife Mary, but at the same time Richard noticed an elderly, cloaked gentleman sitting alone in an atmosphere of complete tranquillity. It was Professor Sir Albert Richardson, who had been his tutor at the Bartlett School of Architecture 50 years before. Then approaching his late seventies, he had aged somewhat since Richard had last seen him, but his mind was still alert. In fact Richard quickly realised during their exchange of stories that he was still being treated as a student under the spell of the master. Then came the shock – he confided to Richard that he had been invited to Northampton to discuss an exciting commission to design Bernard Sunley's mausoleum. Later that afternoon, Richard took Bernard aside to inform him that he had decided to resign as he could hardly compete with Sir Albert. Bernard had innocently forgotten that he had invited two architects to discuss the same commission and they were both at this 'mad hatter's tea party' for the same purpose. Unhappily, both Bernard and Sir Albert died shortly afterwards and the mausoleum was never built.

Richard thinks the late Felix Fenston was probably the greatest of all property 'impresarios'. He is convinced that Felix had little appreciation of architects' drawings – he remembers one occasion when he appeared to be completely immersed in studying drawings held upside down. Multi-million pound projects calculated on the back of an envelope were almost daily occurrences at Felix's house in Hill Street where activities commenced at the break of day and ended in the early hours of the morning. For example, Felix once promoted an enormous scheme which could not be built unless backed by a huge amount of institutional finance. Richard was asked to prepare impressive plans and to be present at Hill Street for a meeting with a syndicate of property managers representing institutional funding groups. Richard relates that, on occasions such as this, Fenston's brilliance outshone all others and the massive, oak-panelled boardroom provided an ideal backcloth to his performance. In addition to Richard, a number of professional experts were present who had prepared figures and feasibility reports to encourage the institutions to agree to the funding. I am told that Fenston's board, which included the late Prince Radziwill and other expert property men, found themselves at this meeting short of a director. Felix wanted someone present who had considerable fund experience but who was not necessarily acquainted with the property. George 'X' was apparently the perfect choice; he knew little about the scheme, spoke little but yet would be a charming, quiet, co-opted member of the gathering. He was allowed to sit in at the meeting, at his own request, provided he did not utter a single sound. After three hours of discussion and explanations by Felix, everyone expected a unanimous 'yes' from the chairman of the syndicate and his colleagues. But, to everyone's astonishment, they decided against the scheme. Utterly shattered and bewildered, Felix insisted on seeing the syndicate's chairman to his car. He obligingly confided to Felix that they had all been pretty worried about the gentleman in the corner who did not say a single word – perhaps because he had something to hide. It may well be, however, that even the institutions did not have the courage to embark upon such a large undertaking.

*

Once, when I lunched with Fitzroy Robinson, another leading architect, at his offices in Portland Place, he complained that architects spend little time indulging their skills at a drawing board these days. Instead, they must do administration work, fill out forms, make application for town planning consents, give evidence at Public Inquiries and deal with claims by contractors. A man gifted with artistic flair, Roy has designed many important buildings in France and the UK, including Angel Court, an outstanding modern office building, close to the Bank of England, and Queen Anne's Mansions for Land Securities. His practice has also received a Civic Trust Award for designing Chailey Heritage, a home for handicapped children in Sussex.

Roy has had many interesting experiences in his professional life – amusing and happy, as well as bitter and sad. With all the frustrations he has suffered during the course of a project, he has one cherished memory. During the 1950's he was commissioned by Mr Benson Greenhall, a colourful character if ever there was one, to design a hotel on what was then a remote island in the Caribbean called Grand Cayman. Roy set off on a four-day trip involving four different airlines and finally touched down at Georgetown. He stepped off the small Vickers Viking aircraft – the only passenger to do so – to be greeted by a smart looking Caymanian dressed in white overalls. He lifted Roy's suitcase out of the baggage hold and led him to the airport building – a structure 20 feet x 10 feet consisting of four poles supporting a thatched roof. Inside there was a bench and a green filing cabinet. He put Roy's case on the bench, opened the cabinet and took out a hat on which were written the words 'Customs Officer'. Roy told him he had nothing to declare whereupon he was asked: 'Will you be wanting a taxi?' 'Yes', Roy replied. The man took off his Customs Officer hat, returned it to the filing cabinet and brought out another displaying the words 'Taxi Driver'. He led the way to a large and ancient limousine. Remembering that the next day was a Sunday, Roy enquired if there was any fishing to be had. Ertis Ebanks (which Roy later discovered was his name) promptly replied: 'Of course, sir, I will arrange some for you and will call for you at 10.00 a.m.' Ertis duly turned up as promised, wearing yet another hat with the word 'Fisherman' boldly written on it. For the next few days, Roy spent most of his time sitting on the beach designing, between swims, a new hotel to sit on the edge of a five-mile stretch of coral sand – the most beautiful he had ever seen. When his task was completed, together with his client plus a boy who carried a crate of empty beer bottles, he set off to choose a suitable site. They found a splendid spot and paced out the site from the plans, marking the corners of the proposed hotel by sticking empty beer bottles in the sand. Five months later a contractor from England went out to Cayman, found the beer bottles and erected the building exactly in the right position. The memory is precious to Roy because the job was such fun from start to finish – bureaucracy conspicuous by its absence, no town planning permission, no building regulations and no building inspections. It also gave him one glorious opportunity in his life to design and build just what he wanted, subject, of course, to his client's approval.

*

When I first met Eric Miller he seemed a pleasant, bright young man, keen and very ambitious, of good appearance and quick wit. Eric worked hard and well for the Peachey Property Corporation and became friendly with his chairman and managing director, George Farrow. And, over the years, Eric matured to become an effective senior executive. Suddenly George Farrow had a series of heart attacks and was obliged to leave the company and live abroad for health reasons. He was replaced as chairman and managing director by Eric Miller. With drive and entrepreneurial ability, the new chairman carried out many successful Peachey transactions, including the building of the Churchill Hotel in Portman Square. I sold him Lowndes Lodge, an attractive block of flats facing the Carlton Tower Hotel in Knightsbridge, and I believe the penthouse has since been occupied by prominent Middle Eastern oil magnates. My firm was also involved with Peachey in connection with the sale of the Carnaby Street estate. After conducting intensive negotiations with Eric, I had authority to purchase the estate for him at £3 million prior to its sale by auction. He promised to sign the contract the same evening, but I heard nothing further from him. As a result of the bidding at the London Auction Mart, my late partner, Ted Stringer, knocked the property down to Peachey at an increased price of £3,400,000. His action or rather, inaction, had cost his company an additional £400,000 but in fairness to Eric, if the sale room had not been well attended, he might have done better. He was prepared to take the gamble. By the time of the Carnaby Street deal he was fast becoming a public figure, much in the news, being appointed a magistrate, acquiring a private plane and developing a flamboyant lifestyle. Our paths were destined to cross again.

Cyril Smith, managing director of the British Rail Property Board, had instructed my firm to deal with a proposed commercial development on their behalf of a site called Euston Square, adjacent to Euston Station, in conjunction with Douglas Marriott of Douglas Marriott, Worby & Robinson, the architects. After several years' work, agreeing the plans, preparing a viability report and obtaining town planning consent for a series of office buildings, Douglas Marriott and I, accompanied by my colleagues, John Cook and Donald du Parc Braham, were instructed to present the scheme to the 'top brass' members of the British Rail Property Board. These included Robert Lawrence; Edwin Phillips, a director of Lazards; George Ridley, Trustee of the Grosvenor Estate; Cyril Smith and Ray Haxby. The scheme was approved and the Property Board invited selected developers to tender – with a provision that the successful development company took over and retained the same consultants who were advising the board on the scheme. Peachey, in conjunction with a financial group, had set up a joint company to consider British Rail development and this joint company won the scheme. The financial group later withdrew but Eric convinced the Property Board that Peachey could undertake the development alone.

In private life he continued to live extravagantly, becoming more involved with politics and parties. He was also a director of Fulham Football Club and developed more and more outside activities so that it became increasingly difficult to make appointments with him. Then he decided to terminate the appointment of Douglas Marriott, Worby & Robinson, and to appoint Colonel Richard Seifert, as the latter was better known to him. After McAlpines had started to build the scheme it became evident that Eric Miller was in difficulties. There was some doubt whether, as developers, they could meet payments due to the various contractors and consultants. In a desperate attempt to keep work going on this huge project, Eric convened monthly meetings in what is known as the Library at the Churchill Hotel. All those involved sat round the table and the meetings would include Eric representing Peachey; Ray Haxby of British Rail; Richard Seifert, the architect, with his assistant; Jack Neary of Banks Wood & Partners, the quantity surveyors; representatives of Matthew Hall Mechanical Services, and of Pell Frischmann & Partners, consultant engineers; and, of course, representatives of the contractors. Eric Miller requested Dick Seifert to record the minutes and asked for comments from each of the consultants in turn. He had a fiendish sense of humour, making jokes which were hardly appropriate for a serious meeting – although I must admit that most of us round the table rather enjoyed his amusing but pretty basic banter. On one occasion, when Eric as chairman announced the date of the next meeting, Jack Neary said politely that he would be unable to be present. Eric turned to him and said: 'What the hell do we pay you for?' and Jack politely added that he would be abroad on that particular date. Attempting to be a little facetious, I piped in and said: 'Mr

Chairman, wouldn't it be possible for the meeting to be convened abroad?' to which Eric replied: 'If you don't mind Eddie, I shall make the jokes here.' On another occasion, when Dick Seifert was shaking his head expressing doubt, Eric exclaimed; 'Richard, if you shake your head any more, it will fall off.'

Eric was notorious for not keeping appointments. Sir Edwin McAlpine – now Lord McAlpine – told me that he had an appointment to meet Eric at Euston Station to view progress on site, but, knowing the chairman's habits, he was resigned to possible cancellation or postponement. When he joined us for a meeting at the Churchill, Sir Edwin mentioned that he had already bet his co-directors that Eric would not turn up. On arrival at Churchill's, when questioned by Sir Edwin, Eric asked: 'Didn't you see me? I was sitting in crane number three.' Although Eric had entrepreneurial ability and could be kind and amusing on occasions his lifestyle overtook him somewhat. A Board of Trade enquiry took place regarding his activities and criminal proceedings had been rumoured. Before he was questioned on misuse of his company funds, British Rail carried on the Euston Square development themselves. It is sad that with all the promise of a thoroughly successful career, Eric Miller found himself in impossible difficulties due to his own indiscretions and he eventually committed suicide. When Euston Square was completed, John Cook and Peter Shaw of my firm had an anxious and responsible time letting such a huge office complex. Cyril Smith had retired as managing director of the British Rail Property Board to be succeeded by Bobby Dashwood. We eventually concluded a spectacular letting to a single tenant on a full repairing and insuring lease at £3 million a year plus outgoings. It was a happy ending to a large project which had been fraught with difficulties for Bobby Dashwood and Ray Haxby of the Property Board and their consultants.

The grandiose scheme to reconstruct Victoria Station for British Rail did not have a happy ending. Although it could have been extremely exciting and profitable, British Rail's first duty was to maintain railway services for the commuters which necessitated building in stages over a period of 15 years and the enormous loss of interest on the capital invested made the development unworkable. Howard Lobb, the architect who led the team with Professor Nathaniel Lichfield, the planner and other consultants, gave me three minutes finally to address the directors of the British Rail Property Board. I enjoyed announcing: 'I have been given three minutes to discuss a scheme estimated to take 15 years and I would like to curtail the time of both'.

*

The topping-out ceremony is preserved by building contractors as the climax to the construction of a modern building when the highest point has been reached with the last block of concrete. Fables and superstitions connected with the origin of this pagan custom are obscure and are said to date back to ancient times. It is a good excuse for a party to mark the achievement and good work carried out by contractors and their workmen, architects, engineers and quantity surveyors. The high spot of the ceremony is when a klaxon horn sounds for the workmen to knock off for a pint of beer all round. A topping-out also usually involves local dignatories such as mayors, local councillors and VIPs who assemble to partake of drinks and choice food. An invited mayor often makes a speech to thank the workmen and all others connected with the project and to bless the building. Should the building be completed on time, the developers or financiers backing the enterprise are likely also to shower blessings on the contractors. In these days of high-powered advertising and public relations, the topping-out function is used to introduce the location of a new building which will shortly be available for letting. For this purpose, the Press are invited to the party and a press handout issued which lists the attributes of the building. I have often regretted accepting invitations to topping-out ceremonies of partially completed skyscraper buildings which I felt obliged to attend. Many of these took place on cold, rainy days when shivering visitors are invited to climb perilously up flights of muddy concrete stairs without handrails in a panting effort to reach the top floor. Lifts have usually not yet been installed. In recent times many of the leading building contractors have introduced a more civilised and sophisticated method of organising topping-out functions by holding a first-class, catered, champagne luncheon party on the ground floor, leaving it to courageous officials to ascend the heights seen and heard by visitors on the ground floor through the medium of close-circuit television.

Sir Robert McAlpine, the contractors, related to me an occasion when, the formal speeches concluded, arrangements were made for the guests of honour to press a button to sound the klaxon horn to signal the hoist operator to send the skip skyward. Meanwhile, the men on the job were told to stop work and make their way to the canteen on hearing the signal. The ex-army man operating the hoist obeyed the last order. The Pipe Major, in full regalia was blowing his lungs out with 'Scotland, the Brave'; grand tune as this may be it is not calculated to engender a love for music when played 15 times on the trot on a bagpipe. The hoist operator, having downed his pint, finally dashed down many flights of stairs in Olympic style, pressed the magic button and watched the skip proceed on its flight to enable the ceremony to proceed to a happy ending. I remember being invited by the late Bernard Sunley to a topping-out ceremony on an important building near St Paul's Churchyard in the City. The Lord Mayor of London, in full regalia, accompanied by the Sheriff, trudged up numerous flights of unfinished concrete stairs to the top storey only to find that their host, the irrepressible and fun-loving Bernard Sunley, was not present to receive them personally. It was rumoured among the guests that he might be indisposed or was perhaps suffering the after-effects of a heavy, festive night out and unable to face such a strenuous climb the following morning. His son, John Sunley, deputised for him, carrying out the honours with distinction. I am sure no discourtesy was intended by big-hearted Bernard, although some members of the Common Council of the City of London may have raised an eyebrow or two.

*

There are two families named Wingate in the property industry – and neither is connected or related to the other. Harold Wingate and his son, Roger, of Chesterfield Properties, have been described in an earlier chapter. The other one is Maurice Wingate, who came to this country from central Europe and, in his early days, set up a factory in Edmonton to make mirrors. He was very bright and as a result of his own industrial experience established the Angel Trading Estate at Edmonton and started to build factories – his first venture into property. He later formed Wingate Investments, which became a quoted public company. Maurice was an effusive character and lived with his wife, Bella, in an attractive house facing Hampstead Heath, with a minstrels' gallery, situated a few doors from the house of the famous artist, Frank Salisbury. In partnership with others, he acquired the shares of the Fore Street Warehouse Company – a textile firm – in Fore Street, which was to become the famous 'Route Eleven' on the rebuilding of this part of the City of London after wartime bombing. No doubt Maurice realised that, by taking over the company, he could take advantage of a building lease on the site which was to be acquired by the City of London Corporation for the development of Route Eleven. He was thus able to obtain, as an alternative site, a City Corporation lease on St Alphage House. Maurice Wingate died while delivering an address at his company's Annual General Meeting. His son, Stephen, then assistant managing director, took over the Ellis Birk, the solicitor, became chairman. In later years, the Wimpey Construction Company acquired control of Wingate Investments and assisted by Trevor Burfield, they are jointly completing the construction of an office building situated in a depressed area, adjacent to Aldgate on the fringes of the City. The Minories development has provided an extensive office complex and just under 200 dwelling units – built by the Guinness Trust, a charitable housing association – to rent to those in social need. Stephan Wingate, however, is staging a comeback on his own account and has arranged to buy back from Wimpey the name of Wingate Investments and other development sites.

18

FACTORY BUILDERS

*

Many leading building firms have over the past decade created in-house industrial divisions to supervise their industrial projects. Similarly, pension funds and other institutional investors have tended to include a percentage of industrial property within their total property portfolios. There are a few outstanding men, however, who have devoted their energy almost exclusively to the specialised field of building factories and warehouses – one of the most prominent being Nigel Mobbs. He runs the international factory group, Slough Estates. Like his father, Gerald, he has a strong sense of national and social responsibility. A former chairman of the British Property Federation – an organisation which is affiliated to the Confederation of British Industries – Nigel is also chairman of the Charterhouse Group, part of a merchant banking organisation whose policy is to provide capital for industrial firms with growth potential. He is also a vice president of the British Chamber of Commerce. Slough Estates, of which he is chairman and chief executive, started big and have grown bigger – unlike other concerns which had small beginnings.

After the 1914–18 war the company acquired from the Government a 600-acre site in Slough, including many disused army vehicles. About 8,000 people were employed – nearly half the population of Slough – repairing and selling the vehicles and, to speed up progress, the work force was retained, taken off piece-work and a 40-hour, and a five-day week was introduced without anyone suffering a loss of earnings. It was a highly successful experiment in productivity. The company then diversified into constructing other industrial buildings. In addition to being factory builders the founders of Slough Estates pioneered the concept of providing social amenities on industrial estates – a concept they successfully repeated in England and in various parts of the world. They believed, as early as before the last war, that social and sporting activities were necessary to ensure the welfare and health of workers in the factories they built. The company has built trading estates in Birmingham and elsewhere in the UK, followed by others in Canada, Belgium, France, Germany, Australia and America. Among its tenants are leading international industrial companies. Slough Estates is now one of the largest and most successful industrial development companies in the world. The asset value of factories built totals more than £380 million. Among the company's strong and experienced board is Ronald Diggens who is well known to me. He is also chairman of the public company, Allnatt London Properties and of the Guildhall Property Company Limited – both of which have concentrated on building factories and warehouses. Ron has run these companies successfully with the able assistance of Leslie Smith, his first lieutenant. More recently he has felt obliged to relinquish some of his responsibilities and has resigned from the chair in favour of Leslie Smith, but still remains on the board.

*

Another company which has concentrated principally on industrial development is Brixton Estate. Its current property portfolio worldwide is worth more than £150 million. Started almost by accident in 1924, the company was founded by the late Percy Meighar-Lovett. Succeeding his father as head of a Hatton Garden pearl business, Percy decided to diversify by acquiring a number of petrol stations. After inspecting a petrol station site at the corner of Brixton Road and Camberwell New Road, he was persuaded by the agents, Savills, to buy six acres at the rear of the garage. The site had been developed by the Compagnie Générale des Voitures de Paris as a taxi-cab garage and workshops, but the company had failed and the premises had been empty for several years. Meighar-Lovett was attracted by the fact that he could use as payment French francs owed to him by Cartiers in Paris. He could not remit the money to England through normal channels because of French currency regulations then in force. The deal was done and the company was formed with the obvious title of Brixton Estate. No new development took place for a while as, in 1930, Meighar-Lovett nearly went bankrupt in the worldwide crash as he was once more owed money by French pearl dealers. He weathered the storm to continue developing property, including some factories and an office block, and the company went public in 1935. In appreciation of the way in which the principals had handled the development of the Napier Aero Engine Works at Acton, west London, to avoid labour troubles, they were presented with a silver replica of the Schneider trophy – given to Napiers to commemorate the building of an engine at Acton Works to power the Supermarine Napier, forerunner of the Spitfire.

Percy suffered two heart attacks during the 1950's and it was decided to bring in Harry Axton to take over from him. When Harry arrived at Brixton Estates there was a staff of nine. He thought the company needed a logo to give it an identity. Members of staff were offered a prize of 10/– for ideas, but Harry Axton did not like any of the entries and asked his wife for a suggestion. Mrs Axton produced the idea that the logo should be the shape of the Brixton Estate and this is still the company's identity. Harry paid his wife 10/– and another 10/– to the runner-up on the office staff. His advertising agent told him later that the agency would have charged a design fee of £5,000.

In the mid-1960's the board agreed to seek development opportunities abroad. Harry Axton decided to expand in Australia. The Melbourne office of Jones Lang Wootton provided a young man to escort him round an industrial site and Harry asked him whether he had walked round it himself. It was an unwritten rule that no scheme would be considered by Brixton Estate without the managing director seeing and walking over it. The young man assured Harry that he had walked over the site and, in accordance with precedent, Harry set off to do the same. Within two minutes he was up to his knees in mud and returned to the car to convey his thoughts to the young man in no uncertain manner. They made for the nearest shop to buy a pair of socks and, in his agitation, the young man drove into another car. His misfortunes were not yet over – he was involved in yet another traffic accident before the end of the day. Despite this, Jones Lang Wootton are still the official valuers to Brixton Estate.

Percy Meighar-Lovett and I found we had a fair amount in common from the moment we met. I started as a rifleman in the Territorials and he began his army career with a commission in the Rifle Brigade. He had joined the special reserve from the Officers Training Corps at Trinity College, Cambridge, when aged 20, and he had served in the First World War. Percy was socially minded and became chairman of the Nuffield Nursing Home Trust, BUPA and other causes, and his successor, Harry Axton, followed him as chairman of the former. His chief love, however, was his former regiment and he remained chairman of the Rifleman's Association for a quarter of a century. He once invited me to a Brixton Estate directors' dinner and I found myself sitting among many former Service chiefs. Completely outranked, I almost felt I should spring to attention. Sitting next to me was Field-Marshal Sir Francis Festing and I believe the deputy chairman of the company at that time was Sir Gervais Tennyson d'Eyncourt. I think Percy's policy was unique in having a senior board of eminent Service chiefs to adjudicate on principles and policies and to criticise the activities of the managing director – without interfering in any way in day-to-day business management.

Harry Axton, the present deputy chairman and managing director, tells me that in his early days with the company board meetings were run like an Officers' Mess and exactly at noon, Sir Gervais Tennyson d'Eyncourt, would rise and pour drinks for those present. As the drinks tended to be rather large, Harry says it paid to organise the agenda with difficult items at the end rather than at the beginning. Incidentally, Harry is a keen yachtsman and his boat Alpha II took part in the disastrous 1979 Fastnet Race. He ended up in southern Ireland with minor damage to the boat and to his own head. He was much amused when, on the day it became known that there was no news of his boat, Brixton's shares went up 3p and, on the announcement in the *Daily Telegraph* that he was safe in Dunmore East, they fell 4p!

Another leading developer of industrial property is Percy Bilton. A great character, he is a bright and clear-minded gentleman of 84 and still at the helm. When Percy was 14 his father died. He went to a technical school in Liverpool and then obtained a local job with a lubricating oil manufacturer. Within a year he was in a laboratory learning the lubricating oil business and he became head chemist at the early age of 18. He then joined Costains at Liverpool. By working at the same desk as Costain for three years he learnt a great deal as Percy Costain was the dynamo striving at that time to put Costains into a higher league. Percy Costain drove a 'Tin Lizzy' Ford but Percy Bilton and other members of the staff thought it was a Rolls Royce. Percy Costain moved to set up business in London and left Percy Bilton to settle the final account on a building estate near Middlesbrough. It was Percy's job to negotiate with Dorman Long, the steel contractors, bearing in mind a Costain instruction: 'Go and do your best to get £5,000 to settle all our claims.' The secretary of Dorman Long challenged Percy's authority as he was then only 23. But Percy assured him he had full authority and whatever they agreed would be honoured by Costains. He eventually settled the bill at £17,500, thinking he had done a good job and that he would get a bumper bonus. He was destined to be disappointed. All Percy Costain said was: 'Go back and finish the job and I will then give you a bonus.' Percy tells me he received only one £50 bonus for three years' work – he says it was like the Americans' 'fifty minute egg – very hard and tough.'

He decided to start on his own account, marketing his oil against Esso, Shell and Castrol. This period was apparently the hardest time of his life. As his brother was a book-keeper and cashier with Costains in London, Percy asked him how many houses they were selling and whether they were making a profit. When he heard the size of the profits, he was determined to have a go at building property. Percy persuaded Jim Bloomfield, one of Costain's foremen, and his brother, Fred, to join him to form his first company, the London & Provincial Building Company. He had hardly any capital and, after much searching, he found a small piece of land at Mitcham, Surrey, big enough to build 22 semi-detached houses. He knocked at the door of a caravan on the site to ascertain the owner and was surprised when an old man inside said he owned the land and would accept £1,200. Percy paid him a cheque on the spot for £120, wrote out a contract and deliberately avoided inserting the clause 'subject to contract' as he felt the deal was too good a chance to miss. He bought the property in his father-in-law's name, agreed to pay his father-in-law £6,000 on paper (although the cash did not change hands) and he then deposited the deeds in the bank and asked for an overdraft of £4,000. He got it because his references from his oil business were good. The houses were built and sold after being advertised in the *Standard* and the *Evening News* and Percy went on to build several other housing estates. Percy divided his oil business into two – his brother taking part while he began the southern section of Vigzol Oil Company at Greenwich. In 1962 he sold the company to Amoco for £1.25 million and decided to put the proceeds into property development.

When it became known that Percy had done this deal and had bought Ealing Golf Course, Major Allnatt – Founder of Allnatt London Properties – invited him to dinner. A thrifty man, the Major did not entertain Percy in a four-star hotel. Curious to know the reason for the meeting, he asked the Major: 'It is very nice of you to have invited me, but I am sure you have something in mind.' 'Yes', said the Major, and he pulled out his last balance sheet showing he had made £93,000 the previous year on factory sales and rentals. He said: 'I wonder if you would lend me £10,000 at ten per cent interest.' Percy replied he would think it over. But he says wryly that he could have done with a loan of £10,000 at ten per cent himself at the time. Seeing the success of factory development, Percy decided to enter the field himself. He recalls a further meeting with Major Allnatt when he remarked: 'Do you know, Bilton, the thrill I get when I have sold or let a factory? The next morning, I treat myself to a new razor blade.' Percy restrained his mirth to ask: 'How many shaves do you normally get from one razor blade?' 'Ten,' he replied, but even if I have only had three shaves with the old blade, I discard it and treat myself to a new one.' Although a highly successful business man, the Major was somewhat eccentric. From this point onwards Percy developed a large number of factory estates and built up his company, Percy Bilton Limited, concentrating on property development and civil engineering. He is still chairman of it and the company now possesses a property investment portfolio valued at about £118 million.

*

Nathan Brown is another developer who has concentrated exclusively on building industrial property. An engineer by training, at the end of the war he set up a manufacturing company in Manchester which was highly successful. Orders poured in for the company's products and its existing factory on the outskirts of the city was inadequate to meet the demand. When Nathan Brown began to search for a larger factory, he discovered that industrial space of the type he wanted was extremely scarce. After almost giving up hope of finding suitable factory premises, he approached – as a last resort – the liquidator of a 20-acre disused factory complex to see if he would rent him part of the property. The answer was 'no', but the liquidator asked Nathan Brown to make an offer for the entire complex. His first reaction was against the idea, but he could not understand why, with such a shortage of manufacturing space, no one else had acquired the site. A visit to the local planning office, however, produced the answer. The area had been designated 'green', with a temporary wartime planning consent for additional buildings. No doubt this had scared off potential purchasers. Nathan decided to take the plunge and made an offer for the entire site. With the prevailing shortage of factory space, he felt it would prove impossible for the planning authority to refuse an application to develop the site for industrial purposes. The seed was sown to produce a successful industrial property developer. Nathan's hunch proved right and he got his planning consent. He then gained first-hand experience of restoring and converting existing buildings into modern self-contained industrial units, all of which were speedily let. Impressed by the financial possibilities of letting industrial space, he sold his engineering company, let the factory unit it was proposing to occupy and proceeded to develop factory sites in other areas. Nathan Brown's company was eventually acquired by Harold Samuel and it was to become the industrial division of Land Securities Investment Trust, the world's largest property company. Nathan remained chairman and managing director of the division until his retirement.

*

Ronald Lyon is a pleasant and considerate man and, when I met him socially, he never gave the impression of being a property tycoon with aggressive energy and urge to build an empire. It is difficult to forget the magnificent Ascot parties he arranged during his hey-day. He is a perfectionist and at these parties every detail was taken into consideration for the comfort of his guests.

His career as an industrial developer began after the war in a somewhat unusual way. Leaving school at 16, he started making small, sectional garden sheds at £16 each. Immediately after the war timber and other building materials were available only through licences and were in short supply. In order to obtain supplies – albeit secondhand – he bought a number of war surplus buildings for their material content. This led to him buying Nissen huts and other buildings direct from the Government and entering into contracts to dismantle redundant wartime camp sites so that the land could be returned to its owners. The business grew until he was not only buying ex-army huts for their content but was also reconditioning and selling them on – both in the UK and overseas. The business, which was based in Suffolk, continued to expand. He dealt in large steel buildings – mainly ex-Government aircraft hangars which were in great demand for use as factories, warehouses and even as hangars for civil and foreign government use. There was an acute shortage of steel to manufacture new buildings at the time. He therefore started his own steel fabrication workshops to adapt and recondition the hangars. At 22 he secured his largest contract to date – to fabricate 26 large steel buildings for a major Canadian client, just outside Toronto. This established him at a very young age as a steel fabricator in both home and export markets.

His energy, enterprise and enthusiasm led him on to build industrial estates. He probably developed and built more than 2,000 factories, large and small, throughout the UK and Ireland in the ten years leading up to 1974. He undoubtedly made a considerable contribution to industry and his tenants included many leading firms. For speed of execution he set up in-house teams of architects, surveyors, engineers, town planners and solicitors and, in most cases, carried out industrial developments – even the largest ones – without the assistance of any outside consultants. He also set up his own construction and contractors' plant companies to speed up and improve the economics of the construction process. He soon controlled 11 regional offices in the UK – including several in Scotland, where he made a major contribution to areas of high unemployment by bringing in new industry. His organisation spread overseas to France, Germany, Spain, Singapore, Hong Kong, Indonesia and Australia. Ever practical, Ronald Lyon directly controlled every aspect of his company business. Because he designed and built industrial estates in-house, he could provide factories and warehouses more quickly than most other contractors.

Despite building up such a prosperous company and giving valuable help to industry, his firm came to grief during the property and secondary banking crisis of 1974. Because the holding company, Ronald Lyon Holdings Limited, was a private company in which Ronald Lyon personally held the majority of the shares, he had given personal guarantees to support about £52 million worth of the total borrowings of the company which, by early 1974, amounted to about £85 million. The borrowings were all secured against the properties, sites and work in progress – all of which were valued at £150 million. Nevertheless, the property crash was so severe that, when eventually sold, some of the properties failed to make a price sufficient to cover their mortgages. Ronald Lyon found himself in an impossible position. He was liable to be 'called' for a considerable sum – if not the entire £52 million he had guaranteed, certainly for more than £10 million at a time when the market was on its knees and his company was in liquidation. In the event the banks were both lenient and practical and allowed him to hand over his remaining assets to a trust for their benefit in settlement of liabilities under all his guarantees. Thus, in the summer of 1975, he walked empty handed from what remained of his empire – relieved of debt and not officially bankrupt. Following the sale of his properties, many millions have been repaid to the banks and their patient attitude has paid off.

Ronald Lyon has broad shoulders and it is impossible to keep a good man down. In 1975 he obtained financial backing to start a house building venture in the Middle East. He started a company in Dubai, he prospered and soon extended his activities into Qatar and Saudi Arabia. In recent years he has restarted his operations in England by forming the

Arunbridge Group in London. Already it is project-managing a huge industrial complex in Wembley and Ronald Lyon is masterminding the huge development on Vauxhall Bridge known as the Effra Creek and the 'Green Giant' which at Michael Heseltine's request are subject to an architectural competition. I am sure it is everyone's wish that Ronald Lyon should prosper once again and make a renewed contribution to industry.

From a fund of stories concerning his career, here is one of them. A property was being offered for sale by tender and the owners, not entirely satisfied with the first result, decided to go out to tender again, inviting only the three highest bidders – one of which was Ronald – to make a final bid. Knowing he was in competition with two other prospective buyers, Ronald was prepared to increase his offer by another £50,000, but was worried that he might be out-bid. Although anxious to secure the property, he could not make up his mind on the final figure which he had promised to convey to the auctioneer by 11 a.m. on the day the tenders were due in. Thinking of making an offer of £1,650,000, he was on his way past the Monument for a site meeting when his car was held up in a traffic jam next to the Monument itself. On it, he noticed a plaque commemorating the date of the Great Fire of London in 1666 and he made up his mind to telephone in a bid of £1,666,000. His bid was successful as he just pipped the under-bidder whose offer was £1,665,000. This is a practical example which illustrates that valuation is an art and not a science.

*

Just after the war in 1947, when I was concentrating hectically on building up my practice, I met Godfrey and Elsa Bonsack, a charming couple who hailed from central Europe. Godfrey was a talented artist, full of ideas and enthusiasm, and Elsa had an outstanding talent for interior design. Godfrey has flowing white hair, and is full of *joie de vivre* and Elsa is like a slim china doll, perfectly and elegantly dressed. I was fascinated by the layout of their studio flat in Chelsea for, instead of dividing the rooms with walls, they had used wrought iron gates to give an impression of light and space without inhibition. Having taken a flat on the top floor at 50 Park Street, Mayfair, I had no time to furnish it in my bachelor days, so I entrusted the task to Godfrey and Elsa. The furnishings included an original Bonsack flower painting above the fireplace.

With his artistic flair for invention, Godfrey started to design what became known as Bonsack baths – double baths and others of unusual shapes and sizes. The business grew enormously and eventually joined forces with Bradley of York, a joinery business which also built gliders and planes. Mr Bradley's son was educated at Gordonstoun and the firm decided to present a glider to the school. The Duke of Edinburgh expressed interest and arrangements were made for him to visit the plane and glider works at Slingsby, York. Godfrey considered this an ideal opportunity for the Duke to be introduced to the concept of Bonsack baths, although this was not scheduled on the Royal tour. A disconcerted Duke of Edinburgh said: 'What a terrible design', pointing to a double bath. Godfrey, the irrepressible, though unhappy to see the Royal reaction, jocularly asked if he could exhibit a notice above his shop: 'By Disappointment to his Royal Highness.' This amused the Duke, who confided to Godfrey that he was a shower man, took exactly three minutes to have one and never paid attention to his bathroom. Godfrey has since sold his interest outright and there is a department featuring the famous Bonsack baths in Harrods.

*

One day, without any appointment, I received an unsolicited call from Irving Feist, a fine American gentleman staying with his good-looking blonde wife, Dorothy, at Claridges. He wore the most English of bowler hats and told me he and his wife – both of whom were crack shots – were in England for their annual grouse-shooting expedition. He was a tall, robust figure with a strong, engaging personality, and he was also a high ranking member of the Boy Scout movement, representing the United States at jamborees in various parts of the world. He told me about Feist & Feist, his practice in New York and New Jersey, real-estate brokers, and said he wished to compare our respective practices. We exchanged views about modern covered shopping centres and found we had a great deal in common – including our moral outlook on professional duty. We became friendly – both commercially and socially – and I visited America to see some shopping centres managed by his firm and to meet his son, John.

I learnt that Irving was highly respected in the States and knew several developers personally. We decided to form a link to enable my UK clients wishing to invest in the States to be referred to his office and vice versa. At the time, my practice was considerably smaller than it is now and I was reluctant to lose my key partners on permanent secondment to New York. I was also concerned that the American real estate-market appeared volatile and speculative and less stable than that of the UK. Most of the leading UK agents had not, by then, established themselves abroad. In order to minimise the risk which I was nervous of taking at the time, I managed to set up a consortium – British Canadian and American Real Estate Consultants (BCA) – with offices in Canada, in conjunction with Feist & Feist, Goddard & Smith, Healey & Baker and Jones Lang Wootton around 1960. This was rather a one-off, remote control arrangement, perhaps doomed to failure because no one firm undertook total responsibility. We had impressive meetings with Irving Feist, George Bourner, Aubrey Orchard-Lisle, Douglas Tovey and Noel Taylor, but when it came to it, all of us were reluctant at that time to make repeated journeys to North America as we were all profitably engaged with UK business. The consortium's main project was with Bill Zeckendorf – regarded as one of the most fabulous US property developers and, in his own country, as a 'visionary'. The building with which we were all involved was the United Nations Plaza, a skyscraper office and apartment block, adjacent to the UN's headquarters in New York, well conceived to provide accommodation for delegates attending the assembly. When the property market declined, Bill ran into difficulties meeting his enormous commitments and loans. I am sure all the British participants in BCA enjoyed our friendship with Irving Feist. He was a man of enormous energy and, apart from his personal involvement in many hectic negotiations, he and his wife also conducted a full social life. The members of the consortium were treated royally when we visited New York. His sudden death after a severe illness in 1978 was a sad blow. Several years previously we had terminated the BCA office in Canada which had proved to be unworkable.

I will never forget one of my business trips to New York. There for three weeks, I called on most of the leading property operators and brokers, starting with breakfast meetings. I met many owners in New York, among whom was Irving Brodsky. The introduction was arranged through two New York agents who conducted me to his office to meet him. Brodsky owned a modern skyscraper in the centre of New York which I was endeavouring to purchase for important clients in London. The agents, acting jointly, informed me that their client was important and influential and that I should neither bargain nor question the price as he would refuse to deal with me if I did. I walked into his office and he asked if I was able to make a decision. I replied that I had full authority to do so. He then said, to my amusement: 'I am accustomed to making decisions and I only have to report to one source, God.' Then he said: 'And I have a hungry wife.' I told him that this should not cause problems because my wife was on a diet. He talked for a long while about the attributes of the building. I said nothing, continued to stare at him and noted that he reduced his own price on two occasions without my putting forward an offer. He then showed me a concealed television set built into the top of his desk of which he was obviously proud. I told him I had never seen one like it before and he seemed to be more enthusiastic about the television set than about the deal itself. Our deliberations continued with a further meeting at the Pierre Hotel where my wife and I were staying. Brodsky and I were joined for that meeting by one of the agents concerned, Gerald Sklan, a prominent real-estate financial expert who, at that time, was with Easton Dillon, the New York financiers. Friendly back-chat was going on which I thought would never end and I could see Pamela patiently waiting for me, sitting alone at the other end of the hotel lounge. In an attempt to terminate the discussion I said that my wife was waiting for me and I made the fatal mistake of pointing her out. Spontaneously, Brodsky walked over to

Pamela, gave her a hearty slap on the back and said: 'What do you want to do, honey, booze?' Pamela has had a very sheltered and conservative English upbringing and was staggered by this ungallant approach. Worse was to come. Although we had nothing in common socially with Brodsky, it was taken for granted that we would celebrate the proposed transaction. So, we invited him and Gerald Sklan to join us for dinner at El Morocco, the leading night club in New York. In the early hours of the morning, Brodsky persuaded us to visit a dimly lit nightclub in a basement called 'Eddy Condens'. It was full of smoke, blaring saxophones and couples dancing on a small dance floor. I remember that the Twist was in vogue and I was a little annoyed when our host said to a rather palefaced, tough-looking hostess in the club in an undertone: 'Teach this limey how to twist.' This stirred my British pride and I danced the Twist as I have never danced the Twist before – or ever will again – knocking over several chairs and lifting the hostess off the floor. Unfortunately, when I came back to London, Irving Brodsky called off the deal and sold his building to an American company.

The late Sol Atlas was a fascinating American property dealer I met in New York and at a subsequent Annual General Meeting of Dollar Land Holdings in London. He was short, wore sporty grey suits with enormous checks and chewed a large cigar as he spoke with a rather slow deliberate drawl. In 1967 I was instructed, together with accountants, Peat, Marwick, Mitchell, to report on the properties and management of the somewhat tangled affairs of Dollar Land Holdings. The circumstances surrounding this company were incredible and unique in my experience.

Sol Atlas was the main shareholder of a private company which owned a huge shopping complex, known as the Cross County Shopping Center, covering nearly 80 acres in a prominent position in Yonkers, a few miles outside New York City. It also owned a small shopping centre of less importance in British Columbia. Cross County Shopping Center, built before covered air-conditioned centres became fashionable, was an open shopping concourse. It contained 14 main blocks, two major departmental stores – Gimbels and Wanamakers – two Woolworths, 54 shops, banks, restaurants, a children's playground, filling stations, an eight-storey hospital and office block with car parking for over 5,000 cars. The other property, known as Southgate Shopping Center, was in Chilliwack, British Columbia, serving an isolated community about 70 miles from Vancouver. Sol exchanged the shares of his company for shares in Dollar Land Holdings Ltd which was floated on the London Stock Exchange in 1960 based on a questionable report by agents in USA and he became one of the largest shareholders. The flotation was sponsored by persons of good standing in the city, but the original London directors all resigned. The Company's prospectus included, of course, the two shopping centres. Sol G. Atlas Realty Inc was retained to manage the Cross County Center for an agreed fee but the management agreement was cancelled a year later. The prospectus also provided that another company, registered in the Bahamas, should act as consultants on future acquisitions. The company later defaulted on payments due to Dollar Land Holdings, and after action was taken it was struck off the Bahamian Companies register. After the flotation there was a legal dispute when Sol claimed that his wife retained rights over an access road to the Cross County Shopping Center. My subsequent investigation produced evidence that the valuation on the company prospectus was excessive. Due allowance had not been made for a new assessment of real-estate taxes and a vital detrimental clause in the lease to Gimbels Departmental Store had not been mentioned. Worse still, we could not contact the North American valuers concerned.

It was found that structural problems existed at Cross County causing movement and settlement. The centre had been built on marshland which had been reclaimed by tipping and, therefore, substantial sums had to be allowed for additional maintenance or structural improvements if the directors ever contemplated modernising the centre by covering the shopping concourse. The difficulties of sponsors increased when the company lost its management on site and the centre could not be managed from London. An arrangement was made to join joint managers – Joseph Tankoos Jnr, a well-known property man in New York, to deal with properties in the States and Elliot Yarmon, a Canadian estate agent to handle the properties in Canada. Each purchased a parcel of shares to establish confidence and they then proceeded to acquire a large number of additional properties and part interest in properties for which substantial fees were paid. The board of Dollar Land and some of the shareholders were not satisfied with the results – suspicious that the managers had conflicting interests as directors of the company and as practising real-estate brokers.

I went to America to try and sort out the problem. When I arrived in New York, I was met by a Rolls Royce with an internal telephone, driven by a uniformed chauffeur on the instructions of Joseph Tankoos Jnr. I declined an invitation to stay at the Del Monico Hotel – owned by Tankoos – as I thought this was inappropriate. But I learned from him his latest, successful sales gimmick to increase the hotel's popularity. One day, I was discussing Dollar Land affairs with him in a New York restaurant when he suddenly got up from the table and walked across to two attractive young ladies, handed them his Del Monico card and said: 'You have been awarded a free entrance prize to the Pretty Girls' Dance at the hotel.' I thought this an effective compliment as well as a clever means of increasing his turnover. He held Pretty Girls' Dances at regular intervals. It appeared that no agreement had been reached regarding the road over which Mrs Atlas claimed rights and that, reluctantly, Dollar Land's directors had agreed to pay her a specific sum. Contracts had been exchanged but completion had not taken place and Dollar Land's solicitors were instructed to take proceedings for specific performance of the contract. It had apparently been held up because of proposals to build another store on land adjacent to the shopping centre. Having visited all the parties concerned, I rendered a full report on the company to be circulated to all the shareholders in London. My recommendation was that all Dollar Land's properties should be sold to enable the unfortunate shareholders to receive back some of the capital they had invested. I advised the company to employ American agents to dispose of the properties and took no further part in the affair. The realisation of the properties was obstructed by legal proceedings and injunctions for over ten years, but may have ultimately been resolved by my good friend, Hugh Brackett, the former City of London surveyor who had the temerity to become chairman of the company.

*

A few years ago FIABCI, the International Real Estate Federation, of which my friend, Geoffrey Gay was World President from 1973–75, ran a seminar at the Tower Hotel in London strongly supported by the RICS – its secretary Robert Steel being one of the principal speakers – and well attended by continental brokers and agents. I had great fun addressing the delegates, and although it is hoped to form an international brotherhood, I must admit I have always been somewhat sceptical as to its success because our methods are so different. Perhaps, one day, we will grow closer together. I told the audience that we lived in a strange world. In the UK, a licence is needed for a dog but not for an estate agent; in France, a licence is required for an estate agent but not for a dog. It is probably a question of priorities, reflecting the animal on which the public bestows the greatest affection. I dealt with the image of the estate agent in the UK, describing the complementary roles of valuer, surveyor and auctioneer and pointing out that professional training nowadays, often at university, has converted what was formerly regarded as a business into a profession. I emphasised that it was recognised that the consultant surveyor or valuer in the United Kingdom would act in the best interests of his client even if he had to swallow the bitter pill of advising him not to proceed with a purchase or sale.

In France, West Germany, Belgium, Holland and on the Continent generally, there are few brokers who combine the services of valuers, building surveyors and consultants. With notable exceptions, most overseas firms confine their activities almost exclusively to introductions and brokerage and in some regions they may accept commission from both sides – a practice which is illegal in the UK. Many continental clients seek outside advice from banks concerning property and some large development consortiums have formed subsidiary departments to advise on and execute property tasks which would be a normal function of a UK agent. Accordingly, in France brokers protect their position by securing written contracts from their clients in the form of a mandate appointing them selling or letting agents. It is continental custom generally for client to meet client face to face and not to entrust the broker with complete authority to conclude a deal. I have great respect for the business acumen of the French and this direct confrontation between parties appears to suit the Gallic temperament. Negotiations are much more dramatic.

I had my first French lesson in Paris late in my career when I went there to conclude a lease on offices my firm proposed to occupy as an overseas branch. I was puzzled why I was asked to attend as terms had already been agreed. I was informed by my legal adviser that, although terms had been settled, intensive negotiation usually takes place at the completion meeting when patron meets patron in the presence of their agents and the solicitors. In addition, a notary has to attend to verify that the transaction is above board and that the appropriate stamp duty is paid. My firm's attorney in France was Christopher Mitchell-Heggs, and his colleague handling my negotiations turned out to be a most attractive and elegant French lady – Dr Hélène Annengand – who was also studying at the Middle Temple in London. I must admit that, when we were first introduced, I was pleasantly surprised and a little overwhelmed as in London most of my legal contacts were with pedantic, hard-faced male solicitors dealing with technical points. We both arrived early at the Paris bank where completion was to take place. In complete innocence and without the slightest thought of discourtesy, or attempting to cut out the introducing agent, when we were announced at the bank, I introduced myself to the 'patron', our future landlord, before his broker arrived. I was therefore dumbfounded when the agent appeared as she also turned out to be a good-looking, quite young French lady, and thoughts came to my mind of 'Gay Paris'. I was immediately deflated when this young lady rebuked me severely, but with some dignity and charm, for making direct contact with her client prior to her arrival. I tendered my sincere and unqualified apology in the best tradition of an English gentleman. After what sounded like a heated argument in French, in which the patron and everyone else except me participated, the transaction was completed and everyone solemnly watched me sign the document as if it were the Treaty of Versailles. Due to the presence of these gracious young ladies, an air of romance filled the office and I was about to suggest a celebration party. However, I swiftly changed my mind. Immediately I had signed the lease, the young lady agent placed in front of me her firm's account for commission for the introduction. Being accustomed to a more modest scale of charges, I thought for a moment that I was suffering double vision. I later learned that this was normal practice in Paris and I must admit that it is a perfectly sound one – it certainly brought me down to earth! In the

UK we usually submit accounts some weeks after a negotiation has been completed, except perhaps in the case of small transactions. In fairness, we are probably just as eager to collect our fees as anyone else and no-one can dispute that commission is legally payable the moment completion takes place.

During one of my journeys to Paris, I visited Howard Ronson, a bold ambitious man with a modern outlook. I was impressed with his apartment and intrigued by his two tiny dogs in contrast to his well proportioned figure. My immediate reaction was that he was a playboy but I found he was on the ball, had strong views and a complete grasp of the intricacies of development. He did not have a happy time in the family building business in the UK which he left at a young age, became a local resident in Paris, lined up some key sites in the heart of the City on his own account and carried out several highly successful developments. Howard has now turned his attention to New York where he has had almost instant success and the property market there may well suit his temperament.

*

David Goldstone is a shrewd, logical Welshman who is a solicitor. He is a team man, a keen and competitive squash player, has sat on the World Football Association Council and is chairman of Cardiff City Football Club. He has devoted much of his time to dealing with flats and is chairman and managing director of Regalian Properties which owns about 4,000 flats in the London area. Like other experienced property men, David Goldstone and the Regalian board have the necessary expertise to take a long-term view and to employ qualified agents to deal with maintenance and management of their buildings.

In recent years many insurance companies have ceased investing in residential property because rent control and other legislation has resulted in uneconomic returns. They – like other landlords – often found themselves in conflict between duty to their own policy holders and shareholders and their wish to exercise lenience and sympathy towards unfortunate tenants finding it hard to make ends meet. Not all landlords are altruistic – during my career, I have met all types. And I have come to the conclusion that not all landlords are bad and not all tenants are good! Around 1977–78 insurance and property investment companies began to sell off blocks of flats. A few property speculators, some of whom were of doubtful standing, seized the opportunity to buy residential property obtainable at comparatively low prices because rents receivable were regulated and therefore low. The speculators figured they could in time make a capital profit by selling a long leasehold interest to each tenant of a block and carry the risk of those tenants who were not in a position to buy. This procedure became known as a 'flat break-up' scheme and, although I have not been involved personally in such transactions, I was recently asked by solicitors to address a newly formed tenants' association of a good class block of flats in north-west London.

The block had been purchased speculatively by one of William Stern's companies which went into liquidation during the property crash. The liquidators were prepared to recommend a sale of the freehold for just over £1 million and a building society had tentatively agreed to provide mortgages for individual purchasers. At a tenants' association meeting I suggested that as many tenants as possible should offer to purchase their flats at a discount below the normal vacant possession value. Unfortunately a long delay ensued and the association members were unable to agree. I could not, therefore, put forward on their behalf a concerted offer to purchase and in the meantime a speculator acquired the freehold. While the tenants were still deliberating, an unnamed Iranian purchaser had stepped in and acquired the block over the heads of the association – thus providing a profit to the original purchaser. Although the buyer had signed a contract and paid a deposit, he was unable to complete on time because of an embargo on capital remitted from a foreign bank on the due date. Agents acting for him negotiated a staggered completion and arranged bridging finance with a merchant bank to enable the Middle East buyer to complete; only on condition, however, that he produced within three weeks signed contracts from a number of tenants in the block to recover the whole of the finance required. I attended another tenants' association meeting with David Sayers of my firm. Sales were arranged to 34 tenants within three weeks at an average price of £50,000 – representing a 50 per cent discount on the estimated open-market value. We had thus managed to convert disaster into benefit for many of the tenants. David Goldstone has told me he thinks 'break-up' is an unfortunate term as the process need not be a destructive exercise. Where legitimate purchasers are prepared to take a reasonably long-term view and are willing to resell to tenants at fair discount prices, it becomes a case of buying wholesale and selling retail. A purchaser has to take the risk of tenants refusing to buy and he must then hold the remnants of a block for an unknown period. But there are speculators who are disreputable and who neglect repairs and maintenance of the buildings they buy.

There are many bizarre stories from West-End blocks of flats where wealthy Oriental tenants have purchased expensive apartments but have not yet become accustomed to English habits and etiquette. I know of a case where, innocently, live snakes were brought into a flat. There was a restriction in the lease against dogs, but there was no bar against reptiles. In another important West-End block, tenants complained bitterly of an unusually strong smell of Oriental cooking pervading the lift-shaft. The reason was revealed when a barefooted cook, employed by one of the occupants, entered the lift containing several other tenants in order to visit his master on a lower floor.

19

THE ENTERPRISE OF AN ANCIENT DUKEDOM

*

In the United Kingdom there are few private individuals who own large estates and even the well-known ones who reach the headlines in the Press are usually involved in companies in which the public and institutions are also shareholders. In central London, the Crown Estate ably managed by Sir Oliver Chesterton and Richard Caws, the Church Commissioners and the Trustees of the Portman, the Howard de Walden, the Cadogan and the Grosvenor Estates are among other large well-managed estates of high repute. The pension funds may in future be taking the place of the past inherited estate owners. In recent years, due to increased salaries and corresponding pensions, the large pension funds of the Coal Board, the British Steel Corporation, the Electricity Supply Board, the Gas Board, the Railway Board and a whole host of others, including many insurance companies who manage large funds on behalf of a number of smaller pension funds, have recently become extremely large owners of property. In addition to direct ownership of property, many of the pension funds and insurance companies also own large blocks of shares in quoted public property companies. In 1981 the Coal Board alone were reputed to have £500 million in direct property ownership.

One of the most outstanding estates is the Grosvenor Estate, which has a most fascinating historical background. The Duke of Westminster's family can be traced back to Hugh Lupus, who was a nephew of William the Conqueror, and the name 'Grosvenor' is derived from 'Le Gros Veneur' meaning 'Chief Huntsman', the title accorded to Hugh Lupus. It is interesting that the names of many of the streets in Mayfair, Belgravia, Pimlico and Chester have historical connections with past members of the family and their associates. It is recorded that Sir Thomas Grosvenor married a Miss Mary Davies, Heiress of the Manor of Ebury, Davies Street off Berkeley Square; Ebury Street, Belgravia, Lupus Street, Pimlico and many others are examples. The family are quite remarkable as, although the estate is one of the oldest Dukedoms in the country, unlike some estates satisfied to continue their survival by opening their historic homes for admission to the public, the Duke of Westminster's Estate is a virile organisation making a vital contribution to the economy and the environment by carrying out a large number of modern property developments in various parts of the country and in competition with other developers. I have been fortunate to know George Ridley, who was for many years one of the Trustees. An astute adviser and a man of exceptional ability, George started his career as an assistant forester on the Duke of Westminster's Eaton Estate in Cheshire. The agent was then Major Basil Kerr, whose task – apart from that of managing the Estate – was to be a friend and confidant of the landowner. The Duke was a very fine imposing figure and the Major was outstanding in his appearance, his dress and confident demeanour. One morning, I am told, George Ridley was instructed to appear before him at the Estate Office and was warned that, as the sub-agent for the Chester Estate had died, the interview would be in connection with a new appointment. The question and answer session which ensued between the Major and George went as follows:- 'Do you know anything about urban property?' 'No, Sir'; 'Do you know anything about property construction and maintenance', 'No, Sir'; Do you know anything about property rental?' 'No, Sir'; 'Do you know anything about rates and taxes?' 'No, Sir'; 'You'll do, I want you to take over the Chester Estate – start next Monday!'

It is largely through the shrewd advice of George Ridley, without any professional qualifications, that the Estate in Mayfair and Belgravia, Scotland, Chester and elsewhere is still thriving. He boldly decided to develop an area of the north-west of Scotland known as the Reay Forest Estate where unemployment was rife. The Estate redeveloped the harbour at Kinlochbervie to boost the local fishing industry and provided public transport and other industries to revitalise the area. Because he wished to ensure that the assets of the Estate were widely spread, taking a long-term view George negotiated the purchase of a large industrial estate in Canada requiring a heavy injection of capital for its development. At about the same time the second Duke died and, as a large amount of Estate Duty was payable, George arranged for the Canadian scheme to be developed in association with Laings, the contractors. A joint company, Grosvenor Laing Development Company, was formed for the purpose. Apart from selling less valuable parts of the London Estate, such as Pimlico, George and his other Trustees were able to hold on to the extremely valuable empire of Mayfair and Belgravia intact. They also carried out an extensive redevelopment programme in Eaton Square, which is recognised as one of the most fashionable residential estates in London. The Trustees of the Estate have always employed first-class advisers and their skilful management of the London Estate is a shining example to town planning authorities.

When I first came in contact with the Grosvenor Estate, the Chief Surveyor dealing with the London operation was Geoffrey Singer, a chartered surveyor who for many years was trained by Arbour Rutter Waghorn and Brown, whose offices were at 1 Mount Street, on the corner of Berkeley Square. Geoffrey Singer was a very able property manager for the Estate in London. He had a keen sense of humour and thoroughly enjoyed his job during the property boom when he was able to serve the

Estate well by securing maximum prices from those who wished to acquire long leases of commercial property to carry out developments. I remember Geoffrey asking me if I knew a certain property speculator whom he had never met but who had the temerity to address him in a letter as 'Dear Geoffrey'. He was writing in connection with a proposed purchase of a lease of a corner site near Eaton Square. Geoffrey considered his mode of address impertinent and he told me, with a knowing smile, that he intended to charge the party in question an extra £100,000 on the premium for his lease for such an indiscretion – and he carried out his threat. Geoffrey sometimes lunched at the club which I patronised for a time in Grosvenor Street. The proprietor, Rico Dajau, was often hard up and Geoffrey used to joke that, after signing the bill, he had to rush back quickly to the Grosvenor Office in Davies Street or the bill would reach the office before he did. When I met him after his retirement at a lavish lunch laid on by the 'Old Guards' – the older members of the profession – he looked round at the impressive array of foods and wines and remarked: 'Another example of meals on wheels.'

Upon Geoffrey's retirement Jimmy James was appointed surveyor to the London Estate and, when he became a Trustee of the Estate in 1971, another chartered surveyor, Stanley Coggan, formerly with John D. Wood & Co, assumed responsibility for the management of the Estate's London properties. Jimmy James, president of the RICS for 1980–81, told me that it took Geoffrey 11 weeks to make up his mind whether or not the Estate should engage him. Geoffrey, with his customary candour, admitted to Jimmy, some years later, that he had in fact preferred someone else who had turned down the job. Jimmy also informed me smilingly that he can deny the rumour that Geoffrey's blue pin-stripe suits came from a bale of cloth which fell off the back of a lorry going round a corner in Eaton Square during the war. He has also scotched the rumour that Geoffrey retired prematurely because the last suit from the bale had worn out.

George Ridley still acts as adviser to the Estate of the second Duke's widow, but retired as a Trustee in 1971. He arranged for a joint company with Laings, the contractors, to be set up in the UK and engaged Kenneth Eyles as general manager of the Grosvenor Laing Development Company. Kenneth Eyles, previously employed with the Ministry of Works, was an extraordinary man. Schooled in bureaucratic administration procedures of the Ministry for no less than 20 years, he was an extrovert by nature and a forthright entrepreneur. He readily admitted that he sought to make 'profits' for the Grosvenor Estate, a word which was seldom used in the hierarchy of the Duke's advisers. Kenneth's bold and blunt outlook appealed to George Ridley and Kenneth informed me that he was proposing to instruct me and my office to help transform the centre of Chester into a modern covered shopping centre. When questioned by

George on why he wished to appoint me, Kenneth's answer was: 'If he is good enough for Isaac Wolfson, he is good enough for me. He is a poor tennis player, but you have only to stroll with him from his office to Claridges for lunch to realise that to be unknown to Edward Erdman in the property development world is a fate worse than banishment.'

I had the honour to be invited for the first time to lunch at the Grosvenor Estate Office in Davies Street. During the course of lunch, George said: 'We seldom invite estate agents for lunch; you have been made an exception and, if you do not make a success of the Chester Shopping Centre, you will never be invited again.' The Grosvenor Estate owned a large area of land at the rear of the finest shopping position in Chester. The area was approached through a narrow passage at the side of the Grosvenor Hotel also owned by the Estate. The main retailers adjacent to this land were Browns of Chester, a large departmental store belonging to the Peter Robinson arm of Montague Burton. Browns was a highly successful, extensive store at the hub of Chester's main shopping area. Behind the store was a goods entrance abutting on to the land owned by the Grosvenor Estate. The key to developing the rear land was to come to terms with Montague Burton. Browns had to be persuaded to drop their back entrance to basement level and to convert their existing one into window frontage. This was to face the Piazza – focal point of the new precinct. After intensive negotiations direct with Raymond Burton of Montague Burton, I managed to get him to agree to the scheme. I was invited to lunch again!

The public presentation of plans for the Chester Precinct was made by George Ridley and Kenneth Eyles in the ballroom of the Grosvenor Hotel at a champagne reception. There was a model of the shopping complex for guests to see and, the Mayor and everyone in Chester who mattered – and also those who thought they did – were invited. As the planning application had not yet been submitted, the Mayor arrived without his official chain of office. But I remember the Sheriff appearing in full regalia. The precinct model was exhibited in an arcade the following day and the public acclaim which greeted the scheme eased the bureaucratic restrictions and delays of the kind normally prevalent in ancient cities such as Chester. The development has been an overwhelming success. It is an example of carefully blending a new shopping centre with an old street pattern, without detracting from its character or antiquity. When building work was complete, Bob McKenzie, a vigorous member of the practice, and his team of negotiators dealing with shop lettings, had no difficulty in introducing first-class retailers to trade in the new centre. George Ridley afterwards came to an amicable agreement to take over Laings' share interest in the Grosvenor Laing Development Company and he changed the name to Grosvenor Estate Commercial Developments Limited.

After promoting many profitable deals for the company, John Walshe was appointed managing director and Kenneth Eyles became deputy chairman. At the end of 1979 Kenneth retired as deputy chairman to be succeeded by Jimmy James, Trustee of the Grosvenor Estate. John Walshe, with Dick de Broekert and Peter Martin under the direction of George Ridley and Jimmy James, have created a modern development company which is part of one of the oldest estates in the country. GECD competes on favourable terms with other developers and property companies. It has established for itself a reputation for carrying out successful developments in participation with local authorities and builds shops, offices and industrial buildings wherever there is a public need. The GECD team has carried out spectacular developments at Chester, Runcorn, Lewisham, Northampton, Staines, Macclesfield and Wrexham. Unlike some of the older landed estates whose fortunes are declining, the Grosvenor Estate should continue to prosper under the leadership of the present young Duke, who was married in 1978 and who now has a family.

*

Local Town Planning Officers are about as popular as football referees and although I jocularly refer to them as 'the blighters', I have a high regard for dedicated planners – many of whom I number among my friends. In our democratic society, it is not always easy for planners to make decisions in the best interest of the community as a whole. They are sometimes frustrated by political party pressure, public participation dominated by individuals with an axe to grind and even opposed by other Government departments. My good friend Sir Dennis Pilcher, when he became president of the RICS, summed up the situation in a few words: 'Town planning is the economic use of land for the social, commercial and religious needs of the community.' The word 'economic' is often the key and some planning authorities impose conditions on developers which are uneconomic and impracticable. The character of a neighbourhood can alter and become blighted if town planning decisions are long delayed.

One example which comes to mind was my meeting many years ago with the late William Webb, an honest-to-goodness Cockney character and a former valuer of the London County Council. Clients of mine had acquired the leasehold interest of a block of shops and flats on the south side of Shaftesbury Avenue. The LCC were the freeholders and William Webb, as a practical man who knew the properties had little depth, said: 'Arrange for your clients to buy the freehold properties in Gerrard Street at the rear of the Shaftesbury Avenue shops and I shall then recommend the Council to carry through a joint development scheme. If we redevelop the whole block, we will clean up the section of Soho containing several seamy night clubs and dubious occupiers.' Under normal circumstances, the purchasers would not have acquired buildings in Gerrard Street as an investment but they did so in this case because the joint development scheme was an attractive proposition. Having acquired the properties and drawn up plans, the planning authority refused to make a decision. I approached the officials time and again over many years, but was informed that no decision would be taken until the future of Piccadilly Circus had been determined. I could never understand why. During the delay, a large number of Chinese traders established themselves in Gerrard Street and, when I last approached the planners, they told me that development was no longer contemplated as Gerrard Street had become the recognised Chinese Quarter, was regarded as part of the London Scene and there would be political pressure if it were disturbed. Reconstruction will become necessary in the future.

Many distinguished men such as the eminent QC, George Dobry, have urged the Government to speed up the planning process. I believe that planning should be outside the scope of party politics. Local government officials, subsidised by the ratepayer, are inclined to become oblivious to the cost of time. Apart from blighting an entire area, planning delays can cost developers thousands of pounds in interest on the capital invested to purchase the land. Painstaking plans representing years of work, expense and effort by architects, quantity surveyors and engineers are often rejected without sympathy. Large-scale property development is not an occupation for the fainthearted. In addition, town planning delays and slow performance by building contractors has made rents in this country less competitive and sometimes encourages multi-national firms to seek other shores.

There have been perhaps 20 different plans in an attempt to change Piccadilly Circus over the last 50 years. However, something has been achieved at last. The improvements to the Circus today are due to a great extent to the untiring efforts of one man, Councillor Herbert (Sandy) Sandford. He moved from Westminster City Council where he served for many years to the GLC to become chairman of the Central Area Planning Committee. Under the former leadership of Sir Horace Cutler, Sandy was the right man for the job as he had been an indomitable fighter who served in the RAF Pathfinders Squadron during the war and had been decorated for his bravery. With the able assistance of Dr John Parker of the GLC Planning Department and of Ian Lacey, Westminster's chief architect, Sandy piloted the new road and improvement scheme for Piccadilly Circus which was eventually adopted. Not only did he have to withstand sniping from the opposing political party but he also faced opposition from many pressure groups who had selfish or commercial motives to prevent the redevelopment and cleaning up of the Circus. They made representations to MPs in some cases supported by the media – under the guise of championing the cause of community and so-called 'culture'. Politicians and government officials are often easy prey for pressure groups who are always given a full hearing in accordance with the democratic principle of public participation in planning decisions. Sandy patiently dealt with all the objectors and sponsored a workable plan to preserve Piccadilly's scheduled buildings, improve the environment and segregate pedestrians from traffic flow. It is hoped that the Circus will eventually be improved on the lines of the continuity of Regent Street and that in future, some of the unattractive parts of Old Compton Street and Soho will also be upgraded. The Electricity Supply Pension Fund is, I am told, investing some £70 million in the reconstruction of the former Trocadero and my friend Barry White has been dashing backwards and forwards to the States to introduce a novel entertainment complex on the site. The bite of the recession and the down-turn in West End retail rents may delay some of the contemplated developments but only temporarily I hope.

*

In the 1930's when I was less civilised and building up my practice, if any members of staff dared to raise the question of pensions, my answer at that time was: 'Pensions are preparation for death – get on with your work and earn some fees during your lifetime.' Later, of course, I was obliged to make a complete u-turn and to arrange an office pension scheme of which, incidentally, I am still a Trustee. The property activities of the large pension funds have become more important in the last few years. Due to the inflationary wages spiral, the funds keep pouring into them and they must be on tip-toes; Hugh Jenkins is outstanding among the pension fund managers I have met. He is director general of investment of the Mineworkers' Pension Scheme and the Coal Board Superannuation Scheme and also serves on the Commercial Property Panel to the Department of the Environment. Bright, able and articulate, he is equally at home with miners' union leaders such as Joe Gormley, Mick McGahey and Laurence Daly as he is with business tycoons and city financiers. The Coal Board Pension Funds have a successful record concerning more than 250,000 employees. Hugh Jenkins, with his able colleagues, runs an in-house team with the knowledge, capability and expertise to undertake the risk of carrying out speculative building developments themselves, instead of investing only in income producing buildings which have already been let. Hugh Jenkins has recently been promoted to investment maestro and Bob Juddery is his successor.

Insurance companies have also become a more potent, if still conservative, force. Several still require a business partner or entrepreneur to underwrite any risk and to provide the expertise and management needed for large scale property development. Others have particularly skilful fund managers who have the expertise to take calculated risks on speculative building. Prominent among these are John Darby and his colleagues, Martin Olley and Jack Abel of the Norwich Union Assurance Society. John Darby was born and bred in Norwich and it is surprising that this insurance company, whose headquarters are 'out in the sticks' should have taken the lead in carrying out spectacular, large scale commercial property developments. The Prudential have an estate department second to none. Over the years, I have known their eminent successive chief surveyors, George Coombe, followed by Fred Waller, Michael Dunnett and Eric Chapman who only recently retired, Michael Mallinson and Peter Green having taken over, Tony Lovell concentrating on development in order to manufacture some of their own investments. Arthur Green and John Crickmay, formerly of the Legal & General, at one time were jointly responsible for the expansion of their property investment department – they were effective partners, Arthur tactful and John blunt. Apart from life funds, a huge property fund subscribed by outside pension funds is now managed by Peter Sim who is ready to invest a percentage of their funds in speculative development as also is Peter Henwood of the Standard Life Assurance Company. Sydney Julian and Gerald Grant of the Pearl Assurance were well respected property managers who have now retired. Stanley Bennett followed them and tells me he would prefer to recommend income producing properties and leave others to take the risks unless an exceptionally well located site turns up.

Many of the leading merchant banks are not adverse to participating in property management themselves, in addition to backing good enterprises. Quite apart from visible earnings, the invisible earnings overseas by bankers in the City which assist the economy and contribute to the balance of payments are often underestimated. The cream of commercial property investments involve many millions of pounds to create and build and can be beyond the grasp of smaller pension funds. A good friend of mine, Norman Bowie, formerly of the Prudential and Jones Lang Wootten, had a brain wave which provided the solution to the problem. After seeking advice from top city professionals, Alan McLintock, the accountant and Ferrier Charlton, the solicitor, he obtained clearance from the Department of Trade and the Inland Revenue to form – under the umbrella of two leading merchant banks, Hambros and Schroders – the first Pension Fund Property Unit Trust. It was headed by Cecil Baker, a vigorous property man of considerable experience. Once Norman had got the first property unit trust off the ground, I thought it was high time for me to promote one. So I approached Jeremy Cotton, Jack Cotton's son, a bright young solicitor and merchant banker then at Rothchilds, suggesting that they formed a trust of their own. Jeremy Cotton is a fast mover and a horseman. He was one of the amateur riders in the 'Mad Hatters' private sweepstake at Plumpton which created much public interest because the Prince of Wales entered the race, almost won it but eventually came second. The proceeds of the meeting went to the Injured Jockeys' Fund.

In due course Jeremy helped me with the formation of a property unit trust, sponsored by Rothschilds in conjunction with Hill Samuel, which was known as the Mutual Property Fund. In the end, each bank preferred to paddle its own canoe and Rothschilds now have their own property unit trust while Hill Samuel has altered the name of the Mutual Property Fund to the Hill Samuel Property Unit Trust. I enjoyed being involved with them, sitting in on all their board meetings in the past in company with Colin Kerr, Eddy Mowle and Clive Ross. The chairman, Douglas Allison, is an experienced investment analyst with the background of an economist and a logical mathematical mind. His pleasant manner gave everyone round the boardroom table the opportunity to pass comment and helped – with charm – to avoid conflict. Audrey Head, his *aide-de-camp*, was a former winner of the Times Veuve Cliquot award for 'A Woman in a Man's World' for which she receives a magnum of champagne every birthday. I have always found her extremely efficient, with a penetrating, fast-moving mind and an uncanny instinct for picking up points which may have been overlooked. Other members of the board included George Ross Goobey, Bill Broadfield, Geoff Morley, George Dennis and Tony Gaitskell. George Ross Goobey, formerly of the Imperial Tobacco Company Pension Fund, is an actuary and mathematician with a special flair to make the correct business decisions. He has a reputation for after dinner speaking and will tell you when asked for his definition of an actuary, that the job is: 'A cross between a bookie and an undertaker.'

One evening, when he arrived at Paddington to catch his train back to Bristol, George found he had nearly an hour to wait. It was tea time, too early to go to the bar, so he found the restaurant and got himself a cup of tea and a packet of biscuits. He was sitting reading his *Evening Standard*, with *The Times* beside his cup, when a fellow traveller asked if he might share the table. He had no sooner seated himself when, without so much as a 'by your leave', he helped himself to one of George's biscuits. George wondered what the world was coming to and debated with himself as to whether he should object. He refrained from saying anything, believing that the best way of dealing with the situation was to ensure that he managed to eat more biscuits than his unwelcome guest. George dipped in and nibbled away quickly at biscuit number two. The traveller beat George to the packet for biscuit number three, but George was not far behind with biscuit number four. There are five biscuits in a packet and George did his best to reach the last one, but the other fellow got there first, ate it quickly, swallowed his tea and departed without a word of thanks. George sat there for some time ruminating about standards of behaviour until it was time to get his train. He got up, picked up his *Times* from the table and underneath it was his own packet of biscuits!

Bill Broadfield of the Unilever Pension Fund, a charming Scot with vast experience, is unlikely to make a reckless decision. Geoff Morley, formerly of the Shell Pension Fund, is a bright and quick-witted individual with the instinct of a wheeler-dealer which is restrained due to his responsibility as a pension fund manager. George Dennis of the Post Office Pension Fund is a talented young economist and Tony Gaitskell is a bright technical man with property experience. I have happy memories of working with the Hill Samuel Property Unit Trust board and they have recently strengthened their management with the full-time addition of Brian Wootton, an experienced chartered surveyor, formerly with Manufacturers Life Insurance Company. Unlike advertised ordinary unit trusts, property unit trusts are confined to pension funds and are unavailable to the general public. Property bonds filled the gap. They allow anyone to invest in property, providing them with a stake in a property investment, linked to a life assurance policy. The property bond business took off when Mark Weinberg, the bright young managing director of Abbey Life Assurance, set the operation into motion on a large scale. The inspiration came from Jeremy Pinckney, a Hambros Bank executive who later built up the Vavasseur Group. Initially, Mark kept putting Jeremy off when he tried to persuade him to start Abbey Property Bonds. He thought they would have a limited appeal, whereas they attracted an enormous amount of money very rapidly. There was additional advantage to the investor in terms of relief on surtax and estate duty. When the tax laws were changed in 1968 to remove both of these benefits, it was thought that property bonds would die a death. In fact, after a year or so sales bounced back beyond their earlier level, demonstrating that investors were anxious to put their money into property. Abbey Life is still the market leader in the property bond field and Hambro Life, which started in business in 1971, now has the second largest property bond fund. Mark Weinberg left Abbey Life at the end of 1970 to form Hambro Life Assurance as a joint venture between Hambros Bank and the various directors who left Abbey Life. Mark's Hambro Property Bond Fund now has assets of something over £300 million. The success of property bonds prompted me to approach the vigorous banker, David Montagu, who arranged a link with the Pearl Assurance Company creating the Pearl Property Bond Fund.

*

I have always enjoyed dealing with Morris Saady, a stimulating individualist with a ready wit who was involved in some important office developments in London and subsequently in America and the Trade Centre in Switzerland. He telephoned me one day and in his inimitable style said: 'Your office is becoming like the casbah; you made me an offer for one of my properties subject to acceptance by twelve noon, you later increased the offer subject to acceptance on the following Friday by five o'clock – have you a bloody stop watch in your office?' The lively partner who heads the investment department, Michael Fowler, and his able lieutenant, Tony Trump, who is almost a human computer, tell me that to protect pension fund clients, they sometimes find it necessary to adopt these tactics to avoid influencing a last-minute competitive over-bid.

*

I found David Montagu a forceful and active merchant banker. During his career, he has been chairman of Samuel Montagu & Co, the Orion Bank and later moved to Merrill Lynch, the international share and commodity brokers.

David is on the board of a number of companies with which I have had dealings, including London Weekend Television. Having been awarded a franchise, the company – which included on its board Robert Clark, the Hon John Freeman and George Ross Goobey – entered into a building lease on a large South Bank site close to the Festival Hall. Arrangements were made for the building to be financed in advance by the Coal Board Superannuation Fund, London Weekend Television taking back a lease in order to provide £4 million – the estimated cost of construction. Town-planning consent had been obtained to build comprehensive studios on the lower floors with a tower block above, restricted for use as administrative offices ancillary to the television industry.

The brilliant architect, Alan Roberts, of Elsom Pack Roberts Partnership, journeyed to America to visit the most up-to-date studios to ensure London Weekend received the best and most modern layout and equipment for its new building. The technical specification, combined with rising building costs, pushed the estimated total cost of the project to £8 million – double the figure which had already been promised. The board was in a dilemma. It knew that the only method of raising more finance would be to sub-let the upper floors in the tower block at the maximum rent for general office use. But the only planning consent it had was restricted to the television industry. Restrictions on building offices for general use applied at that time to central London. A prerequisite for London Weekend was an Office Development Permit to be obtained from the Department of the Environment. The matter was of such extreme urgency that David Montagu himself decided to accompany me in a taxi for a personal interview with Philip Daniel, the Department of the Environment executive dealing with Office Development Permits. After we put our case, the Department agreed to modify the existing town-planning consent and this was later ratified by the local planning authority. Thus the upper floors of London Weekend's tower block were let to produce an income which justified the Coal Board Pension Fund investing £8 million instead of £4 million. I have a feeling that, if this arrangement had not been made, London Weekend might not have been operating at the present time.

Two men who left professional practice and set up successful public property companies developing commercial buildings were Joseph Gold, chairman of Centrovincial Estates and Jack Rose, chairman of Land Investors Limited. Centrovincial Estates became a property company in 1959. In his early days Joe was a vigorous, hard-working estate agent who followed me at Dudley Samuel & Harrison, the fertile training ground for young negotiators. Today he is a more relaxed, smiling figure who has enjoyed his success. The company has built and owns a large number of shop and office properties and has also carried out many developments overseas. Joe completed one of the last spectacular developments on the corner of New Bond Street and Grafton Street, containing shops, offices and flats above. The corner shop is occupied by Ted Lapidus, the continental boutique, and one of the shops in Grafton Street is the home of Wartski, jeweller to Her Majesty the Queen.

Jack Rose's Land Investors is also a highly successful public property company. Its portfolio includes industrial and office property in good locations. Jack is an extrovert with ready wit, but he also possesses an interesting and unusual aspect to his character. Although a keen commercial man, he is an academic, fascinated by the technicalities of his profession. He enjoys mathematics and has produced a number of books and valuation tables, with interest rates and calculations to assist other members of the profession.

Another prominent developer is Alec Coleman. Jovial, optimistic and always smiling, I think he has much to smile about as he was shrewd enough to arrange a timely sell-out on a share basis before the property crash. Alec is an individualist from the Midlands. There he concentrated on speculative house building and then came to London and expanded into commercial property. He operated abroad, too – one of his spectacular deals involved an extremely large office development in Boston in the US, which he carried out in conjunction with Central & District Properties. Alec is socially minded and now lives a quiet life with his wife, Eileen, concentrating more on charitable causes than business.

*

I had many occasions to meet the late Colonel John Trevor – known as Jack – who was one of the great personalities of the property world. In 1930, he founded the firm of J. Trevor & Sons in Coleman Street in the City of London and now of 58 Grosvenor Street in the West End. Jack was a vigorous and energetic man who cultivated a large personal clientele. A member of the Territorial Army, he served in two world wars and gained the rank of Honorary Colonel in the Seventh City of London Regiment. He also supported many charitable causes and his skills as an auctioneer were very much in demand at charitable functions. He raised £1 million for charity through auction sales during his career. His first wife was a member of the family which controlled J. Lyons & Co. Lyons entrusted Jack with a great deal of its insurance business and his office built up a reputation as fire and loss insurance assessors. After the death of his first wife he married an attractive young American called Georgia. Cynics did not expect the marriage to last due to the difference in ages, but they were wrong – after Jack's retirement in 1971, he and Georgia lived happily together in the south of France until his death in his 98th year. Keen and alert, he retained all his faculties to the end. Just before his death in 1978 he was invited to attend a luncheon of the old guards in the profession – including myself – and he sent an amusing telegram from Cannes apologising for his absence because he could not obtain 'a babysitter for his French poodle.'

Several well-known members of the profession graduated in the offices of J. Trevor & Sons including Basil Samuel, Walter Flack, Marcus Leaver, John Hines and Leslie Stenning. Marcus Leaver was an able negotiator who eventually founded his own successful practice. His untimely death following an illness resulted in his colleague, Alfred Essex, becoming senior partner of the firm which is still flourishing as Leavers of Bruton Street, Mayfair. John Hines set up his own practice after the war following army service. A capable agent with expert knowledge of provincial and suburban shopping centres, John dissipated his energies by becoming involved in Town & Commercial Properties whose shares were quoted on the Stock Exchange. During the property boom he arranged mergers with other companies, created a large amount of loan stock and encountered difficulties during the crash. However, undeterred, he has restarted his professional practice in Brook Street, Mayfair.

*

Joseph Levy is a likeable, down-to-earth, genuine cockney character, bubbling with success and confidence. During the war he was awarded the British Empire Medal for his actions in the Fire Service and he has since received the MBE for his charitable work. Happily married, he always likes to tell how he met his wife, Ninot. He made a foursome with a friend on a blind date! Ninot's hobby is painting while Joe's is developing property and his charitable foundation. Their son, Peter, is a fully qualified chartered surveyor and is a partner in the practice of D.E. & J. Levy with the old faithfuls – John Bodie, Walter Swindon and Derek Glancy. Joe and his late brother, David, received their early training and inspiration from the famous Jack Phillips, the estate agent and developer, before forming their own practice as D.E. & J. Levy. Although they served in the Fire Service during the war, they managed to keep their office open and had the foresight to appreciate the future possibilities of bomb sites and other buildings. In addition to selling many key sites to clients on the cessation of hostilities, they formed a partnership with Robert Clark, a shrewd Glasgow solicitor, who had previously arranged some finance for them. The keen but cautious Robert Clark and the sparkling, ambitious Levy boys with their knowledge of property proved to be a very successful partnership. In the early days Robert Clark worked more behind the scenes than in the limelight and was better known for his connection with Associated British Cinemas.

Unfortunately David Levy died suddenly in 1952 at a young age but before his death he and his brother secured an insignificant company – the Stock Conversion Investment Trust – and transferred into it the properties they had acquired. They then skilfully built it into one of the most successful public property companies. Joe Levy joined Robert Clark on the board of Stock Conversion and he was instrumental in carrying out perhaps the greatest achievement of his career – the development of the massive Euston Centre. He had purchased a 12-acre site within a comprehensive area zoned by the London County Council for road improvements such as the construction of an underpass to relieve traffic congestion at the junction of Euston Road, Marylebone Road, Tottenham Court Road and Hampstead Road. The site carried a town-planning consent to build offices. Joe had retained as his consultant his friend, Sidney Kaye, the architect.

Joe succeeded in making an arrangement with the LCC whereby Stock Conversion would attempt to acquire all the ownerships within the area by private negotiation on the understanding it would dedicate to the LCC parts of the land required for road improvements. Stock Conversion would also reimburse the LCC if the Council was forced to use compulsory powers in the event of the company's failure to acquire any of the interests. Full credit is due to Joe and Robert Clark for undertaking the huge risk of buying out a large number of tenants and owners on an extensive site to complete their development jig-saw. Because of the magnitude of the site and to avoid being held to ransom by one or two owners hearing about Stock Conversion's intentions, Joe approached a number of estate agents to act on his behalf. It would probably have taken a local authority years to carry out such a huge undertaking and it is to Joe's everlasting credit that he adopted a broad view and arranged for his company to pay some of the owners well over the odds to ensure that no one could hold up the scheme. Joe was taking a calculated risk on the value of offices in a yet unproven area, although his confidence was, no doubt, boosted by the Government of the time placing a ban on new office building. The Euston Centre development, when eventually built, is an outstanding example of what can be done by a local authority willing to work in close co-operation with private developers.

Stock Conversion then acquired important sites in Piccadilly Circus, including the Trocadero, hoping to carry out a similar development at the same time as adding Piccadilly road improvements. Joe, however, became tired of the delays, difficulties and political implications so Stock Conversion sold its interest in the Trocadero. Joe now devotes a great deal of time to charitable activities. He has strong, sentimental feelings for his former principal, Jack Phillips. When the Old Curiosity Shop came up for auction Joe resolved to emulate the action of Jack Phillips, who purchased it for £2,000 in 1925 to ensure that the ownership of this memorial to Charles Dickens should remain in British hands. Joe bought it at the London Auction Mart in 1972 for £70,000 and now proudly holds it in his charitable foundation.

20

WATCHING THE CABARET

*

I am reminded of an amusing incident when friends of ours, Aubrey Orchard-Lisle and Bunty, invited my wife, Pamela, and I to cocktails at their town house in Aldford Street, off Park Lane. Sir Charles Clore and Jack Cotton were present, as well as Betty Beaman, who was a life-long, loyal friend of Jack Cotton. After dinner at the Mirabelle we adjourned to the Pigalle in Piccadilly. I remember the excitement of the head waiter when he saw the two tycoons in question. He immediately sat us at the most prominent table adjacent to the stage where a cabaret performance took place during the course of the night. The stage was constructed on an electrically-propelled rising platform. Suddenly the music struck up, the stage rose to almost the same height as our table, the curtains parted and floodlights displayed – almost at eye level – 18 pairs of cheap, bright, green patent shoes worn by a troop of coloured dancers, clad in evening dress with top hats and walking sticks, doing a tap dance routine. This prompted me to remark to Charles Clore: 'Those look like Phillips fashion shoes.' Phillips was one of the companies he had merged into his huge Sears footwear empire. Clore possessed a dry sense of humour and quick wit and in a flash he replied: 'These look like Greenlees.' The retort was a thrust at Sir Isaac Wolfson, chief of Great Universal Stores, who had just taken over the footwear group of Greenlees. Another Clore comment I shall never forget occurred when he pushed past me at a crowded cocktail party at the Dorchester. Charles said: 'I wish I had your figure', and I replied: 'I wish I had your money.'

One of my favourite quotations is: 'Personal friendship is not a sound basis for business, but good business relations sometimes result in personal friendship.' The latter was the case with Aubrey Orchard-Lisle and me. Aubrey became a personal friend following a large number of transactions I carried out with him and his firm, Healey & Baker, where I was acting on behalf of vendor clients and Aubrey was acting in his advisory capacity as property consultant to the Coal Board Pension Fund. He has been a Governor of Guy's Hospital since 1953, is now its chairman and is also chairman of the Advisory Panel for Institutional Finance in New Towns. He is a director of the National Bus Company and was honoured for his public service in 1973 with the CBE. He joined Healey & Baker in 1926 and is now senior consultant. A man of high standing in the profession, he thinks much and talks little and his thoughts are often riveted to business matters. His brother, Mervyn, tells of the time they both lunched at the House of Commons and were walking through Westminster Hall. Mervyn paused and said to Aubrey: 'Do you realise that Warren Hastings stood on this very spot when he was being impeached by Parliament?' There was a pause and Aubrey replied: 'No, but how did you settle that deal with Montague Burton this morning?' Mervyn did not pursue the history of Westminster Hall, needless to say.

*

Noel Taylor of Jones Lang Wootten is a good friend of mine as also was his late brother Eric. Their father, A.C. Taylor, was also well known to me and was a typical professional city surveyor. Noel and Eric joined the office straight from school in 1938 and Noel tells me that were it not for the fact that his father was a close friend of Sydney Wootton, his first day at the office might have been his last. The office routine was explained to him by Percy Paice, an outstanding character, who led him into the basement and instructed him on how to copy plans. Percy stood aghast when in the afternoon he came to check on Noel's progress. For the purpose of distinction, part of the original plans were coloured pink and other parts blue, but Noel's copies were all pink. Percy thought Noel was either completely stupid or was a mischief maker who should be dismissed on the spot. As a newcomer, Noel was understandably diffident about volunteering the fact that he was colour blind. Forty years later Noel offered Percy a lift to the City. Percy sat quietly with his seat belt firmly fixed. When Noel asked him whether he remembered his first day at Jones Lang Wootton, Percy replied: 'Never forget it, sir. I have been watching you tonight and, amazingly, you have not yet crossed any red traffic lights.' Percy was a rare character who put service and loyalty to the firm above everything and, having retired after 50 years, he returned once again and remained a stalwart in the practice until he died still in harness in 1979. Eric and Noel Taylor rejoined the firm in 1945 after serving in the army and revolutionised the practice by opening branch offices in various parts of the world. In 1946 there were about 30 JLW partners and staff in two offices – in the City and West End. Now, JLW employs about 1,000 people.

During the property boom several London estate agents like Jones Lang Wootton foresaw the possibilities and made an early reconnaissance overseas, setting up offices abroad as a forerunner to encouraging their British clients to enlarge their boundaries by investing in other countries. However, most of them could not permanently spare their leading partners, who have remained based at headquarters in London with an occasional flight abroad. A few shrewd developers were successful abroad, particularly those who set up local offices on the spot. But several companies found themselves in difficulty at the time of the crash in 1973 because they were not sufficiently conversant with local conditions, and they were hit hard by currency restrictions. Companies with a good UK asset base overcame these restrictions by persuading their banks to guarantee a 'back to back' loan with foreign banks. Those developers who survived the crash are now more cautious in connection with development overseas.

*

Having told stories about many friends in the profession who are members of other firms, I do not think I can be accused of being immodest if I mention a few of my Edward Erdman colleagues. We cannot claim the distinction of being as old-established as other London agents and surveyors as I only commenced the practice of Edward Erdman & Co in June 1934. From 1939–45 the office ceased to operate as I and nearly all the other members of the firm were called up at the outbreak of war. At the end of 1945 I was joined by nine former members of the firm when I re-opened the practice and, since then, we have grown to a total staff of about 300, with offices in the West End and City of London, Glasgow, Paris and Amsterdam. An association has been formed with Arthur Rubloff, one of the largest realtors in the USA, with headquarters in Chicago and offices throughout America; a link has also been set up with Jules Vaisse with offices covering France.

Well after retirement age, I received an unsolicited approach from a certain public conglomerate to join their board as an active executive to concentrate on the development of their extensive property portfolio. I was taken by surprise, had no thought of retiring from the practice and therefore made it clear to the chairman that I could not leave my colleagues with whom I had life-long association. The chairman of the conglomerate then offered unusually attractive terms – not only to me but to all the partners in the firm. Although negotiations reached quite an advanced stage, the younger partners feared their professional independence might be jeopardised and, because of this, I called off the proposed transaction. But the approach triggered off thoughts that perhaps I had reached the age when I should retire from the firm to give the younger partners more opportunity to progress. Over a long period the legal machinery was completed which resulted in my retirement from the practice and my being retained as a consultant. The life-long founder members who had worked with me from the early days of the practice, Eddy Mowle and Stanley Behrens, came to the conclusion that if I retired, they would do likewise. The remaining founder member, the late Ted Stringer, became senior partner until his tragic and untimely death. Ted was a sportsman, a good team man and a first-class administrator. He was a former president of the Incorporated Society of Valuers & Auctioneers. Alice, his widow, was devoted to him and has attended many ISVA functions to present prizes in memory of her husband. After Ted's death the firm's Management Committee elected John Cook and Colin Kerr joint senior partners.

Well before I retired in 1973 I came to the conclusion that John Cook, whom I had had the foresight to engage as a junior clerk over 30 years before in 1947 at a salary of £4 a week – with the added precaution of one month's trial – had developed the ability and confidence to become a senior partner of the firm. As a broad hint, I sent him a copy of a light-hearted book, signed with my compliments, entitled *How to Get Your Boss's Job*. Among the quips in the book was the advice: 'If you wish to succeed, the first thing to remember is that your secretary's pad is to write on and not to sleep in.' John was born in East Anglia and has always been socially minded. He was a young member of the Round Table and Toc H and is now a JP sitting at Great Marlborough Street, Horseferry Road and Bow Street Courts. He has conducted many exciting negotiations in the central area of London. It was he who concluded the letting of the office complex adjacent to Euston Station which he handled with the assistance of Peter Shaw on behalf of British Rail Property Board. This was a sensational letting to one firm at £3 million a year which, at the time, was a record figure.

Colin Kerr, the joint senior partner, came from a real-estate family as his father was a surveyor. His early hobby was rugby, but when the nominations for joint senior partners appeared Colin emerged from the back row of the pack and his hobby now is leading the team from 6 Grosvenor Street. As a person, he is keen, ambitious and full of energy. Colin held a commission in the Army while John Cook held one in the Navy and together they form an ideal combined operation – Colin spearheading the attack and John ensuring that the ship is moving forward on an even keel. Like John, Colin is a happy family man. His wife, Françoise, has a captivating French accent; they have two sons and a daughter and live in an attractive house near Hampstead Heath. Colin is occasionally able to drag himself away from the practice for a game of golf or weekend sailing, which is his real passion.

Colin's speciality is putting together large and complicated development schemes. In his early days, he was highly successful in South Wales. The redevelopment of Merthyr Tydfil's central area was involved and complicated; what is more, in those days travelling to Merthyr could take up to five or six hours, depending upon rail connections. On one occasion he remembers missing a connection at Pontypridd for the inevitable evening meeting with the local Planning Committee and he cast around for some means of transport which, at that time of day, was almost non-existent. Eventually, a taxi company was found, but the only vehicle they had available was a hearse – they had diversified as undertakers! Undaunted, Colin had the novel experience of arriving in Merthyr on time, in a hearse. He got the scheme through and, since then, has helped to resurrect several Welsh towns by promoting development schemes in Cardiff, Newport, Pontypridd, Aberdare, Ebbw Vale, Mountain Ash and Barry.

*

In 1947, I had difficulty in securing the right type of office boy for my practice. I therefore wrote to the headmasters of various schools, including the Archbishop Temple's Boys' School in Lambeth, offering a job to a bright school leaver willing to start as an office boy at £2.00 a week, with the possibility of becoming a negotiator and an estate agent in the future. Archbishop Temple's produced Ronald Presley. When he first joined us no-one realised that he would eventually become one of the leading partners in the firm. Ronald is a great family man, has a pleasant wife, Frances, and four sons. A keen sportsman, he is particularly interested in tennis and was an active player in his early days. He is a member of the Surrey County Lawn Tennis Association, is currently chairman of the LTA's Commercial Committee and also chairs the Committee considering the development of a National Training Centre. In 1978 he visited California as a member of the LTA to witness the finals of the Davis Cup. He played in the *Evening News* Lawn Tennis Tournament and has captained tennis teams in Paris. At one time the firm, as a social event, held an inter-departmental table tennis championship in the basement. Through Ron's contacts, we were able to invite as guests on that occasion the English table-tennis captain, Ron Crayden, and Diane Rowe, the English lady champion. They gave some exhibition games against members of staff and even when Ron Crayden played seated in a chair against our champion, he was able to win the match!

Some years ago, Ron received a recommendation via a senior secretary to the director of one of the leading City merchant banks to act and advise a property company in Ipswich on the sale of their sole freehold asset. His name had been put forward to the Annual General Meeting of the company and he was asked to journey to Ipswich to meet the chairman. It was duly arranged that he would meet this gentleman in the White Horse Hotel. Over coffee, he learned that the shareholders in the owning company were seven ladies, several very elderly and all related through marriage. The chairman himself owned only three shares. To help Ron in what was to be a difficult task the chairman then drew him a plan showing exactly where each old lady would sit at the board meeting following lunch. He also told Ron which one had more shares than the others and who was likely to comment on the figures. Ron tells me that he was worried in case he failed to memorise all this in a very short time. His worries were unfounded. After some persuasion, all the ladies agreed to allow Ron to market the property privately. He finally said that he must have a complete vote of confidence to proceed and to the chairman's astonishment, all seven complied. The property was eventually sold and Ron was told that the ladies were satisfied with the result and the final division of the spoils. Ron certainly has a way with the ladies – an important attribute in these times of sex-equality!

*

It is not only Ron Greenwood or Brian Clough who receive reflected glory by choosing the right team. Thirty years ago, I engaged the services of Donald de Parc Braham at the princely salary of five guineas a week. In 1980, he became Lord Mayor of Westminster and has proved to be a match winner. Apart from conducting many transactions for the firm, he has also managed to find time to take a vigorous part in community affairs, to marry Tanis and also to become a member of the MCC and innumerable other committees and charitable organisations. I have watched him develop from an eager, ambitious, slim young negotiator into a more generously proportioned, tolerant, benign character as a result of the patience required to chair many committee meetings at Westminster City Hall.

Donald mentioned to me one of his memorable experiences as a City councillor. Apparently, councillors can be telephoned during the weekend by their electors and, one Sunday morning, Donald was 'phoned by an agitated woman who lived in a nearby road. She said she had a difficult problem and could he call to see her that evening. An appointment was made and Donald called at 8.00 p.m. She lived in a nice maisonette and he was duly ushered into a comfortable living room and sat down. His hostess was an attractive woman of about 35 and wearing a skirt and jumper. Donald started the conversation: 'Now, what is the problem?' Without hesitation, she lifted her jumper and pulled down the front of her skirt exposing the whole of her stomach. She pointed to a rather prominent scar and said: 'What do you think of that – do you think it disfiguring and should a surgeon have left me in that condition?' Donald jumped up hastily, took half a dozen steps backwards and said that he didn't think a local councillor was the man to help solve this particular problem. The distraught lady replied that as he was both a councillor and a surgeon, she thought he would be ideal for the job. Donald said he was not a surgeon but a surveyor – a slightly different profession. 'Oh no', said the lady, 'Your name definitely has the letters FRCS, Fellow of the Royal College of Surgeons, after it.' 'Oh no', said Donald, 'It has the letters FRGS, Fellow of the Royal Geographical Society.' With much confusion all round, the lady hastily adjusted her skirt and Donald retired politely but quickly from the scene.

During Donald's term of office as Lord Mayor, I was impressed to see a large, official limousine outside the office early in the mornings, bearing the insignia of the Westminster City Council with the numberplate 'WE 1'.

The gold-braided mace-bearer seated next to the chauffeur would, with ceremonial grace, open the car door for Donald who, adorned in his regalia, dashed upstairs to inspect the post prior to attending his next function.

*

In addition to arranging the sale, purchase and management of property, the firm has a large valuation and survey department. Although a skilful property negotiator must be a good valuer and have some knowledge of building construction, there is an enormous gulf between the temperament of a negotiator and a highly technical valuer and surveyor who does not handle sales. The valuer, by nature of his work, is usually somewhat uncompromising and, once he has fixed a firm principle in his mind, it is difficult to persuade him otherwise. Such a man is Louis Ashley, a sound and dedicated professional valuer who, although of diminutive stature, is cast in the bull dog breed. After passing his RICS examinations he became a surveyor in the valuation department of an East London local authority. He then moved to the more glamorous atmosphere of the West End, but this failed to soften his caution and professional stability in dealing with high-flying property speculators who sometimes cause him dismay. He has been involved in innumerable debates – both heated and pleasant – with clients and sometimes with me. He has never faltered and, though he may not have endeared himself to clients, he is highly respected by his colleagues who have developed a sort of love-hate relationship with him. Lou has always expressed his opinion and made his recommendations without fear or favour and, even if some clients did not agree with his views, his judgement has often rescued them from possible disaster. There are other equally skilled valuation partners in the firm such as Jim Collingwood, Ian Hayward and Colin Knott, with a team of assistant valuers. But, despite the expertise of his senior colleagues, Lou ensures that no report leaves his department unless it has been scrutinised by him. There is a good spirit in his department – his partner colleagues recognising his vast experience and graciously acquiescing to this double scrutiny which is a safe-guard for everyone. I was amused when I asked for Lou Ashley recently that his staff referred to him jocularly as the 'Ayatollah'.

*

During my working retirement – despite being told by a good friend that I was crazy – I accepted an invitation from Alan Bailey to join WPHT Housing Association (formerly the World Property Housing Trust). It was set up in 1969 with the help of several eminent architects, surveyors and other professional men and was supported initially by charitable donations from the commercial property world. Later, it changed its name – perhaps inadvisedly – to WPHT Housing Association because of unfounded prejudice in some narrow quarters that it was too closely connected with commercial property concerns. Due to the operations of some housing associations, the 1974 Housing Act, which was conceived to try to 'tidy up' housing associations generally, was no doubt justified. But it has forced voluntary associations to become bureaucratic in complying with Government regulations. Having devoted a large part of my professional life to seeking commercial sites for entrepreneurs, I thought I might carry out a similar exercise finding housing land for WPHT to provide homes for the needy. It was harder than I anticipated as first. Each site had to be registered with the Housing Corporation (the governing body of housing associations) which could have allocated the area to another association; also we could only purchase at the District Valuer's figure. In addition, some local authorities wished to own all available land themselves on political grounds. This seemed short-sighted because our work was complementary to theirs and WPHT normally allocated half the accommodation to be built for the local authority to ease their urgent waiting lists.

Almost by accident, on the departure of the then chairman, Peter Anker, for Canada, I found I had inherited his job. WPHT has a first class team of voluntary members and experienced officers led by Mark Cato, the chief executive, a good administrator and vigorous worker who seldom takes 'no' for an answer. I have cultivated many new friends on the voluntary committees, many of whom are retired professional people keen to help try to solve the housing problem, and I am always on the look out to recruit new members of good standing who are on the 'free transfer list'. It is not easy to build homes for those in need. To get a project off the ground is laborious, first registering it with the Housing Corporation, seeking agreement with the local authority, gaining town planning consent and approval of plans, preparing specifications, submitting tender forms to six builders with double scrutiny by the Department of the Environment, the Housing Corporation and/or the local authority. All of this causes enormous delays, frustration and increased costs. Unavoidable hold-ups provide scope for journalists to print sensational, inaccurate articles in local newspapers – read avidly by disgruntled home-seekers – accusing housing associations of inefficiency and negligence. One national newspaper even went to the lengths of showing a photograph of a tenant in an alleged dilapidated room with the plaster falling off the ceiling. A retraction and an apology were eventually given to WPHT, confirming that the pictured property was not her flat. When projects are completed, the effort seems to have been worth while. It is a delight to share some of the happiness of the new tenants – some elderly, some disabled and others who have been rehoused from almost uninhabitable rooms. When Hugh Cubitt recently became chairman of the Housing Corporation, he announced the abolition of the red tape 'double scrutiny' but associations have not yet been able to test the benefit owing to Government cuts.

21

PUBLIC RELATIONS

*

Advertising relations have become a major force in the modern industrial and commercial world. In my young days I felt strongly that a professional man should not employ a PR firm to puff up his ability but should be judged purely on his skill and performance. Likewise, I advised clients in the old days not to incur unnecessary expense having glossy brochures prepared as this might give the wrong impression that a good property was becoming difficult to sell or let. Events have overtaken me, however, and the infectious selling style, which I suspect has emanated from America, has now become one of the facts of life and PR firms have secured a strong and perhaps impregnable foothold in the property industry. When launching a large property-development scheme today, provision is usually made, as part of the overall costs, for a PR firm to deal with publicity and promotion. To be fair, since the early days PR firms have developed specialist techniques dealing with property which are different from marketing consumer goods such as slimming products, cosmetics or cereals.

An amusing incident occurred in connection with the letting of a prominent shopping complex in Birmingham. The development had been well designed and constructed but the first lettings had not taken place. Our clients were understandably anxious as interest on their large capital outlay clocked up with no rental income to offset it. We were acting jointly with Healey & Baker, represented by Peter Winfield and Paul Orchard-Lisle. The clients were a consortium and refused to be satisfied by the assurances of Peter Winfield, Bob McKenzie of my firm and I that we were confident that the shops would let and that we could secure the rents we had forecast. The consortium became impatient, consulted a PR firm and our clients presented – as a *fait accompli* at our next meeting – their intention to adopt the proposals suggested by the PR men. The joint agents thought the proposals original, but we considered them totally wrong as a medium for letting shops. Despite our protest, a full page advertisement appeared in the *Financial Times* (see photograph) and which displays a scantily clad girl with the caption: 'Who's going to clothe 20,000 women a day in Birmingham?' Peter Winfield and I were not stricken with terror that we might be picked up by the porn squad but, without consulting Mary Whitehouse, we felt that such an advertisement was totally unsuited to contain the names of professional firms. We both refused to allow the names of our respective practices to appear on such an advertisement; and in any case, we felt that a gimmicky advertisement of this type would not encourage hard-headed multiple retailers to be interested in a shopping centre in Birmingham. The other suggestion made by the PR firm at the same time was that a letter be sent to the chairman and managing directors of retail concerns, advising them that an attaché case would be delivered to them on a specific day containing something to their benefit. A plastic attaché case was specially designed with a spring inside so that, upon opening, a raised model of the shopping centre appeared. These ideas were novel but costly, and it is questionable whether any shop letting was concluded as a result; in fact I am told that one recipient telephoned for an assurance that the attaché case did not contain a bomb. Our confidence in the scheme was justified as it was eventually let and has proved most successful.

In recent years, there has been a growing tendency for stockbrokers and estate agents to obtain publicity for their firms through the medium of the national Press – in some cases initiated by the PR consultants. Many of the principal firms of good standing who carry out a large volume of transactions are able to provide the public with reviews of the market, useful statistics and market trends which form a valuable guide for investors. Some firms, however, manage to supply what purports to be a report on market conditions purely as a 'plug' to get their names into the newspapers. The use of large-scale publicity over the last few years has become more pronounced and I believe the future trend is likely to be centred on television. This has not yet developed to any extent, so far as professional firms are concerned, because there is not yet an atmosphere of trust and confidence between professional men and TV producers. There are cases when professionals have appeared on programmes, had their words cut and, in their opinion, were distorted and felt discredited without justification. There is, therefore, a reluctance by company executives and professional people to appear on TV. The time may come, however, when TV production staff could inspire more confidence and be relied upon to broadcast factual information without political or other bias. In the future, it may be that directors of public companies and professional men may be selected as spokesmen for their good looks and persuasive delivery before the cameras.

Television is an effective medium when used constructively. An instance of this was when the BBC approached the Incorporated Society of Valuers & Auctioneers and asked for help in producing one of six television programmes to be called 'Jobs with Prospects'. Clifford Tippett, then president of ISVA, liaised with the RICS and a television film on estate agents and surveyors was produced for showing on the BBC for fifth and sixth formers. The theme in the first part of the film was house sale, survey and valuation and obtaining mortgages. Two firms of agents were selected to feature in the programme – Robert Duff & Partners of Pall Mall and Baxter, Payne & Lepper of Bromley, Kent. Both gave a good practical demonstration of the duties of the estate agent and surveyor and illustrated what happens in their daily work, both inside and outside their offices. For the second part of the film my former practice was invited to show how a large, modern, covered shopping centre is formulated, designed, completed and let. The Elmsleigh Centre at Staines was selected as an example, starting from the time it was a vacant site, moving on to showing how plans were prepared and how meetings took place between various parties to culminate in a joint scheme between Grosvenor Estate Commercial Developments Limited (the developers), BP Pension Fund (the financiers) and Spelthorne Borough Council (the local authority). The film featured formulation and approval of lay-out plans, forecasting the cost of construction against estimated rental income, completing construction work and commencing the agents' letting campaign. The various practical stages of the project were carefully portrayed and our development and letting team of David Allen and Peter Fineman were filmed at site meetings and in our office. David Allen was seen sitting in his office conducting negotiations with Terence Courteney, the property manager of Chelsea Girl, a fashion multiple with 120 branches in the UK. David explained the good location of the shop within the new centre, surrounded by attractive neighbouring shops likely to attract a large volume of trade. Terence was impatient to know the rent and terms and, when David said: '£25,500 per annum on lease for 20 years with five-year upward rent reviews', Terence Courteney replied: 'Very expensive.' David enjoys a practical joke and told him: 'I have a new technique of encouraging clients to pay the rent we quote', producing a toy revolver and pointing it directly at Terence. The producer immediately shouted 'cut' and the sequence was edited from the film. The Elmsleigh Centre comprises 40 shops, a supermarket, a 30,000 square feet office block, a multi-storey car park and 26 flats designed in sympathy with and scaled to surrounding older buildings. The development was officially opened by the Queen.

Some years ago, I met Alan Bailey, an interesting man, a thinker, a writer and a PR expert. He had a company called Kimball Bailey & Partners which developed a flair for and expertise in dealing with marketing and promotion of property developments. One of the reasons for this was Alan's former experience as one of the under secretaries at the RICS. Apart from writing for the leading papers, he and his team of good-looking young ladies, known as 'Bailey's Angels', became prominent by arranging Topping Out opening ceremonies and press conferences. Alan was involved in many other activities – he is a talented cartoonist – and, apart from running his PR company, much of which he was able to delegate to 'Bailey's Angels', he became chief executive of the World of

Property Housing Trust from its inception for ten years. Now a consultant to Kimball Bailey, he continues his varied activities in the property world. He was also responsible for setting up Placemakers Luncheon Club which is run from KBP's offices in Kensington.

Inexperienced journalists reporting property transactions are notorious for publishing inaccurate information. But there are a few with specialised knowledge of property who are skilful and up to date and, in fact, sometimes appear to obtain information even before a deal is concluded. An extremely talented young man is Oliver Marriott, who, as a journalist, was given leave from the *Sunday Times* to write a book entitled *The Property Boom* published in 1967. It contained a thorough analysis, crammed with accurate facts and figures which could only have been produced after considerable research by a skilled professional journalist. It was not always complimentary to individual developers who had the drive and initiative to rebuild many of the bombed sites in London and elsewhere. Oliver is a 'do it yourself' man and, having assimilated the possibilities and the problems of the property market, he became a director of Town & City Properties and more recently, chairman of Churchbury Estates Limited, the public property company. Perhaps Oliver will emerge as one of the tycoons of the future.

Another able and experienced journalist is Bruce Kinloch, the property correspondent of the *Daily Telegraph* who writes some interesting and well-informed articles in the property columns. He seems to have a habit of obtaining information in advance of the other correspondents. After the war, when he served in the Navy, he resumed his career as a journalist and worked for the *Evening Standard* and the *Daily Express* prior to joining the *Telegraph*. Before concentrating on property, he wrote the food and wine column in the *Standard* and he is recognised as a connoisseur of these subjects. I was present at the Placemakers Luncheon Club when Bruce Kinloch was the guest speaker introduced by Colonel Michael Barton, the public relations man. Ironically, Colonel Barton is an ardent slimming fanatic with an interest in a gymnasium and keep-fit club in St James's. In contrast, the proportions of Bruce's figure are somewhat generous. I remember he opened his amusing address by saying: 'Whenever I give a talk, I always remember ABC, XYZ. ABC – Always Be Careful, and XYZ – Xamine Your Zip'. Some of his more pungent remarks may not have been appreciated by everyone at the lunch – particularly by some of the older, more staid members of the property industry – but I found his speech humorous and entertaining. It did not prevent me as a member of the Panel of the ISVA voting him Commercial Property Journalist of the Year. During the past few years many property journalists on national newspapers have changed, but the evergreen Gerald Ely of *The Times* has been writing consistently accurate articles for as long as I can remember. Baron Phillips and others are now writing for *The Times*, whose reporting is of a high standard. Similar standards apply to the *Estates Gazette* which is regarded as the official 'Bible' of the property world and produced with accuracy by the editor Ernest Speller and associate editor, John Clayton. The *Estates Times*, with its punchlines and entertaining photographs, edited by Adam Murza, I regard as the modern book of revelations of the real estate world.

*

Morris Leigh and his son, Geoffrey, are two entertaining characters who run a successful public property company, Allied London Properties Limited. Not long ago I was involved in the multi-million pound sale of a large covered shopping centre and offices, built by Allied London Properties in an important position in a well-known London suburb. It was quite an experience and I am convinced that one of the reasons for the Leighs' success is – although they are jovial and introduce humour into their negotiations – father and son retain tight control on all their operations. Despite the advice they receive from well-known professionals, they study every word of small print in every document which passes through their hands. They operate from two separate houses, rather like the House of Lords and the House of Commons. When I visited the chairman, Morris, I was impressed by the elegant town house in which he conducts his business. It is similar to an ambassador's private residence with a splendid staircase leading to Morris's tastefully furnished office on the first floor. I was charmed by my warm reception and, having discussed the price offered and enjoyed an extremely pleasant discussion with the chairman over tea and biscuits, I felt I had more or less done the deal. I was totally mistaken, however, as Morris then remarked that he would call his 'MD'. I was a little mystified because I had assumed that he was referring to his doctor. Instead, he was referring to the managing director of his company, none other than his son, Geoffrey. While the house occupied by Morris gives the impression of being a beautifully furnished private residence, the house in the adjacent thoroughfare occupied by Geoffrey is the office 'factory', with papers and plans everywhere and a keen staff operating at high pressure. In response to the telephone summons Geoffrey appeared in his father's office and greeted me with a handshake and smile. When the chairman informed him of the proposal to sell their property and the price we had discussed, Geoffrey immediately 'pooh-poohed' the whole idea and said that unless £1 million pounds more was offered, he could not recommend the sale to the board. I felt a bit deflated as, until he had arrived on the scene, I felt the price had almost been agreed. But the proposed purchasers – a pension fund – finally accepted the increased price and the deal was done.

I gained the impression that the chairman and his MD conducted their negotiations very successfully on the lines of one injecting the honey and the other getting tough. I had another surprise in connection with these negotiations as, although the company employed eminent solicitors, Morris and Geoffrey both appeared personally at the purchasers' offices with their lawyers and went through the terms of the contract themselves in order to conclude the transaction. After completion had taken place, I had to see some clients with one of my colleagues in Grosvenor Street and, as he was delayed at a meeting and I could not park outside the office, I drove round the block in my car several times, circling Davies Street and Brook Street and passing the main entrance of Claridges. By a coincidence, Morris and Geoffrey Leigh were celebrating the transaction at a special luncheon. With his usual sense of humour, Morris walked out of Claridges, stopped my car and said that if I drove round again he would tell my wife I was seeking to pick up a lady for improper purposes. I enjoyed the joke and retorted that I had heard they were lunching at Claridges and that I was driving round in an effort to catch them at the entrance to collect my firm's commission. Morris asked me to submit our account and it was paid immediately with a footnote which read: 'I have much pleasure in enclosing a cheque in settlement of your account and congratulate you in dealing with such difficult clients with such ease!! Perhaps we can do this once a year for the next quarter of a century. Kind regards, as always, Morris Leigh.'

22

YOUNG TYCOONS

*

Many years ago, my wife Pamela and I were invited to dinner with Nigel and Joyce Broackes, who were then living in Holland Park. They were a charming, entertaining and courteous couple and two things stand out in my memory. First, Nigel looked remarkably young and relaxed – although he was acclaimed already as a tycoon – and second, he had a very good-looking wife. Even in those early days, he had acquired the house next door for expansion. His career has been outstanding; he had a good family background, was educated at Stowe, and I would attribute his success to the ambition to be a leader in the financial world, coupled with an ability to harness to a clear-thinking commercial mind a very broad general knowledge. He has an uncomplicated mind and an easy style which inspires confidence. After National Service as a cavalry officer in the Hussars, Nigel started his business career with a firm of Lloyds underwriters. He soon left, acquired a few houses and carried out several small but successful flat conversion schemes. A limited inheritance, small by today's standards, caused young Nigel to take a stake in various business ventures – plastics, toys and hire purchase – but some of these proved unprofitable and his most successful early venture was property development.

At the age of 21 he had already gained valuable and varied experience of business. His social life brought him into contact with many young men of good standing and ambition and, as a result of his contacts, he was able to acquire a stake in an investment trust which owned property. The trust soon acquired an interest in a firm of estate agents where Nigel was able to set up an office to gain experience of real estate. The investment trust eventually became Trafalgar House Investments Limited and Nigel forged business links with Commercial Union Assurance Society which, at that time, had relatively limited property interests. By an ingenious exchange of shares with Commercial Union, Nigel acquired an inactive company which owned several of the best sites in London which were ripe for development. This brilliant deal was perhaps the foundation of his outstanding success. In 1963 Trafalgar House Limited was floated on the Stock Exchange as a public company, with Nigel as managing director at the age of 28. Not content to confine his activities to building flats and commercial property developments, he soon formed a holding company and the Trafalgar House empire was born. By clever timing and making the right moves, he created a contracting and construction division by acquiring the shares and merging the interests of several leading contractors. Perhaps one of his most fortunate acquisitions was Bridge Walker, together with the services of that dynamic character, Victor Matthews – a man who has always been ready to undertake both work and responsibility.

Victor Matthews, now Lord Matthews, is a practical man of the building industry. Formerly with Trollope & Colls, who are noted for their high standard of work, he ran his own construction business under Bridge Walker which carried out a number of contracts on behalf of Trafalgar House. When Nigel Broackes became chairman of Trafalgar House in 1969, Victor became the Group's chief executive and then deputy chairman. The Group expanded by taking over Cementation Limited – the contractors – the Cunard shipping line, a number of hotels including the Bristol and the Ritz and the *Evening Standard*, *Daily Express* and *Sunday Express*. The amazing success of the Broackes/Matthews partnership may be due to the difference in character and style of the two individuals. Nigel is a young and suave ex-cavalry officer with an extraordinary flair for finance; Victor, on the other hand, is older and a practical team man who has been on the shop floor in the past and has mixed with the men doing the job. He served in the Royal Naval Voluntary Reserve throughout the war and is down-to-earth, blunt and vigorous.

During his career, Nigel has found the time to run a charitable housing association for the needy and to do other social work. He is interested in sculpture and art – a preoccupation which he perhaps inherits from his mother, who was a talented artist. After completion of the Trafalgar House offices and the Bristol Hotel, facing the Ritz in Piccadilly, he commissioned Elizabeth Frink to design a bronze horse and rider to stand outside the building. He also acquired from Dame Barbara Hepworth one of her last important works, the 'Family of Man', comprising the nine large abstract bronze figures on display in Hyde Park. They have been loaned to the nation. Victor Matthews was a good amateur soccer player and cricketer in his young days and, as chairman of Express Newspapers, he has actively sponsored many charitable causes. Trafalgar House employs a large number of people and is a prosperous company which contributes to the UK's earnings overseas. In 1978, Nigel was honoured by the Guardian as the 'Young Businessman of the Year' and he has since been chosen by the Government to become chairman of the Urban Development Corporation dealing with the rehabilitation of London's Docklands. Victor was created a Baron in the Queen's Birthday Honours List in 1980 and he takes his place in the House of Lords.

Sir Charles Clore was a major shareholder in the Ritz Hotel and he was concerned that the majority shareholder, Sir Guy Bracewell Smith, no longer had his heart in it. The hotel was losing money weekly and Sir

Charles and his colleagues had no time or expertise to run an operation of that kind. I happened to be well acquainted socially with the late Sir Guy. He was a charming man, but had become lonely and depressed after the death of his American wife, Helene, to whom he had been devoted. After leaving the services, Guy had inherited the Ritz from his dynamic father – another Sir Guy – a tough Yorkshireman who was chairman of Arsenal Football Club and other companies. The Ritz, like its sister hotel in Paris, is world famous and in the past many of the most illustrious people in the world have stayed there. It has also featured in many novels but, as an organisation, it was living in the past and, when I inspected it, it seemed that little refurbishment or alteration had taken place for 40 years. The tourist boom had not yet commenced in London and a large percentage of the suites and bedrooms, which were without air conditioning and double glazing, were unoccupied. In addition to this the Grill Room, formerly one of the most attractive features of the Ritz, was empty and derelict as Sir Guy had hopeful negotiations in hand to let it as a casino to Lady Birley. It was said that the casino venture was to be backed by Sir James Goldsmith, but the proposed transaction did not materialise. The kitchens in the basement, extending from one end of the hotel to the other, were outmoded and, when I discussed the matter with Guy, he admitted that he was no longer interested in running the hotel and wished to sell his shares as soon as possible. Plans were produced showing how the frontage could be let as shops, how the Grill Room might be let as a casino and how the number of bedrooms could be increased by adapting existing large bathrooms and wasted corridor space. Armed with this information I called personally on leading hoteliers in London, all of whom expressed interest in acquiring the Ritz. Most of them, however, were short of the finance required to acquire the shares and, in addition, to improve the property. The capital outlay required was huge.

I came to the conclusion that the best bet was Nigel Broackes. His company controlled its own contracting division which could carry out the refurbishment, and his ownership of Cunard could increase the hotel's occupancy rates. I also suggested to him that it might be possible to tunnel under the road in order to link the kitchens with those of his Bristol Hotel opposite, thus using one set of kitchens to service both hotels. I had a pleasant meeting with Nigel and Victor, who expressed interest, and when I informed Sir Guy that Trafalgar House was interested he was pleased. He had been concerned that the Ritz – as part of the establishment of this country – should pass into the hands of hoteliers of good standing. After several meetings and negotiations on price, a figure was formally agreed by the board who were controlling shareholders and I attended a meeting with the respective merchant banks, Rothschilds and Hill Samuel at Sir Guy's offices in the Park Lane Hotel and at the Panel of the Stock Exchange for approval. The only further action required was for the merchant bank formally to acquaint all the minority shareholders in order to give them the opportunity of seling their shares at the same price agreed by the board. I left the meeting late in the evening expecting Hill Samuel and Rothschilds to send out the appropriate circular within 48 hours. At this point I received an unsolicited enquiry from solicitors on behalf of undisclosed clients who wished to inspect the hotel. It was improper for me to reveal the sale prior to the circular being released to all shareholders, the Press and the Stock Exchange. I therefore decided to fix an appointment three days ahead in expectation that the circular would have been circulated before then enabling me to cancel the appointment. Unfortunately a slight revision of the circular was required by the merchant banks and the Press announcement had not appeared by the morning I was due to meet the gentlemen in question. I was therefore obliged to meet the prospective purchasers, take them into the Marie Antoinette Room in the Ritz for coffee and make frantic telephone calls to the merchant bank to ascertain whether the circulars had been despatched. At last, after going backwards and forwards and swamping the gentlemen with coffee, I was relieved to learn that the circulars had been sent by hand to the Stock Exchange and to the Press. I could then disclose that the hotel had been sold. I apologised most profusely for making the appointment, trying to explain why I had acted as I did, but I am not sure that they understood and, when they left, they seemed rather displeased, and I must admit to being extremely embarrassed. Under the able management of Trafalgar House who have refurbished the hotel tastefully, the Ritz should regain its past glory, but they would have to sell a colossal number of steaks in the former Grill Room to justify the rent now paid to them by the casino.

*

At a recent luncheon party, I sat opposite Gerald Ronson and his attractive wife. He is a rugged individualist who, at a young age, has made a considerable impact on the industrial and property worlds. Born a Londoner, with both feet on the ground, he has a keen sense of humour and no time for superficial culture, making no pretence regarding commercial etiquette of past decades or red tape. Instead, he is keen to get down to the basics of modern trading. He is a worker who wants results today and gives the impression that he will get them. He runs the Heron Corporation, one of the largest private companies in the country, and has gained varied experience of both industrial and financial matters. The activities of his company include petrol retailing, motor and vehicle and motorcycle distribution and sales, a housing development division which has built and sold more than 1,000 new homes during the last year, a consumer products department marketing clocks, radios, cassette re-corders and cutlery, a travel division and a large commercial property department under the management of Tony Royle, who has an exceptional flair for large scale development. Heron has a big portfolio of properties and has carried out important developments in Cardiff, Manchester, Paris and elsewhere and has been selected as developers in partnership with the Coal Board Pension Fund to develop a 50-acre site in Southampton. Gerald Ronson has already made his mark on the commercial world and he may well prove to be one of the leading industrialists of the future.

*

Not long ago I met Sir Donald Gosling, known to me as Don, in a plane bound for Nice. I was impressed with his relaxed style, his sense of humour and unassuming manner, and I could not help thinking that his fantastic business success and knighthood had not changed him from the time we first met. I was taking a holiday and he was spending a weekend on his yacht, *Brave Goose*, which enables him to cruise where he likes. However, as he is a shrewd businessman, during the year the yacht is chartered to foreign tourists. As a boy he had a childish whim for the sea, although he was born in London from a non sea-faring background. Against his parents' wishes, he joined the Navy when only 15 and saw war service in the Mediterranean. He enjoyed naval life so much that he was disappointed to leave in 1949 when the services were reduced. One of the reasons for his success is that he is a hard worker, a disciplinarian and an opportunist. While walking down Charing Cross Road he decided to blow into the Westminster City Council to see if he could get a job. He was engaged as a trainee surveyor at a weekly salary of £3. 5s od, to survey every street in Westminster and to record the state of the City's ironmongery – lamp posts, name plates, sandbins and other items, because all previous records had been destroyed during the war. However, fate decreed that he should not remain in the profession.

In his official capacity he received a chance call from a young ex-soldier, Ronald Hobson, who thought that car parking would become a serious problem in London. Ronald had secured a bombed site on nominal terms in Red Lion Square in the Borough of Holborn which he wanted to use for parking over 100 cars. He required town-planning consent and sought guidance from Don on the way to make formal application. Ron was bewildered by the number of authorities which had to be consulted even in those days and Don's limited but useful knowledge of local government procedures helped. Don immediately appreciated the possibilities and Ron Hobson and he got along well together. Within a short time Ron had won the battle for his first car park and although trade was not brisk even at 1/6d per day, with a free car wash thrown in for five day's parking, he was not put off and soon opened a second park and sought more – always with his new friend Don, who remained in the background and continued his training as a surveyor. As the parking business developed with the additional potential of petrol filling stations, so did the friendly partnership. In 1953, Don 'burned his boats' and joined Ronald full time. Their lack of capital (£200) was made up by the tremendous effort they both put in working at home, around the clock, seven days a week, looking for new sites. To this day, they both maintain 'it was fun'. Their keenness and hard work resulted in the formation of National Car Parks, which began by renting at nominal rents a few disused bomb sites and which is now a vast enterprise with a turnover of more than £30 million.

Don and Ron are diligent workers who have had no difficulty in getting on well with people and with their staff. NCP is now the largest organisation of its type in Europe and, apart from having created a large number of jobs, it has also spawned substantial construction projects. I am told that the company sells more than 100 million parking tickets a year in the UK and it also operates in Germany, Denmark, Holland, Austria and Italy. Ron is good at managing people and has a quick eye for a suitable site. Don tends to concentrate on the technical and town-planning sides. He makes the point that if London and other cities are to remain prosperous and attract spending power, it is inevitable that there will be traffic and a lot of it, and local authorities must continue to improve roads and access, but car parking can be provided by the private sector without burdening the public purse. National Car Parks have helped ease traffic congestion in various parts of London by developing car parks under Cadogan Square, Cavendish Square, Brunswick Square, Bloomsbury Square, Finsbury Square and many others.

An enterprising man in more ways than one, Don has become chairman of Palmer & Harvey, one of the largest wholesale confectionery and tobacco firms, and has also acquired an interest in Lovells, the building contractors. He keeps his first love for the sea alive through the White Ensign Association – a registered charity giving professional advice to officers and men leaving the Navy and the Royal Marines. He is also a Patron of the Fleet Air Arm Museum, of which he is a Trustee and Appeal Chairman, and he was knighted for these charitable services to HM Forces. Still only 50 years of age, Don is always cheerful and full of fun, though he admits that car parks and petrol pumps present problems of some magnitude. Don and his partner are typical entrepreneurs, ready to undertake other enterprises. They formed a hotel section which developed the Montcalm and Portman Hotels at Marble Arch and others in London. It always tempts them to erect buildings adjacent to their car parks, and Don tells me that some years ago they became involved in operating a utility, low-priced hotel opposite Finsbury Park in north London known as The Alexandra National. The price for bed and breakfast was 30/–. An immediate decision to sell The Alexandra and everything in it was taken one Christmas Eve after the manager telephoned head office to say that someone had stolen all the turkeys. A second telephone call informed them that the chef had left and the hotel was full. The late hours of Christmas Eve were spent driving around Smithfield Market to find 40 turkeys and then someone to cook them!

Apart from Sir Don Gosling and Oliver Marriott, some of the younger men who may prove to be tycoons of the future include Geoffrey James of the Illingfield Group, Stuart Lipton of Greycoat Estates and the bright Peter Jones of Trust Securities with his fabulous Stockley Park project. There are many other young success stories and despite the cynics, the opportunities in this age are just as plentiful as in the past, perhaps more so today when so many people devote more time to leisure. Successful personalities only appear with hindsight and I am quite sure that among the present younger generation, many new ones will emerge.

CONCLUSION

*

I hope that the lighter anecdotes in this book have proved amusing; but also, on a serious note, I hope that stories about the personal achievements of a few enterprising individuals have brought out the importance of people, how their personal success has directly or indirectly benefited others, and how some men have an inherent ability independent of their degree of scholastic training. I believe that achievement is related to the inspiration, enterprise and work of people and that they do more for the community than faceless companies, government departments, trade unions, the media or machines. I have enjoyed meeting many people with enormous purpose and ability, some pleasant and some a trifle difficult; but for the most part, integrity has prevailed. In our democratic society, I have had the freedom to choose my clients and it would be boring if the State itself ever became the only client. It is our task to endeavour to discipline ourselves with unselfish christian principles in order to maintain and enjoy the luxury and freedom of democracy.

INDEX